ISRAEL
AND THE WESTERN POWERS

1952–1960

ZACH LEVEY

ISRAEL
AND THE WESTERN POWERS

1952–1960

The University of North Carolina Press / Chapel Hill and London

© 1997 The University of North Carolina Press

All rights reserved

Manufactured in the United States of America

The paper in this book meets the guidelines for permanence and durability of the Committee on Production Guidelines for Book Longevity of the Council on Library Resources.

Library of Congress

Cataloging-in-Publication Data

Levey, Zach.

Israel and the western powers, 1952–1960 / Zach Levey.

p. cm.

Includes bibliographical references and index.

ISBN 0-8078-2368-6 (cloth: alk. paper)

1. Israel—Foreign relations. 2. Military assistance, American—Israel. 3. Military assistance, European —Israel. 4. World politics—1945–1955. I. Title.

DS119.6.L49   1998

327.5694—dc21   97-12363

CIP

r97

01 00 99 98 97   5 4 3 2 1

Chapter 1 appeared in abbreviated form as "Israel's Request for a Security Guarantee from the United States," *British Journal of Middle Eastern Studies* 22, no. 1 (1995): 43–63.

Chapter 2 appeared in abbreviated form as "Anglo-Israeli Strategic Relations, 1952–1956," *Middle Eastern Studies* 31, no. 4 (October 1995): 772–802.

Parts of Chapters 3 and 7 appeared in "Israel's Pursuit of French Arms, 1952–1958," *Studies in Zionism* 14, no. 2 (1993): 183–210.

For my parents, David and Beverly Levey

CONTENTS

PREFACE

This book seeks to fill a large gap in the history of the formation of Israel's foreign policy during the 1950s. The existing literature does not deal systematically with the strategic aspects of Israel's relations with all three Western powers—the United States, Britain, and France—during this period. With few exceptions, previous studies have focused either upon Israel's relations with only one power over a more limited period of time or upon specific issues in Israel's foreign and defense policies. Furthermore, there is no study of Israel's policies toward the United States, Britain, and France during the 1950s based upon archival material. This work is based upon recently declassified documents released in the archives of Israel, Britain, and the United States. Such material makes feasible a hitherto impossible analysis of both the debate over and formation of Israeli policy. Thus in addition to a large number of documents of the Foreign Ministry in the Israeli State Archives, access is now available to the diaries of David Ben-Gurion and Moshe Sharett, the protocols of meetings of the Central, Foreign Affairs, and Political Committees of Mapai (the largest and dominant party in the Israeli political arena), and the archives of Ahdut Ha'avoda and Mapam (smaller parties to the left of the moderate socialist Mapai). In some cases, such as that of negotiations between Mapai and Ahdut Ha'avoda and Mapam over the formation of the government in 1955, only the archives of those parties can afford insight into the direct connection between ideology and party politics and the formation of Israeli foreign policy.

Although the archives of the Israeli Defense Ministry and Defense Forces remain closed to the public, declassified documents at various locations in the United States, the Public Record Office in Britain and, to a much more limited extent, French foreign policy documents shed a great deal of light upon Israel's bilateral relations with those countries as well as upon the details of arms transactions in which the Israeli government was involved. In London,

British records describe Israeli arms transactions with not only the United Kingdom but also the United States and France. Thus, through documents of the Public Record Office at Kew, in Surrey, we can learn about the Near East Arms Coordinating Committee and efforts the United States, Britain, and France made toward arms control in the Middle East in the framework of the Tripartite Declaration.

Yet the material available in the archives of the United States, Britain, and France is also subject to limitations and restrictions. The release of documents on the foreign policy of the United States by the State Department has thus far not kept pace with the target date of publication (thirty years at classified status), and documents dealing with certain politically sensitive matters under the purview of the United States Central Intelligence Agency have been unobtainable.

That the documents at the Public Record Office at Kew have been released on schedule in accordance with Britain's thirty-year law governing the opening of material to the public greatly enhances the value of this archive as a research tool, but the diminished role of Britain with regard to the Arab-Israeli conflict from the 1950s suggests that these documents are of correspondingly diminished centrality to future research in this field. The French archives have thus far not released documents on anything approaching the scale of their American and British counterparts. The use made in this study of French documents is limited to the bound volumes released by the French Foreign Ministry; these do not contain much that sheds light on either Israeli foreign policy or French-Israeli relations.

My work focuses upon Israel's relations with the Western powers during the periods preceding and following the Suez-Sinai conflict of 1956, and I have accorded the military moves of late October and early November 1956 only cursory treatment. Other authors have dealt extensively with those military operations, and I have left to them the task of detailing the progress of those campaigns. My narrative, based upon an extensive rather than a selective use of declassified documents, affords a comprehensive view of historical processes, a view made possible only through a complete review of both the Israeli diplomatic records and the internal debates of the political parties in Israel that underlay Israeli foreign policy. Further, I seek to present an even more thorough historical picture by comparing these Israeli documents with the records of those countries that dealt with Israel as a foreign power.

I am grateful to the late Professor Dan Horowitz, who pointed me in the direction that my work eventually took and whom I consulted frequently before his untimely passing.

I owe gratitude to Dr. Yehoshua Freundlich and Mr. Gilad Livne of the Israeli State Archives, Dr. Tuvia Freeling and the staff of the Ben-Gurion Archives at Sde Boker, and the librarians and staffs of the Israeli Labor Party Archives at Beit Berl, the Archives of Ahdut Ha'avoda and Mapam at Yad Tabenkin, the John Foster Dulles Papers at Princeton University, and the Truman Institute in Jerusalem. I am also obliged to the Eshkol Institute and the Shaine Foundation of the Hebrew University in Jerusalem, both of which provided research grants. The editors of *Middle Eastern Studies*, the *British Journal of Middle Eastern Studies*, and *Studies in Zionism* kindly granted permission to use some material that first appeared in those journals.

Former Israeli officials were generous with their time and offered their own valuable perspectives on the period I studied; I owe special thanks to Gershon Avner, Pinchas Eliav, Walter Eytan, Mordechai Gazit, and Yehoshafat Harkabi.

I would like to acknowledge the warm support and the advice of Professor Steven R. David of the Johns Hopkins University and Professor Ira Sharkansky of the Hebrew University. Their support included but went far beyond their comments on and insights into drafts of my work. I am also grateful for the support extended me by Professors Abraham Diskin and Yitzhak Shichor, former chairmen of the Department of Political Science at the Hebrew University, and to Professor Zvi Gitelman of the Department of Political Science at the University of Michigan in Ann Arbor. And I would like to thank warmly my former advisers at the Hebrew University, Professors Uri Bialer and David Ricci, both of whom worked with me patiently during my time as a doctoral candidate in Jerusalem.

Finally, I wish to acknowledge with gratitude the consistent support and encouragement extended me by Lewis Bateman, my editor at the University of North Carolina Press.

ISRAEL
AND THE WESTERN POWERS

1952–1960

INTRODUCTION

This book examines Israel's relations with the United States, Britain, and France from 1952 to 1960. The point of departure is the end of the brief period during the early days of statehood, when a policy of ideological nonidentification between the Eastern and Western blocs was the lodestar of Israel's foreign relations. This study demonstrates that adopting a clear Western orientation in foreign policy did not afford the Jewish state a set of alternatives within the Western camp. The principal goal of Israel's foreign policy was the creation of a strategic relationship with the United States, the leader of the free world, a goal that, during the period covered in this book, Israel did not achieve. The fact that such a relationship could be realized neither before nor after the Suez crisis of 1956 forced Israel to attempt to augment the country's security through ties with the other Western powers involved in the region, Britain and France.

Yet while Israel's leaders wished to forge bilateral ties with the United States based on an American-Israeli defense treaty, they did not contemplate such an arrangement with either Britain or France. Why this was so and in what manner this should change our view of Israel's policies during these years is the basis of this book. Indeed, while the Israelis envisioned strategic support equal to the substantial economic aid already coming from America, they sought relations with Britain and France based only upon a modus vivendi with the regional interests of, and the purchase of arms from, those two powers.

ISRAEL'S FOREIGN POLICY ORIENTATION

During the early period of Israeli statehood, there existed, at least in theory, a choice among pro-Soviet, pro-Western, or nonaligned orientations. The inevitable tilt toward the West spelled the end of a relatively short period of nonalignment.[1] Thus in the ideological context of orientation, my research assumed a Western direction in Israeli policy from the beginning of the period under study.

Ideologically, Israel leaned clearly toward the Western democracies and the values that the free world espoused, in terms of both the nature of its regime and its view of the international system. Yet the Israelis understood that the Western camp that they aspired to join was not monolithic. As we will observe, Israel had to deal with its Arab neighbors as well as find its place among three Western powers whose capabilities, global roles, and regional policies were at variance. To speak of Israel's Western orientation is not to suggest that there existed an ideologically based choice among Western targets analogous to that between a pro-Soviet or pro-Western direction. Referring loosely to a "French orientation" versus an "American orientation" in 1950s Israeli foreign policy confuses the motives behind Israel's pursuit of ties with all three Western powers. Israel's leaders, rather than pursuing closer relations with one or another Western power because of inherent ideological differences among them, based their desire that Israel's closest ties be those with the United States primarily upon strategic and material calculations. Policy makers felt they could best maintain an independent position in foreign relations through military aid, which the United States was in a position to provide and which would complement the economic support it gave Israel.

Freedom of military commitments is usually accompanied by a stance of nonalignment between ideological blocs. In the case of Israel, however, leaving behind nonalignment was not accompanied by a willingness to assume such commitments. Instead, as we will see, Israel's leaders talked repeatedly to various Western powers about an Israeli contribution to defense of the Middle East in a framework that would not be contractually binding upon Israel. The Israelis wished to receive in return a substantial level of military aid or at least the chance to purchase the arms that would enable them to maintain what they viewed as the correct balance of power between themselves and the Arab states.

THE BACKDROP OF DEFENSE AND DEVELOPMENT

The Tripartite Declaration of May 1950, signed by the United States, Britain, and France, announced a coordinated policy of control of arms to the Middle East and included a strongly worded guarantee of the territorial status quo.[2] From 4 June 1952 the Near East Arms Coordinating Committee (NEACC), an intergovernmental body, administered Tripartite arms policy. Ostensibly, the three Western powers coordinated their arms policies in order to control the Arab-Israeli conflict and to channel the military attentions of the states of the Middle East into anti-Soviet defense plans. In fact, from a very early stage narrower regional interests, especially those of Britain and France, created such discord in Western efforts at coordination as to cause an eventual breakdown of the workings of the NEACC. At the same time, of the three Western powers, the United States was the least willing to provide military hardware to the parties in the Arab-Israeli conflict, except—and Israel viewed this as highly dangerous—such arms as might be granted in the framework of a regional pact under Western auspices.[3]

Israel's security was subject to American and British regional considerations, dictated at the height of the Cold War by the challenge of Soviet expansionism and the spread of communism. The strategic response from Washington and London took the form of plans for regional alliances to stem the Soviet threat. The Truman administration's last major initiative was the Middle East Defense Organization (MEDO), designed as a small-scale North Atlantic Treaty Organization (NATO), the important components of which were to be the United States, Britain, France, and Turkey.[4] Since the "Palestine question" threatened to ruin American relations with the Arab world and disrupt oil supplies to the West,[5] the United States left Israel's situation deliberately vague.[6] Ultimately, the MEDO failed because the Egyptians, whom the United States and Britain considered central to the idea, refused to participate.[7] Nevertheless, the Eisenhower administration, which entered the White House in early 1953, renewed efforts to woo Egypt into a Western defense arrangement and continued these efforts until early 1956.

For President Eisenhower, the Arab world was a significant area for containing the Soviet Union. To Eisenhower, the Arabs offered assets; Israel was only a liability.[8] The tone of the policy toward Israel of Eisenhower and his secretary of state, John Foster Dulles, became clear to the Israelis early on. The State Department cast aspersions upon Israel's Western orientation and as late as 1954 attempted to "paint Israel red." Israeli defense minister Pinhas Lavon's gloomy appraisal was that it would be "impossible to accomplish anything with this administration."[9] In fact, although the United States refused to assume the role of purveyor of arms to the Jewish state, Washington extended considerable economic support to Israel from the time of its establishment. The scope of this assistance warrants a brief recounting here, as it greatly contributed to Israel's perception that it must base its Western orientation upon an American strategic commitment equal to such support.

About 10 percent of the capital Israel imported during the first decade of its existence stemmed directly from the United States.[10] Israel was on the verge of economic collapse in January 1949 when the Export-Import (Exim) Bank agreed to extend $100 million in credits to finance the export to Israel of U.S. equipment, materials, and services.[11] The significance of this first loan was especially poignant. The first credit installment of $35 million went toward increasing the country's food resources as rapidly as possible in order to feed the large number of immigrants entering the country.[12] A U.S. allocation in 1949 of $25 million in order to alleviate overcrowded conditions in Haifa and Tel Aviv through construction of fifteen thousand housing units heightened both the fact and the Israeli perception of dependence upon America. Israel carried out additional projects with U.S. aid: the development of the port of Haifa and industrial development in textiles, chemicals, metals, and building materials.[13]

The United States authorized a further Exim loan only in 1958, and the sum of $24.2 million was a disappointment to the Israelis, who had in 1955 applied for $75 million. However, American aid to Israel in the area of agri-culture (extended through surplus commodities) from the Mutual Security Program and Public Law (PL) 480 from 1949 to 1958 was $196.5 million,[14] and it thus accounted for approximately 7 percent of all of Israel's capital imports during this period.[15] U.S. support in other areas was also significant. Between 1952 and 1957 the United States provided Israel with a $70-million assistance package for industrial development that included the expansion of Israel's power infrastructure and transportation. Point Four programs ac-counted for only 2 percent of all U.S. government aid to Israel during this first decade. However, the sum of $15.3 million which this 2 percent repre-sented was responsible for the launching of 173 development projects, as well as facilitating the training of 525 Israeli technicians in the United States.[16]

The Israelis wished to achieve an American strategic commitment to the Jewish state at a level similar to this economic aid, but the Eisenhower admin-istration felt that its economic support obligated Israel to desist from its vehe-ment protest against the American policy of arming certain Arab states against Soviet aggression and exercise the utmost restraint in its defense against Arab violations of its territory and civilians. In mid-1954, Dulles expressed the view that although the United States had assisted the Jewish state economically and politically, Israel had evinced "a most disappointing lack of reciprocal trust."[17]

Israel's desire to remain free of binding ties with any foreign power made the acquisition of arms vital, so that the Jewish state could "take care of itself." Israel's leaders viewed the procurement of arms as increasingly urgent, due to the unwillingness of the Western powers to include Israel in their plans for regional defense. The Israelis prefered not to join a defense pact, yet being excluded from plans for regional defense was dangerous not only because of the arms the Arab states would receive in the framework of such arrangements but also because the West would not guarantee Israel's security against threats posed by either neighboring states or the Soviet Union. The regional configuration that in Israeli eyes became increasingly threatening by late 1952 but especially so from early 1954 also made arms procurement a vital concern.

Expressions of Israel's persistent concern on this score abound. For example, in July 1954 Teddy Kollek, director general of the prime minister's office, noted that Israel had survived the critical period in arms procurement during its War of Independence only to find itself in similar straits: "It is clear to me that the fundamental issue which we have to deal with today is not foreign policy. The change in the balance of power which we can expect in the years to come forces us to stress arms acquisition and is liable to throw us back to the crisis situation from which we emerged several years ago."[18]

In truth, arms procurement did not proceed on its own but was a major element in the formulation of the foreign policy of Israel. The dominance of this factor in Israel's foreign relations is evident in the diaries of Israel's two most prominent leaders of that period, David Ben-Gurion and Moshe Sharett. Ben-Gurion devoted a considerable part of his personal records to the detailing of arms acquisitions, underscoring the centrality of these transactions. The increasingly hostile regional environment in which Israel found itself explains why arms deals so occupied Israel's policy makers on a day-to-day basis and also underlines the importance of a careful delineation and tracing of these transactions based on recently declassified documents. Arms were the focal point of Israel's relations on the strategic plane with all three Western powers. Between 1954 and 1956, Israel also attempted to obtain a security guarantee from the United States, but Israel's leaders viewed such a guarantee as a poor substitute for arms and hoped that the major advantage of a guarantee would in fact be the granting of arms by the United States.

We shall see that the Sinai campaign of 1956 altered the view of Israel as a regional and military factor but did not itself fundamentally change Israel's relationship with the Western powers. The advent of Soviet involvement in the region and the arms the Soviet Union provided Egypt and Syria meant that obtaining arms from the West remained a crucial element in Israeli foreign policy after as well as before the Sinai campaign. The fact that the United States was unwilling to provide Israel with the arms it required either before or after the Sinai campaign forced Israel to deal with Britain and France. This book explains the circumstances that brought both Britain and France to sell arms to the Jewish state and the trepidation Israel's leaders felt regarding the long-term viability of these arms supplies. Israel considered the arms purchased from Britain and France temporary surrogates for arms from the United States. Israelis hoped that they might replace their dependence, especially upon France, with a supply of modern arms from the United States in the framework of a strategic relationship with that power.

1

THE QUEST FOR A SECURITY
GUARANTEE FROM THE UNITED STATES

1954–1956

From late 1954 to early 1956, Israel tried to obtain a security guarantee from the United States. Of the three major Western powers, the United States figured most centrally in the eyes of the Israeli leadership, as both Israel's economic and military-strategic circumstances created the perception that the survival of the Jewish state depended upon the United States.[1] As early as 1950, Israel's leaders were convinced that the chances of obtaining vital economic aid from Washington stood in direct proportion to their willingness to obligate themselves to a military alliance with the United States. In fact, the United States never asked Israel for military assistance, and the American refusal to forge military ties with Israel or to grant a security guarantee forced Israel to cultivate closer ties with both Britain and France in order to obtain arms.

Despite a clearly Western orientation, Israel did not possess alternatives.

Israel could not choose among ties with one or another Western power. Its position harked back to the admonition of Pinhas Lubianker (Lavon) in 1947 that orientation meant "our readiness to maintain relations with anyone willing to have relations with us, with all those holding the keys of decision. . . . There is only the wretched position of a dependent nation [that] must follow any power willing to have it."[2]

In January 1951, Henry Morgenthau Jr. (an American Zionist leader and former secretary of the treasury) spoke with Israel's Prime Minister David Ben-Gurion and reported that "there is no doubt that the present Israeli government is absolutely on our side in the East-West struggle."[3] Indeed, by 1952 Israel had departed from a policy of nonalignment between East and West and adopted a political strategy that stressed the creation of a de facto link with the West.[4] In practical terms, this move from nonalignment was the result of a number of decisions the government of Israel made in November 1951 aimed at ensuring military, economic, and strategic assistance from the West. The Israelis wished to obtain such support in the form of "facts without pacts," direct and bilateral arrangements with the Western powers but especially the United States.[5] As we will observe, however, the Republican administration that entered the White House in early 1953 did not want closer ties with Israel.[6]

Ben Gurion insisted that Israel establish close ties with a power that would provide the requisite support, and he prefered that this power be the United States.[7] Israel applied to the United States for arms at the beginning of 1950[8] and continued to attempt to secure arms until French arms in mid-1956 temporarily obviated the need to petition Washington. The refusal of the United States to sell Israel almost any arms at all forced Jerusalem to concentrate increasingly intense procurement efforts upon Britain and France. Yet while the bilateral arrangements Israel sought with those two countries were limited to arms transfers, this was not true of relations with the United States. America's centrality to Israel meant that its leadership was willing to consider ties with the United States of a nature not contemplated with either of the other two Western powers. Thus Israel's view during the early 1950s that the strategic balance in the region was tilting rapidly in favor of the Arabs brought the Israelis in late 1954 to seek a security guarantee from the United States.

The request for a security guarantee was an approach Israel was unwilling to consider earlier in 1954 and thus constituted a revolutionary shift in its policy.[9] Both Ben Gurion (who was in retirement at Sde Boker from the end of 1953 until early 1955) and Moshe Sharett (foreign minister under Ben-

Gurion and also prime minister during the period of his absence) feared that application for a security guarantee would merely highlight Israel's isolation. Both men agreed that the chance that the United States would grant Israel a security guarantee was slight, and both thought that even if the United States did grant Israel such a guarantee, it would in reality commit the United States to little and would mean only a vague American pledge to prevent the destruction of the state of Israel.[10] As we will observe, their assumption was correct. Nevertheless, the increasingly threatening regional configuration that confronted Israel from early 1954 on prompted the Israelis to pursue a security guarantee from the United States.

THREE APPROACHES TO A SECURITY GUARANTEE

The desirability of a security guarantee from the United States became a matter of consensus in Israel, if obtainable on the nonbinding terms to which Israel aspired. On 1 June 1955, Prime Minister Sharett told the Knesset (Israel's parliament) that Israel sought a "mutual defense and security treaty" from the United States.[11] Sharett and the Foreign Ministry had coordinated this formula with Ben-Gurion but, in fact, among Israel's leaders there were three approaches: those of Ben-Gurion, Sharett, and the Israeli embassy in Washington. The main differences in these three approaches lay in the degree of restraint to which each of their proponents thought Israel should obligate itself in the face of increasing provocations on the part of its Arab neighbors. Employing these approaches as an analytical tool, this chapter will trace the attempt and failure to obtain a security guarantee from the United States. Whether a more "activist" or less aggressive policy was in retrospect the more correct will not be ventured here.[12]

Briefly summarized, the first approach was as follows: Ben-Gurion saw advantages in a security guarantee but was concerned that it would limit Israel's ability to act independently when its own regional interests were at stake.[13] He feared an American "mandate" or "custodianship" and the possibility that Israel's sovereignty might thus be compromised.[14] But a defense treaty with the United States held out the prospect of purchasing American arms, which were more attractive to the Israelis than arms from Britain or France. Only the British Centurion or the American Patton, for example, could provide the answer to the tanks Egypt received from the Soviet Union beginning in late 1955, and the British would not sell Israel the Centurion. In terms of air power, the British Hunter, American F-86 Sabre, and the French Mystère-4 could all cope with Egypt's Soviet-supplied MiG-15, but the British would not sell Israel the Hunter and French jets were subject to American offshore procurement regulations. Furthermore, the United States could extend long-term credit, whereas Israel had to pay for arms from Britain or France in full, in cash, and with little possibility of credit.[15] It was mainly for these reasons and especially after the Czech-Egyptian arms deal in September 1955 that Ben-Gurion was willing to consider a security guarantee. However, he viewed Israel's right to strike at its Arab neighbors in retaliation for terrorist raids as inviolable. If Israel had to choose between retaining this right or relinquishing it in order to obtain a security guarantee, then freedom of action would prevail.[16]

Although Sharett also regarded the supply of American arms as more urgent than a security guarantee,[17] he believed that Israel's chances of obtaining both arms and a guarantee were in direct proportion to its willingness to refrain from frequent, large-scale retaliatory raids. Sharett based his efforts to secure U.S. support of Israel increasingly upon attempts to present his position as more sensitive to Washington's regional policies than that of Ben-Gurion and therefore deserving of American consideration. Furthermore, he hoped that achievement of a security guarantee would enable him to stay the activism of which Ben-Gurion was the main proponent.[18]

High policy was in the hands of Ben-Gurion and Sharett, the two most powerful protagonists in the struggle between the moderate and activist camps over the policy of retaliation.[19] Yet the documents make clear that the Israelis formulated their policy regarding a security guarantee largely upon the basis of information provided by the Israeli embassy in Washington, which was early on convinced of the need to overcome obstacles created by not only the U.S. State Department but also its own government.[20]

Here was the third approach: Sharett's circumspection must be juxtaposed with the eagerness to obtain a security guarantee that the embassy in Washington demonstrated. Sharett placed greater emphasis than did Ben-Gurion upon the achievement of a security guarantee, but he doubted the feasibility of obtaining one and in early 1955 agreed only reluctantly to the embassy's urging that Israel make a formal request. Sharett considered the idea that the Americans might so obligate themselves "a complete illusion" and did not want Israel to debase itself by supplication for a guarantee that would not be forthcoming.[21] Those in the Israeli foreign service who felt that the enthusiasm of Israel's ambassador to the United States, Abba Eban, and the embassy's first minister, Reuven Shiloah, was unfounded shared Sharett's reservations as well as his view that the embassy in Washington consistently led the Foreign Ministry to think that relations with the United States were closer than they actually were.[22]

Sharett did not implacably oppose the policy of retaliation, a fact important in highlighting that there were indeed three approaches. In truth, his position on activism was somewhere between those of Ben-Gurion and the staff of the embassy in Washington. Sharett on more than one occasion took to task Israel's representatives abroad for not appreciating that Israel had to retain the option to retaliate in response to violations of its territory or civilians. For example, in May 1955 Israel's ambassadors to the United States, Britain, and France convened at the Foreign Ministry for consultations, and the three ambassadors urged that Israel end completely its policy of retaliation. Sharett admonished his subordinates; he as prime minister had to deal with domestic pressures, while they were concerned only with foreign policy. Internal constraints, he told them, made ending the reprisal raids impossible. Sharett also reminded the ambassadors that retaliatory raids at Kibye (1953) and Nahalin (1954) had gone far in forcing the Arab Legion to prevent terrorist attacks from Jordan.[23] As we will see, however, the increasing tendency toward activism with the return of Ben-Gurion to the government in February 1955 moved Sharett closer to the embassy's view that the policy of retaliation reduced the chances Israel might have of obtaining either a security guarantee or arms from the United States.[24]

EISENHOWER AND THE DETERIORATION IN RELATIONS

The advent of the Eisenhower administration in early 1953 did not augur well for Israel. The United States revived the idea of a regional defense organization in the Middle East that would exclude Israel, a move Abba Eban termed both "unjust and inexpedient."[25] But here too Ben-Gurion's and Sharett's views were proximate. Sharett saw advantages in the fact that Israel would thus be able to retain a free hand in foreign policy. The advantages of the absence of binding ties were made all the more salient by the Soviets' resumption in mid-1953 of diplomatic ties which they had broken off earlier that year. Sharett's view of relations with the United States was that Israel would "demand arms for defense but not anticipate the issue of a military-political attachment."[26]

In mid-1953, Israel submitted its first request for arms to the new administration. The request included twenty-five 155-mm howitzers, thirty 105-mm, twelve 3-inch, and twelve 90-mm antiaircraft guns. The United States approved only the last item and refused, for two reasons, to supply Israel with anything but spare parts, small arms, and ammunition.[27] First, Washington was willing to supply arms to countries of the Middle East only in the framework of a regional pact under Western auspices.[28] Second, in the American view, further releases of arms would violate the Western-orchestrated arms balance stipulated in the Tripartite Declaration of May 1950[29] by granting the Israelis a marked superiority over some or all of the Arab states.[30] In September 1953, the figures provided by the U.S. representatives to the Near East Arms Coordinating Committee showed that Israel had 122 medium tanks against a combined total of 216 for the Arab states, while in light tanks the figures were 35 for Israel and 54 for the Arabs.[31] In June 1954, the United States rejected a separate Israeli request to purchase twenty-four American F-86 jets.[32] The Americans considered parity between Israel and all of the Arab states Israeli preponderance, because U.S. assessments took into account the efficiency of Israeli forces and shorter lines of communication. As we will observe, even more significant in political terms was the State Department's view that of the protagonists in the Arab-Israeli conflict, Israel was the more aggressive.[33]

At the end of July 1953, a high-level meeting took place in Jerusalem in order to determine policy in light of the American position on arms to Israel and the Arab states. Generals Mordechai Makleff and Moshe Dayan pointed out that because the United States intended to supply arms to the Arabs, the military balance would worsen even if the United States agreed to sell arms to Israel. Thus the Israelis adopted a policy of protest of U.S. arms to the Arabs; the approach taken was "none for them and none for us."[34] The Foreign Affairs and Political Committees of Mapai upheld this policy in debates in early 1954[35] and accordingly, the embassy in Washington lobbied against the American plan to arm Iraq in the framework of a Northern Tier defense.[36] The Israeli effort was unsuccessful. On 21 April 1954, the governments of the United States and Iraq exchanged letters confirming a program of direct military aid to the Baghdad regime.[37]

Israel's policy makers attempted to assess the scope of the military advantage to Baghdad. The Israelis learned some of the details of America's Iraq policy in two meetings with General Trudeau, United States assistant army chief-of-staff for intelligence, during his brief visit to Israel in May 1954. According to Israeli defense minister Lavon, "On the question of arming the Arab states it was sickeningly clear. In contrast to 'soothing' words we heard from the State Department, he informed us that their intentions were to equip and train two divisions in Iraq. To my question whether their intentions were similar in other Arab states, he answered, simply, that they were."[38]

Lavon and Chief-of-Staff Dayan emphasized Israel's value to the West in case of war, but Trudeau's answer was unequivocal: Israel could not be included in Western defense plans because the Israeli Defense Forces (IDF) would not be able to fight in Syria or Iraq.[39] At most, the Israelis could put up a defense of the Suez Canal in the event the Russians broke through the northern defenses, but the Americans were not worried about that contingency at that time.[40] Nevertheless, the Israelis continued to press the United States to consider some sort of role for their country.

The Israeli campaign against the arming of Iraq strained U.S.-Israeli relations.[41] The State Department expressed displeasure at what it considered an insidious Israeli fight against American-backed collective security.[42] Speeches by Assistant Secretary of State Henry Byroade on 9 April and 1 May 1954 added to the Israeli perception of a belligerent attitude on the part of the Eisenhower administration by questioning Israeli immigration policy (the raison d'être of the Jewish state) and advising the Israelis to give up hope of a peace settlement in the near future.[43]

In July 1954, Secretary of State John Foster Dulles summed up American Middle East policy: "Our basic problem is to improve the attitude of the Moslem states toward the Western democracies."[44] In the eyes of Israelis, such a policy came necessarily at their expense. In mid-1954, Ambassador Eban noted that "during the past year high officials of the United States government have seen fit to criticize almost every important phase of Israel's actions in the public forum."[45] Efforts to impress upon the State Department the gravity of Israel's security situation proved futile. On 12 May 1954, Jacob Blaustein, president of the American Jewish Committee, met with Dulles to express concern at the administration's encouragement of Arab intransigence. Blaustein noted that American policy was making Sharett's position very difficult. The Israeli prime minister was a moderate, he told Dulles, and the United States should "hold his hand." Dulles was unreceptive.[46]

The Israelis attempted to improve their standing with the State Department through the U.S. embassy in Tel Aviv but to no avail. Isser Harel, head of the Mossad (Israel's external intelligence agency), provided Sharett with "further evidence of a hostile attitude. Not so much from [the American embassies in] Baghdad or Damascus . . . as dispatches from [the American embassy in] Tel Aviv on Israel."[47] By mid-1954, relations with Washington had reached a low point. Walter Eytan, director general of the Foreign Ministry, noted that the Americans were again hinting at a link between Israel and communism. Although the Israelis had thought suspicion in that area had been laid aside, the State Department now expressed fresh doubts as to where Israel would stand if put to the (ideological) test. According to the normally circumspect Eytan, the Americans were "preparing a file against us on the matter of communism to be used should the occasion arise."[48] Eytan also addressed the American attitude toward the IDF. "They say that the IDF is a nice army, but they have no use for it in an emergency. And that is worrisome."[49]

According to the embassy in Washington, the American attitude required Israel to submit concrete proposals for Western defense of the region. Shiloah termed this the "constructive approach,"[50] but a skeptical Sharett pointed out to the Mapai Central Committee that, in fact, Israel had nothing to offer the United States.[51] Thus in early July 1954, Eban made an additional attempt to sound out the Department of Defense on a place for Israel in regional defense plans and received a negative response.[52] Israel's security was further threatened when later that month Britain and Egypt reached agreement on the evacuation of British bases in Egypt.[53] The impending removal of what was in effect a buffer between Egypt and Israel was accompanied by affirmation from the United States that with the signing of the agreement, Egypt would receive American arms.[54] These dangers to Israel's security brought Sharett in late August 1954 to agree that the embassy in Washington sound out the United States on the possibility of a security guarantee.[55]

ISRAEL'S REQUEST FOR A SECURITY GUARANTEE

Documents in the Israeli State Archives strongly suggest that the urgings of Eban and Shiloah played a considerable part in the prime minister's decision to pursue an American security guarantee. In early August, Shiloah wrote, "If this embassy had instructions—'devote yourselves exclusively to establishing military ties with the United States'—we could make progress. We have not received open and explicit instructions to proceed in this direction."[56]

On 22 August 1954, Eban told Francis Russell that he was urging his government to seek a bilateral, formal agreement whereby the United States would guarantee to use military force if necessary to protect Israel's borders.[57] This evoked consternation in the State Department. Russell proposed offering Israel a different version of a security guarantee: a unilateral U.S. declaration that would "serve to deter Israel from permitting its dynamism . . . to increase tension"—in other words, facilitate precisely the type of control over Israeli policy that Jerusalem feared.[58] Although Prime Minister Sharett was now convinced that only a security guarantee would assure Israel of military parity with the Arab states, he would not authorize the embassy in Washington to submit a formal request. Sharett realized that if Washington rejected a formal proposal, it would mean the termination of dialogue with the United States on this question, and he did not share the embassy's optimism regarding the prospects of obtaining a treaty. Accordingly, he instructed the embassy merely to "note for the edification of the State Department" that although the Arabs were now to enjoy the benefits of a pact with the West, the Western powers had offered Israel no treaty. Sharett ended on a note of pessimism: The Arabs had precedence over Israel in American eyes; nevertheless, "it will be interesting to see how they [the Americans] react."[59]

Eban presented the Israeli request for a security guarantee to Dulles on 15 September 1954, stating that he was making no formal application, but the ambassador's petition left no doubt as to Israeli intentions. Eban reminded Washington that Israel had no treaty with anyone, stating that "the secretary could draw any implications he wishes from the fact that I was empowered to emphasize this feature of Israel's security position."[60] On 8 October Dulles informed Eban and Shiloah that the United States had rejected Israel's request.[61] Eban's personal disappointment is evident in his appeal to Dulles the same day to redress what he considered a grievance. Dulles's vagueness in earlier talks with Eban brought the ambassador to feel that the secretary of state had now misled him. He protested to Dulles that the secretary's draft

> bears no relation to the lines of your own thoughts expressed in previous conversations. There is no talk of a note in which the United States would reassure Israel concerning her security. There is no mention of any intention to apply military policies in the Middle East in such a way as not to change the balance of power to Israel's disadvantage. There is no talk of offering Israel inclusion in the military aid program, in which the two strongest Arab States have already been offered participation. There is no talk of any approach to a security guarantee for Israel beyond the existing Tripartite Declaration of 1950.[62]

Eban made an obvious allusion to the fact that American policy strengthened the activists in Sharett's government and warned that "Israel would conclude that her survival and security were in dire peril and this would inspire all her policies."[63]

Nevertheless, the embassy did not give up on the idea of a security guarantee. Shiloah made an unsuccessful attempt to convince the Foreign Ministry to rescind opposition to U.S. arms to the Arabs in the hope that this might facilitate the guarantee.[64] Meanwhile, the embassy greeted every word of the administration and the State Department indicating understanding of Israel's position with enthusiasm and relayed this slight encouragement on the part of the Americans to Jerusalem.[65] On 28 January 1955, Eban cabled Sharett that subject to certain conditions, the United States was willing to sign an agreement with Israel, pledging help if Israel were attacked.[66] Such an agreement would require that Israel not expand its borders by force. Sharett consented to submission of a formal request, even though he considered Eban's faith in the prospects of a treaty "misplaced hope."[67]

The prime minister recognized that if the Israelis indeed obtained a security guarantee, it would greatly raise public morale in Israel, stimulating capital investment, providing a boost for Diaspora Jewry, and making the requisite impression upon the Arab states. The danger was that such a document would provide the administration cover for unrestrained arming of the Arabs.[68] But under the pressure of four additional developments, Sharett agreed to a formal request for a guarantee. The first development was an increasing awareness that the United States and Britain might call upon Israel to make far-reaching concessions in the framework of a regional settlement they were secretly planning. The second was the possibility that the American Johnston Plan for a settlement over the waters of the Jordan might also create the demand for concessions unacceptable to Israel. The third was the signing of a Pact of Mutual Cooperation between Iraq and Turkey in February 1955, and the fourth was a domestic challenge to Sharett's course in foreign policy: Ben-Gurion's return to the government as defense minister in February 1955.

The first development came as a result of joint Anglo-American planning toward an overall settlement of the Arab-Israeli conflict. The plan that evolved from these consultations, to which only a few officials were privy, became known as Alpha.[69] The arrangement envisioned territorial concessions on the part of Israel, including Jordanian access to the port of Haifa and a passage through Israel's Negev Desert linking Jordan and Egypt.[70] The Americans and British did not tell the Israelis of the existence of a specific plan for a regional settlement; however, Washington warned Israel in December 1954 that it would expect Israeli concessions.[71]

In October 1953 Eisenhower's personal envoy, Eric Johnston, attempted to achieve an Arab-Israeli settlement of the dispute over the waters of the Jordan

River, the second development.[72] Sharett realized that the Johnston Plan was not only a danger to Israel's security but also a political land mine.[73] The relationship with the United States dictated the greatest possible flexibility in these negotiations. However, Johnston's third visit to Israel in January 1955 caused consternation: there was talk of turning Lake Kinneret into an internationally administered reservoir. Ben-Gurion, still at Sde Boker, warned that Israel could compromise on the amount of water it would receive but not on sovereignty over the lake.[74] Johnston tried to convince Israel that "the utilization of Lake Kinneret was not a Machiavellian scheme on the part of the United States to interfere with Israel's sovereignty."[75] Yet Johnston gave Sharett great cause for concern when, during a meeting on 27 January, he pointed to a map and (reaching well beyond the scope of his mission) asked whether Israel had anything important at Eilat. Sharett feared that Johnston would recommend an Israeli territorial concession in order to curry favor with the Egyptians.[76]

On 31 January 1955, the United States assured Israel that it would not press for internationalization of Lake Kinneret. Sharett decided to ask the Americans for an absolute guarantee against the predations of any third party upon Israeli sovereignty over the Kinneret in particular and Israel's territorial integrity in general.[77] The possibility that the United States might so guarantee Israel's borders provided the prime minister with further impetus for seeking a treaty.

A third development that brought Sharett to agree to a formal request for a security guarantee from the United States was the Northern Tier alliance between Turkey and Iraq, which by April 1955 would include Britain and become the Baghdad Pact. This, feared Sharett, would increase Israel's isolation in both the Middle Eastern and global arenas.[78] Pressure on Sharett to persuade the Americans to provide a "counterweight" to the Turko-Iraqi agreement came from the heads of the United States and Western Europe Sections at the Israeli Foreign Ministry.[79] The Israelis decided to employ the premise of American responsibility for Israel's predicament as the basis for demands upon the United States.[80]

Thus in early February 1955, Sharett instructed Eban to conduct negotiations with the United States toward nullifying the Tripartite Declaration and replacing it with separate agreements with each of the Western powers in order to achieve a redressing of the arms balance in Israel's favor. Sharett explained this to the Central Committee of Mapai: First, in offering to arm Egypt and Syria in the framework of Western defense, the United States behaved as if the Tripartite Declaration did not exist. Second, bilateral relations would facilitate arms to Israel without the need to present "constructive proposals" for Israeli integration into Western defense. This was desirable because, as Sharett pointed out, many members of Mapai objected to such integration.[81] At the same time, Sharett warned Eban not to compromise Israel's right to retaliate when served with provocation.[82] This admonishment demonstrates that, in fact, Sharett's views on retaliation were neither those of his subordinates in Washington nor those of Ben-Gurion. And as we will observe, both Sharett's explanation and the timing of this warning to Eban were poignant.

The prime minister wrote in his diary that the Israelis were in February 1955 still not ready to submit a completed version of a proposal to the Americans, and the first drafts by Eban suffered from defects that could cost Israel more than it might gain. Thus, noted Sharett, Israel could agree to not alter its borders by force but would not forego the use of force entirely. If Israel signed a document whereby it renounced the right to retaliate when provoked, the Arabs would commit aggression with no fear of a response. An agreement with the United States, on the other hand, would call for an American response in case of war but would not obligate the United States in cases of border incidents. The irony, wrote Sharett, was that while seeking assurances against a second round of war, Israel's security would deteriorate irrevocably. Sharett thought it "odd that Eban does not grasp this. The entire matter of understanding the positive value of retaliatory acts—in any case the preventive efficacy of the *possibility* of retaliation—is completely alien to his spirit."[83]

It was thus with acerbity that Sharett greeted a secret message of 16 February 1955 from Dulles praising his policy of moderation in response to Arab border violations.[84] The message included the assurance that Dulles was thinking "day and night" about Israel's security and a hint at the possibility of a guarantee. The prime minister's response to Dulles was an intimation that he himself might authorize further reprisal raids against Syria and Jordan. Sharett requested that the new American ambassador, Edward B. Lawson, warn Damascus and Amman that they were on thin ice.[85]

The fourth development that moved Sharett to press for a security guarantee was his loss of a considerable degree of control over security affairs with the return to the government of David Ben Gurion as defense minister in late February 1955.

On 28 February 1955, Israeli forces left forty-three Egyptian soldiers dead in a retaliatory raid in Gaza. This was a source of bitterness for Sharett, who had agreed to an operation he had supposed would take a toll of no more than ten enemy lives.[86] When Sharett protested to Ben-Gurion that such raids damaged Israel's chances of obtaining a treaty from the United States, the latter responded that first, matters of security were more important and second, if there was a contradiction between the two, considerations of security would prevail.[87]

Although Sharett sought to use the prospect of a guarantee to stay the activists in his government, he refused to deliberately create the impression among the Americans that they might be able to exploit differences between him and Ben-Gurion.[88] On 4 March, in the wake of the Gaza raid, Sharett told Ambassador Lawson, "I am not saying that this incident would have occured had Ben-Gurion been outside the government . . . Ben-Gurion and I are in complete accord."[89]

In fact, the United States embassy in Tel Aviv had in early January 1955 recommended that the State Department pursue a policy that might strengthen the position of Sharett and the moderates in his government.[90] The State Department had not acted upon this recommendation and the situation had now changed radically with Ben-Gurion's return and the Gaza Raid. At the beginning of March, Lawson reported that "the attack was designed to show the United Nations, the United States, and Great Britain that the Israeli government was reaching the end of its rope in following a policy of moderation."[91]

The Gaza raid was a turning point in the struggle between restraint and activism among Israel's leaders. On 2 March 1955, Sharett delivered a speech in the Knesset in which he further emphasized Israel's clearly Western strategic orientation,[92] but he confided to his diary that his foreign policy was sliding down the proverbial slippery slope.[93] The pretense of agreement with Ben-Gurion that he had presented to Lawson contrasted with the intensity of their struggle over the effect of retaliation on relations with the Western powers.[94] Sharett continued to pursue the goal of a security guarantee in the hope that it might provide a solution to both Israel's isolation and his own deteriorating political position. But the prime minister viewed Eban's enthusiasm with skepticism: the ambassador was "galloping" toward a treaty that if rejected would be a "disgrace to the government of Israel."[95]

As the United States and Britain prepared to launch the Alpha plan by taking Nasser into their confidence on the matter, quiet on the Israeli-Egyptian border became of paramount importance to them.[96] Dulles warned that a repetition of the Gaza raid would effect a "reorientation" in American policy[97] and insisted upon an Israeli commitment to end the policy of retaliation.[98] Prime Minister Sharett could not comply with this demand. On 29 March 1955, however, he was able to muster a vote in the government defeating a proposal by Ben-Gurion that Israel conquer the Gaza Strip, noting that such an invasion would destroy whatever chance Israel still had of receiving arms from the United States.[99] But the situation on the Gaza border made it impossible for him to relinquish Israel's right to retaliate.[100] At the end of March, Sharett authorized a final draft of the proposal formally committing Israel to requesting a guarantee from the United States, in the faint hope that this would mitigate Israel's security problem. Sharett's 12 April message to Dulles expressed Israel's desire for "a defense treaty between the United States and ourselves, such as would guarantee the territorial integrity of Israel and assure us an arms supply corresponding to that offered the Arab states."[101]

Sharett's note was an admission that Israel sought a security guarantee as protection not against Soviet aggression but against Israel's Arab neighbors, a position Ben-Gurion would adopt later that year in order to bring the parties to the left of Mapai into his government coalition. Thus while ostensibly still seeking integration into Western regional defense, Sharett argued, "We fully agree that the region's defenses against the possibility of external aggression must be buttressed but cannot contemplate with equanimity this being at the expense of our security and position within the region."[102]

Yaakov Herzog of the United States section of the Foreign Ministry criticized this approach, which in his eyes strayed far from the "constructive proposals" the Americans expected Israel to submit. Israel, he said, should demand military ties along the lines of those the United States had established with Iraq. What Israel was asking instead, Herzog pointed out, was an American treaty aimed against the very countries that the United States sought to bring into a Western alliance.[103]

The Israeli request in any case brought no tangible results. In his answer dated 16 April 1955, the secretary of state noted that the United States had never entered into any security treaty, except in the Western Hemisphere, unless the treaty was directed against communism. In the second place, a treaty would require Senate consent, an unlikely event given that such a treaty would involve the United States in a "highly inflammatory dispute."[104] Dulles extended a faint hope: although the United States would grant a guarantee only in the event that a peace settlement in the region was achieved, in his view such a settlement was at least feasible.[105] As we will observe, this slight chance provided the backdrop in Israel to the continued struggle over security policy as well as to the negotiations over the coalition that would emerge from Israel's elections of 1955.

Abba Eban lent the most optimistic interpretation to Dulles's message.[106] But when in mid-April 1955 United Press International (UPI) published the fact that Israel's representatives in Washington had announced that a treaty was imminent, Ben-Gurion took the embassy severely to task.[107] He did not object to the pursuit of a guarantee but reiterated his refusal to allow the United States to dictate Israel's security policy. The defense minister's unwillingness to permit Washington to dictate Israeli policy was not limited to the subject of retaliation to terrorist attacks. He would not, for example, countenance turning to the United States to force Egypt to comply with the principle of freedom of navigation. Israel would not depend upon American "license" to exercise its rights, and so Ben-Gurion took issue with Sharett's view of a security guarantee.[108] Furthermore, Ben-Gurion did not think Washington should force a peace settlement upon the Arabs. It was not the place of the United States to impose its will upon smaller countries. If the United States signed an agreement with Israel, he reasoned, the Arabs would in time come to terms with the Jewish state.[109]

Sharett was subjected to growing pressure from a number of quarters to resolve the question of relations with the United States. On 12 May 1955, he met with the Mapai contingent of the Knesset's Foreign Affairs and Security Committee. Meir Argov, chairman of the committee, told the prime minister that it was "time to wrap things up." Israel had presented its position and (presumably because no arms were forthcoming) it was time to pursue a more "independent" line vis-à-vis the United States.[110] On 17 May 1955, a mine laid near the southern border kibbutz of Kisufim killed three Israelis. The next day, Sharett, Ben-Gurion, Eshkol, Golda Myerson (later Meir), and Zalman Aran deliberated over the appropriate response.[111] Ben-Gurion pressed for a retaliatory attack along the lines of the February 1955 Gaza raid, whereas Sharett claimed that such an operation would deal a "death blow" to relations with the Western powers. Aran and Eshkol insisted that retaliation was imperative, although they favored a limited response that would not draw the enemy into a large-scale engagement. If it was in the interest of the United States to grant a security guarantee, said Aran, they would do so regardless of reprisal raids.[112] The group voted four to one, Sharett dissenting, in favor of a retaliatory raid the scope of which they did not immediately decide upon. In fact, on 30 May and before Israel responded to the mining incident at Kisufim, the Egyptians fired upon an Israeli patrol near the southern kibbutz of Nirim. Two Israelis were killed, and Israel and Egypt exchanged heavy artillery fire for several hours before the United Nations Mixed Armistice Commission (MAC) brought the sides to cease fire.[113]

Yet the crudest challenge to Sharett's policy of pursuing a treaty with the United States came from IDF chief-of-staff Moshe Dayan. Dayan warned against agreements with any of the great powers, as such arrangements would limit Israel's freedom of action. There was no need for a security guarantee, claimed Dayan; Israel would be ahead militarily for at least eight to ten years. As Sharett noted, Dayan rejected the security guarantee because he wanted war.[114] But as his political position became more precarious, Sharett leaned even more heavily upon the idea of obtaining a guarantee and pressed the Americans for a definite answer. In early May 1955, he sent Dulles a letter detailing exhaustively what the Israelis wanted in a guarantee, ending with a plea of urgency.[115] Sharett complained that neither the United States nor Britain would give him any "new cards" (to employ against his activist rivals) and it should come as no surprise if he were to resign following the upcoming elections.[116]

AHDUT HA'AVODA, MAPAM, AND THE COALITION NEGOTIATIONS OF 1955

The issue of a security guarantee from the United States played a major role in the formation of the government Ben-Gurion put together following Israel's elections of mid-1955. Israel's Western orientation was the sticking point in talks between Mapai and both of its negotiating partners on the left, but on the issue of activism, Mapam and Ahdut Ha'avoda diverged.[117] In 1954, the left-wing Mapam had split into its two original components, the Ahdut Ha'avoda faction emerging as an independent party. Mapam advocated neutralism in international affairs, although in practice this still meant support for the policies of the Soviet Union and opposition to those of the United States, but most members of Ahdut Ha'avoda had by this time moved away from the pro-Soviet line. And although in mid-1955 Mapai negotiated with both of these parties, the differences between the two factions exacerbated the division within Mapai. Sharett was thus in the uncomfortable position of being supported in his policy of restraint by the stridently anti-Western

Mapam,[118] whereas Ahdut Ha'avoda's openly militarist activism made it a willing and natural partner to Ben-Gurion.[119]

Because Ahdut Ha'avoda's leaders demanded abandonment of Israel's quest for American military aid,[120] Ben-Gurion's ambivalent approach toward a security guarantee made compromise with Mapai both feasible and desirable in their eyes, as it would bring the party closer to assuming the position of national leadership to which it aspired.[121] In talks with Ahdut Ha'avoda's Yigal Allon and Yisrael Galili in mid-August 1955, Ben-Gurion expressed deep concern over the nature of a treaty with the United States, telling his prospective coalition partners that in his view, if signed, such a treaty should in no way be permitted to limit Israel's freedom of action.[122] Ben-Gurion's assurances to his left-wing interlocutors placed him in apparent agreement with Sharett's earlier admission to the Americans that Israel sought a guarantee not against the Soviet Union but against its Arab neighbors: "Formally it would be agreed that we would help America if she were attacked, but everyone understands that America does not need our assistance. The guarantee we are seeking does not belong to American treaties against communism. We will not adhere to agreements directed against Russia." [123]

Ben-Gurion's stance facilitated the entry of the militant Ahdut Ha'avoda into the coalition. The meeting between Ben-Gurion and Allon ended in an agreement to disagree and Ahdut Ha'avoda remained firm in its rejection of a security guarantee from the United States. The crux of the matter, noted Ben-Gurion, was that while he *feared* that a guarantee would not be granted, Ahdut Ha'avoda *hoped* it would not be. But when Galili asked Ben-Gurion whether the quest for a security guarantee would be included in the basic policy lines of the new government, the latter replied in the negative. With this, the way was paved for Ahdut Ha'avoda's participation in the coalition.[124] Both sides understood that should a security guarantee from the United States materialize, Ahdut Ha'avoda and Mapam would leave the government. Yet Israel's chances of obtaining a security guarantee from the United States under an activist Ben-Gurion government were not great. Even Sharett was unwilling to comply with the American precondition that Israel commit itself to desist altogether from the use of force as a retaliatory measure. Ben-Gurion was far less likely to cede to such a demand, and the presence of Ahdut Ha'avoda in the government later that year would bolster his activist approach.

In late May 1955, Sharett demanded that Mapai decide upon the principal aims of Israeli foreign policy. Ben-Gurion refused on grounds of the danger that matters discussed in party meetings might be disclosed.[125] Sharett realized that even if his own moderate approach prevailed, the chances of obtaining a security guarantee were slight. Ben-Gurion's refusal to defer to the party made accommodation with the United States over the proper response to Arab provocations even less likely. Accordingly, Sharett told Eban on 3 August to refrain from applying pressure for a guarantee.[126] When Sharett and Ben-Gurion discussed the matter a week later, the former told the latter that as far as he was concerned, a security guarantee was now merely a "catch phrase." There was nothing to be gained, continued Sharett, by bandying the term about in public forums in Israel when the likelihood of a guarantee was so low.[127] The volatile Gaza border, the response Ben-Gurion insisted upon, and the tough approach toward Israel that Dulles pursued all bore out Sharett's gloomy appraisal.

Dulles cabled U.S. ambassador to Egypt Henry Byroade on 20 August 1955 that "with Israel under Ben-Gurion, calm may not last."[128] Meanwhile, the secretary took a hard line; Israel would get no guarantee until a settlement had been reached.[129] On 22 August, Lawson told Sharett that Dulles was about to deliver a speech expressing his views on an Arab-Israeli settlement.[130] But repeated Egyptian attacks again pitted Ben-Gurion against Sharett over the question of retaliation. Anticipation of the secretary's speech as well as an appeal for restraint by Elmore Jackson, an American Quaker serving as a communication channel between Jerusalem and Cairo, moved Sharett to cancel at the very last minute the destruction of the bridges along the Gaza-Rafiah road on 29 August.[131]

The recalling of commando squads already on their way brought Dayan to tender his resignation, with Ben-Gurion threatening to follow. Sharett was forced to acquiesce in an operation against the Egyptians at Khan Yunis, in Gaza, on 31 August 1955, which ended with seventy-two Egyptians dead and fifty-eight wounded.[132] Moreover, Dulles's 26 August speech was unpromising. The day before Dulles had delivered his speech, Sharett had warned Lawson that now his political opponents, including those in Mapai, would point to his policy of moderation and his failure to obtain a security guarantee from the United States and say "we told you so."[133] Now, the Foreign Ministry and the embassy in Washington engaged in a hair-splitting attempt to find positive points in Dulles's speech.[134] Indeed, Dulles did not entirely reject the possibility of granting Israel a security guarantee, but his reference to the need for border changes and the suggestion of a truncation of the Negev left Sharett little cause for optimism. The narrow opening Dulles left was, in Sharett's opinion, only meant to placate American Jewry. Accordingly, on 29 August he cabled Eban that "the entire issue of the security guarantee is without foundation and has been postponed until the coming of Elijah the Prophet because it depends upon border changes, of which there is no chance at all. . . . The only conclusion that can be drawn is that the main intention of the document is . . . to tell the Jews of America what they want to hear . . . while at the same time in fact removing it from the agenda indefinitely."[135]

The embassy in Washington nevertheless again attempted to convince Sharett that there was still a chance for a guarantee. Shiloah protested to the prime minister that Dulles would not have hinted at the possibility of a guarantee merely in order to appease American Jewry; elections in the United States were fourteen months away, and if the positive points in Dulles's speech were found to be devoid of content, then the impact upon the American Jewish community would be severe.[136] Sharett's view of the prospects of a guarantee remained dim despite the exhortations of the embassy in Washington to persist in the quest. The Israeli attempt to obtain a guarantee would probably have died quietly if not for the Czech arms deal, made public in late September 1955.

THE CZECH ARMS DEAL OF SEPTEMBER 1955

Soviet arms to the Nasser regime, which the Soviet Union supplied through Czechoslovakia, brought about a radical change in the Middle East balance of power and were a profound shock to Israel.[137] According to the terms of the deal, Egypt would pay in cotton and rice for some two hundred jets, one hundred heavy tanks, torpedo boats, submarines, and a large quantity of heavy artillery, small arms, and ammunition.[138] As Sharett pointed out to Eban, the main issue for Israel now was arms, not a security guarantee.[139] But Sharett also told Eban that if the security guarantee could be obtained *in addition* to arms, it was still a salient goal, and in his own contacts with the Americans, the prime minister too continued to advance the idea of a guarantee.[140] He still hoped as well that even the prospect of a guarantee might serve as a brake on his defense minister's activist policy once Ben-Gurion became prime minister in November.[141]

At the beginning of October 1955 Isser Harel, head of the Mossad, reported to Sharett that the CIA encouraged the Israelis to strike at Nasser. Sharett's diary entry of 4 October 1955 indicates his complete opposition to a preventive strike. What the CIA told Harel, noted Sharett, did not concur with Dulles's warning to Eban, also issued at the beginning of October 1955, that Israel not attack.[142] Accordingly, on 5 October Sharett told the Knesset's Foreign Affairs and Security Committee that a recent speech by Dulles in which the secretary of state refered to "threatened countries" was not a green light for Israel to go to war.[143]

During the first three weeks of October 1955, the formation of a coalition as well as a temporary illness prevented Ben-Gurion from devoting his full attention to security matters. But on 23 October, Ben-Gurion and Dayan drew up plans for a preventive strike (named Operation Omer) to be carried out at the beginning of January 1956, before Egypt absorbed the Soviet arms. Such an attack would involve taking the straits at Eilat, a move Cairo would not be able to "swallow" as it did the retaliatory raids.[144]

Ben-Gurion's diary from that period has been lost, so no protocol of the defense minister's 23 October 1955 meeting with Dayan is available, but Ben-Gurion's decision not to attack Egypt at this time may have been for two reasons. First, he feared the ostracism of the Western powers, which would not accept the validity of an Israeli strike on grounds of an imbalance in arms. Second, he placed some hope in Dulles's comments at a press conference on 30 October indicating a willingness to consider selling Israel defensive arms.[145] Despite his ambivalence regarding such an operation, Ben-Gurion brought the proposal before the Israeli government at the beginning of November 1955. The government rejected it.[146]

Dulles was well aware of the pressure to which Israel was now subject— a U.S. intelligence estimate of 12 October 1955 noted that "in the absence of convincing evidence of Western determination to preserve the territorial status quo, there is very real danger that Israel will undertake preventive war"—but he remained determined to avoid having to grant a security guarantee.[147] The American problem of policy toward Israel was connected with new problems that the Czech arms deal posed the Western powers. The British urged the United States to join the Baghdad Pact, but Dulles answered that to do so would necessitate granting Israel a security guarantee, because of the reaction that joining the pact would create on the American political scene.[148] This is what the State Department wished to avoid at all costs, and the best the United States would do for the Israelis was to assure them that they were "not without friends and helpless." The secretary suggested giving Israel a firm reaffirmation of the Tripartite Declaration; this was totally unacceptable to the Israelis.[149]

Dulles was prepared to lend "teeth" to the effort to restrain Israel even in its distress. On 20 October 1955, the U.S. National Security Council debated the appropriate response in the event that Israel initiated hostilities. The U.S. Joint Chiefs of Staff opposed American military involvement in the event of an Arab-Israeli war. Vice President Richard M. Nixon favored the employment of an economic blockade, noting that Israel would succumb rapidly to such pressure, and Dulles agreed that this was in fact the only American option should Israel strike at Egypt.[150] When Lawson suggested to the prime minister that Dayan's sudden return to Israel from vacation in late October seemed to portend "preventive action," Sharett disingenuously explained that Dayan was "at that moment in consultation with the cabinet, which was engaged in the unhappy task of deciding which categories of the national budget must suffer diversion of funds for arms purchases."[151]

THE RENEWED ATTEMPT TO OBTAIN ARMS AND A GUARANTEE

On 12 October 1955, Sharett delivered an emotional call in the Knesset for arms to Israel.[152] Eban, meanwhile, told Sharett and the Israeli ambassadors gathered in Paris that key U.S. senators supported granting Israel a guarantee,[153] ostensibly reason enough to continue to press for the treaty. Despite his pessimism, Sharett prepared the ground for another attempt to obtain the guarantee by reiterating at a press conference in Paris on 25 October (during the four-power meetings there) the importance for Israel of this goal.[154]

At the end of October 1955, Sharett met twice with Dulles and asked the secretary of state to grant Israel an unconditional security guarantee. Sharett argued that it was untenable that the Soviet Union enjoy detente with the West in one part of the world while creating danger in another.[155] He wished to resolve the question of the guarantee once and for all and told Dulles that if the treaty were not feasible, Israel would prefer that discussion of the matter be permanently terminated.[156] Dulles did not, at their first meeting on 26 October, explicitly reject the request for a guarantee, but his answer was not encouraging, and it may be assumed that an Israeli leadership under less stress would not have pushed beyond this point. Nevertheless, Eban wished

to keep alive even the slimmest hope of a guarantee and urged Sharett to propose a rewritten version of the Tripartite Declaration, so that the prime minister would not return home empty-handed. Sharett rejected this approach.[157]

On 27 October 1955, Eban reported that Russell had told him not to give
up on a treaty,[158] and in another meeting with Dulles on 31 October, Sharett
again presented the Israeli case. Israel wanted arms that Sharett termed "pro-
nouncedly defensive in nature": antiaircraft and antisubmarine systems.[159] As
for the security guarantee, wrote Sharett, "I repeated that if his heart was not
in it and if it was not a viable question, it would be better for us to stop talking about it, and I moved over to the . . . effect of just talking about a security
agreement on our relations with the Soviet Union, and how we had lost everything there without gaining a thing from the United States." [160]

Dulles's response was a blow to the Israelis. On arms the United States
could give no answer at present. Washington was not sure that the Arabs intended to attack Israel, and Dulles did not think that the president wished to
present a proposal for a security guarantee to Congress for approval. If Sharett
compelled the United States to give a yes or no answer on a guarantee at this
point, the answer would be no. The secretary also warned the Israelis not
to conclude that a preventive war was in their interest; this would compromise their relationship with the United States.[161] In fact, intimated Dulles,
the only thing Israel could count on was the assurance that the United States
would not permit the destruction of the Jewish state. For the Israelis, this was
the unsettlingly ephemeral promise of a "shield for Israel against aggression *if
and when* the armed strength of the Arab states significantly increased." [162]

On 3 November 1955, the new Israeli government under Prime Minister
Ben-Gurion struck at Egypt in order to settle the border dispute at Al Auja.
The one-sided battle left fifty Egyptians dead. Sharett reflected that such a
blow strained the credibility of Israel's image as a beleaguered little country.[163]
Despite the depressing results of his meetings with Dulles and Ben-Gurion's
latest demonstration of activism, Sharett still retained a shred of hope regarding a security guarantee. At a meeting of the Foreign Ministry staff on
8 November 1955, he rejected the demand that the guarantee be removed
entirely from Israel's foreign policy agenda. It would from this point on be
completely subordinated to arms procurement, said Sharett, but it would remain a goal in Israel's efforts in Washington.[164] In truth, American public
opinion did not allow Dulles to remove the question of a security guarantee
from his own agenda, and it was for this reason that Dulles was unhappy at
the prospect of a visit by Sharett to the United States in November 1955. The

State Department considered the visit "a most serious problem. It is obviously an effort on his part to . . . force the administration into a policy of supporting Israel in a manner which will antagonize the entire Arab world and allow the Soviet Union to become dominant in that area."[165]

In order to head off such an eventuality and the inevitable deterioration of the American position in the Arab world, Dulles instructed his subordinates to put pressure on Eban, who could, he believed, have a "moderating effect" on his government.[166] But even Eban took an uncharacteristically militant line when, in early November 1955, he noted suggestions in the American press that now was the time to pressure a "frightened Israel" into making far-reaching territorial concessions. Eban reiterated that Israel would make no such concessions and predicted that he "would not live to see serious changes in Israel's frontiers."[167]

It was in this context that British prime minister Anthony Eden's speech at Guildhall on 9 November 1955 created such alarm in Israel.[168] The speech included an explicit call for Israel to acquiesce in a truncation of its territory. The Israelis feared that this was a blatant attempt to isolate them from the Western world.[169] Ben-Gurion instructed the Foreign Ministry to determine whether the United States agreed with the speech.[170] Eban told the Americans that Israel would not give up the Negev or any part of it. The West could "bless every day" the absence of territorial contiguity that would allow freedom of passage of communist technicians and Soviet arms to the entire Arab world, as well as the establishment of a military command that would operate against not only Israel but also the West.[171]

Thus when Sharett met Dulles on 21 November 1955, he told the secretary that Israel would not allow itself to be cut in half through the Negev.[172] Sharett did not bother to bring up the matter of a security guarantee. Several days earlier, the Israelis had asked Washington for a large quantity of modern arms, including forty-eight F-86 jets, sixty Patton tanks and forty 105-mm howitzers,[173] and Sharett's letter to Dulles on the eve of his 12 December departure from the United States was a further appeal for these arms.[174] Dulles would agree only that Israel should get "something" and answered Sharett in the most convoluted manner possible.[175] The fact that the secretary did not give a clear negative answer to the arms request left the Israelis to believe that at some point arms would be forthcoming.[176]

Meanwhile, Israel on the night of 11 December 1955 launched a reprisal raid across the border on the northeastern shore of Lake Kinneret that left twenty-six Syrians dead.[177] The U.S. embassy in Tel Aviv believed that the sale of heavy arms to Israel was under serious consideration and viewed the Kinneret raid as the height of folly: "Coming on the eve of a U.S. decision on arms availability for Israel, this operation is explicable only as a first class Israeli blunder or a decision to go it alone."[178]

In fact, it appears that the United States did not intend to supply the arms Israel had requested.[179] But because both Ben-Gurion and Sharett believed that there was still a possibility,[180] the Kinneret raid was further proof to Sharett that Ben-Gurion jeopardized such chances by pursuing an aggressively activist policy.[181] The three Western powers placed an arms embargo upon Israel in response to the Kinneret operation. Yet George Allen of the State Department further heightened the impression among the Israelis that arms from the United States might in the future be forthcoming by telling Eban two days after the operation that it was in view of the raid that the United States could not at that moment give Israel an answer.[182]

By early 1956, Foreign Minister Sharett was devoting himself entirely to the procurement of arms from the United States, rejecting further talk of a security guarantee. From early January until late March 1956, the Israeli embassy in Washington made repeated and increasingly agitated applications to the State Department for arms. On 16 January 1956, Sharett again petitioned Dulles for arms, promising that the weapons would be used for defensive purposes only.[183] Several days later, Sharett made sure that Lawson knew it was only arms he was after: "The time for decision has arrived for the United States and Israel. [For Israel] to trust outside guarantees would be irresponsible. In the first place, there is none; if they existed, they could not avail against a swift blitz which could destroy Tel Aviv or Haifa in a matter of hours."[184] As far as Sharett was concerned, the United States could supply arms in secret or agree even only in principle. However, the foreign minister's note to the Americans reflected his deteriorating political position: "The United States must decide in a manner consistent with its traditional sense of fair play and its responsibilities to those nations, large and small, which have chosen to cast their lot with the West. Israel must know where it is going."[185]

FAILURE TO OBTAIN ARMS AND A GUARANTEE: SHARETT RESIGNS

The Israeli embassy in Washington understood that it was pointless to again broach the matter of the security guarantee with either the Americans or Sharett. But Eban saw a final hope for Israel with regard to arms: Israel would prove that the failure of Robert Anderson—Eisenhower's personal envoy, who was preparing the groundwork for another attempt at a U.S.-mediated settlement between Israel and Egypt [186] — was entirely the fault of the Egyptians. [187] Dulles seems to have anticipated this and urged Anderson to do all within his power to achieve a settlement so that the United States would not be morally obliged to provide Israel with arms. [188] On 10 February 1956, Eban confronted Dulles and asked whether Washington was merely delaying or planning to reject altogether the Israeli request for arms. Dulles's response was evasive but essentially negative. Progress toward peace had been made, he said, because the administration had so far not supplied arms to Israel. [189] When Eban met Dulles again on 2 March, the two engaged in recriminations that bore testimony to the ragged state of American-Israeli relations and to the bitterness of the Israelis toward U.S. policy. [190]

On 29 February 1956, Lawson met with Sharett and Ben-Gurion and reported that the latter had been close to tears. There was no mention of a security guarantee, but on arms the Israelis wanted a "yes or no answer. If the answer is no, please let it be now." According to Lawson, Ben-Gurion was very near a decision that would determine Israel's foreign policy for some time (Ben-Gurion's diary from this period is missing; Sharett's 29 February diary entry notes only the fact that the meeting took place and the American ambassador did not elaborate on what he thought this decision might be). [191] Ben-Gurion appealed the same day directly to Eisenhower for arms, noting that "in the absence of a positive response from the United States, we find it well-nigh impossible to get arms from any other country in the free world." [192] Eisenhower on 13 March 1956 noted in his diary that the Israelis wanted American arms in order to turn the United States into "a virtual ally in any trouble they might get into." [193]

Nevertheless, the president wavered momentarily, considered selling Israel jets, then made no reply. On 16 March 1956, Ben-Gurion again wrote to Eisenhower. The answer, which Eisenhower sent only on 30 April, was perfunctory: The president was "not persuaded that it would serve the cause of peace and stability in the world for the United States to accede to your request for arms." [194]

Foreign Minister Sharett felt most keenly of all the failure to achieve a security guarantee or to acquire arms from the United States. He had hoped all along that receipt of a security guarantee and at least some arms from the United States would aid him in opposing the increasing activism that Ben-Gurion pursued. Ambassador Lawson summarized Sharett's position well in a report he submitted in early March 1956:

Sharett's bitterness reflected his reaction to the collapse of his pro-Western orientation and of a foreign policy which placed reliance on the United States. He finds in ashes his basic approach to the problem of Soviet arms to the Arabs, which was one of maintaining a workable defense posture through the acquisition of a minimal number of high quality defensive arms from the United States . . . Sharett is now defenseless against accusations of his opponents within and without the Cabinet who, since October last, have argued that Sharett's moderate approach and trust in the United States would be betrayed.[195]

At a 3 April 1956 meeting of Ben-Gurion, Sharett, Dayan, and Director General Shimon Peres of the Defense Ministry, Sharett's close identification with the failure of procurement efforts in the United States was the subject of sharp confrontation. Ben-Gurion ordered an end to all arms procurement efforts in the United States, even those pertaining to U.S. agreement to arms deals with other countries.[196] Sharett had in mid-March requested that the government allow several more weeks to elapse before making such a decision, in the hope that the United States might provide arms.[197] The decision marked the end of this period, and Sharett resigned on 18 June 1956 over his profound differences with Ben-Gurion.[198]

Ben-Gurion's call to cease contact with the United States on the subject of arms did not preclude efforts on the part of the Israeli embassy in Washington to obtain ammunition and spare parts, and from April 1956 on, the United States affirmed a number of contracts for these.[199] The embassy was greatly disappointed at the failure to obtain more significant armament from the United States and emphasized the importance of these limited shipments,[200] but only in September 1956 did the United States authorize a very modest sale to Israel of five helicopters, twenty-five half-tracks, and some one hundred machine guns.[201] When Dulles met the foreign ministers of the NATO countries in May 1956, he urged the French and Italians to provide arms to Israel.[202] By this time France needed no American urging. Indeed, large-scale arms deals with France meant that during the summer and fall of 1956, Israel focused its attention primarily upon its relationship with France. The Foreign Ministry documents of the Israeli State Archives also indicate that Ben-Gurion during the summer of 1956 had the embassy in Washington attempt to secure American authorization for the sale of F-86 jets from Canada. The United States refused Israel's initial request to purchase twenty-four of these jets in July 1954, as well as Israel's application for the purchase of forty-eight such aircraft in November 1955, in the wake of the Czech arms deal. The United States granted this authorization on 13 August 1956,[203] but the Canadian government agreed to the sale only in late September. By that time, the Israelis had purchased seventy-two Mystère-4A jet aircraft from France.[204] The Israeli Air Force did not want to purchase another type of jet, and in any case, Israel could not afford the jets that Canada now offered in addition to those from France.[205]

The documents also suggest that the embassy relegated efforts to obtain a $75-million loan from the U.S. Export-Import bank to a distant second place on its agenda. After the Sinai campaign, as we shall see, the embassy in Washington was forced to lobby intensively for this vital loan at a time when the embassy staff wished instead to concentrate its efforts upon achieving strategic cooperation with the United States.

CONCLUSION

Three factors characterized U.S.-Israel relations from early 1953 to the fall of 1956. The first is that during this period American and Israeli regional policies were at odds. The second is that failure to obtain either an American security guarantee or arms in no way mitigated the centrality to Israel of the United States. The third factor, which leads us to Israel's relations with the other Western powers, is that Israel's inability to ensure its security with either arms or a guarantee from the United States assured that arms from Britain and France would become a vital concern of Israeli foreign policy.

The disparity in American and Israeli goals is most evident in the fact that the Israelis could obtain arms and a security guarantee from the United States neither by demanding them in order to counter the Soviet threat nor by claiming that only thus could Israel achieve parity with the Arab states. In truth, the Israelis realized that a strategic link with the United States was potentially dangerous, especially if such a connection came at Israel's initiative. This was because to publicly proclaim alignment with America's global security efforts, which were mainly anti-Soviet in nature, could jeopardize Soviet and East European Jewry, whose fate was so important to Israel's leadership.[206]

Yet when during the 1955 coalition negotiations Ben-Gurion stressed to the leaders of Ahdut Ha'avoda that the government would seek a security guarantee from the United States only in defense against Israel's Arab neighbors and not against the Soviet Union, his assurance to them was in fact disingenuous: such a security guarantee would have been a political impossibility for the United States. The Americans were loath to grant Israel even a security guarantee formulated in anti-Soviet terms; the chances of a U.S. guarantee of Israel specifically against the Arabs were virtually nil. Indeed, the Americans in late June 1955 were much impressed by Egyptian foreign minister Mahmoud Fawzi's warning that the United States would do itself "irreparable harm" in its relations with every Arab state if Israel obtained a treaty.[207] Furthermore, the United States during this entire period[208] considered Israel the more aggressive of the parties to the Arab-Israeli conflict; in late 1955 and early 1956 Washington weighed the possibility of severe economic sanctions should Israel launch a preventive attack on Egypt. Moreover, the consistent American view of the arms balance was of a situation favorable to Israel. The United States revised this view of Israeli preponderance in arms only in early 1956, at least three months after the signing of the Czech arms deal.

The Israeli failure to obtain either a treaty with or arms from the United States never diminished the centrality of that power in Israeli eyes. Eban and Shiloah often felt that in order to forge a closer relationship with the United States they had also to overcome obstacles created by their own superiors. They feared that the American refusal to provide arms or a security guarantee would alter the Israeli leadership's view of the paramount nature of Israel's long-term relationship with the United States. In fact, this was not so. Ben-Gurion's position on activism in no way meant that he had retracted his recognition of this fact. His attitude, especially in comparing the reality of arms from France to his continued hopes for arms from the United States, will be demonstrated in all of the following chapters.

The exigency of weapons procurement dictated the cultivation of an arms relationship with both Britain and France. And whereas the Israelis' view of ties with Washington and of American leadership of the free world allowed them to contemplate a treaty with the United States, we will now see that Israel could realistically consider no such arrangement with Britain or France. Although after the Suez crisis, Israel continued its pursuit of a strategic relationship with the United States, both before and after the 1956 conflict Israel acquired virtually all of its armament from France and Britain. Thus the failure to obtain either arms or a security guarantee from the United States clearly illustrates that in its relations with the Western powers, Israel had no alternatives to France and Britain.

2 ANGLO-ISRAELI
STRATEGIC RELATIONS
1952–1956

From 1952 to 1956, Britain sold arms to all of the countries of the Middle East, whereas the United States would sell arms only in the framework of Western regional defense. Thus Israel had to seek arms from Britain, even though its intensive procurement efforts in London during these four years met with very limited success.[1] By the time of the Suez-Sinai campaign in 1956, Israel had succeeded in purchasing twenty-four Meteor jets, a few score old Sherman tanks, most of which were scrap hulks, and two World War II vintage destroyers. The Israelis considered the Meteors nearly obsolete as early as 1952, but they had no choice but to buy them. Moreover, Britain refused to supply Israel with one of the most advanced tanks of that period, the Centurion, although by 1955 the British had supplied forty-one of these tanks to Israel's best-armed rival, Egypt. Indeed, Britain was so careful not to augment Israel's military capability past a limit set by London's policy makers that it refused to sell Israel parachutes on the very eve of British-Israeli cooperation in the Suez-Sinai campaign. This was the result of a consistent British policy of attempting to prevent Israel from developing a paratroop force by objecting to France's sale to Israel of Noratlas transport planes as well as parachutes.[2] Here was a paradox we shall explore, that even while the British sold so little weaponry to Israel, the Israelis had to persevere in their efforts to obtain arms from Britain.

BRITISH ARMS POLICY IN THE MIDDLE EAST

Israel's relationship with Britain was delicate because Jerusalem's arms procurement efforts in London had to be balanced with Israeli policies that were often diametrically opposed to Britain's interests in the Middle East: defense of the British position on the Suez Canal and preservation of influence in Jordan and Iraq.[3] A study of Anglo-Israeli relations from 1952 until the Suez crisis of 1956 must take into account the great degree of ambivalence that characterized this relationship. Sharett's message to U.S. Secretary of Defense George Marshall in December 1950 that Israel was "anxious to contribute as effectively as possible to the security of the region" elicited the admonition that Israel be more explicit about its "willingness to talk with the English" about regional defense. Israel's apparent desire to "let mandate bygones be bygones" was partly the result of an American warning that "if anything should happen there will anyway only be English in the Middle East."[4] A visit to Israel by Britain's General Robertson in early 1951 was to have advanced a British plan for an alliance with Israel, but this plan, which envisioned British bases in either Gaza or Israel itself, evoked the deep suspicions of Prime Minister David Ben-Gurion, who was unwilling to tie Israel to either Britain's defenses in the Middle East or any binding military attachments.[5] Thus Israel rejected this strategic overture on the part of the British.

For Israel, however, the "litmus test" of its relationship with the Western powers was the willingness of any one of them to supply arms, and on this score, Britain claimed to occupy a "middle ground" between the United States and France.[6] Washington considered Israel more than a match for the Arabs in all categories of major offensive arms and the region's potential troublemaker.[7] The British embassy in Washington noted at the end of 1954 the French view that Israeli inferiority in manpower and geography justified steadily increasing French arms sales to Israel, a policy to which the British took exception.[8] Britain's policy was, in its own view, "to build up goodwill generally in both the Arab states and Israel by supplying arms. . . . At the same time we wish to apply this policy with moderation so that the overall ratio between both sides is kept on a reasonable basis and within the practical means of the states concerned."[9]

In fact, the Foreign Office candidly explained this policy to the Israeli military attaché in London in early 1954, noting that U.K. arms sales involved a discussion of each proposed transaction by the different offices involved, with the final decision being at the discretion of the Foreign Office. The Foreign Office thus informed the Israelis that Britain would deal with each of their requests on its own merits and would consider each type of weapon (planes, tanks, artillery, etc.) in light of British figures on relative strengths in that particular category.[10] Such a policy allowed Britain to employ a "carrot and stick" method with regard to arms supplies, as London attempted to influence Israel's policy makers to exercise restraint toward Britain's Arab allies.[11]

There were limits to Britain's leverage over Israel through arms sales. Britain resented France's violations of agreements reached in the framework of the Near East Arms Coordinating Committee,[12] yet the British complained that they were "the traditional suppliers of military equipment to Israel and the Middle East, and could not accept . . . a yardstick decreed by the NEACC."[13] Britain's dilemma was not lost on the Israelis, who thought that the British would continue to sell Israel at least some arms for two main reasons: Britain's fierce competition with France over Middle East arms markets for both political and financial reasons[14] and London's policy of maintaining a military balance between the states of the region.[15] Both of these factors caused Britain's disinclination to impose an extended arms embargo on the countries of the Middle East.

Yet British arms policies remained a major source of concern for Israel. Even when France seriously undermined the NEACC in Israel's favor in 1956, Israel's needs dictated that Britain remain a target for Israeli procurement, especially in the area of armor, because only the United States and Britain produced the heavy tanks Israel wished to acquire. Furthermore, Britain's arms sales in the region made it imperative that Israel increase its efforts to convince the British to limit supplies to Israel's Arab enemies, despite London's objections to Jerusalem's "interference."[16] And finally, the growing potential for conflict between Israel and Britain as a result of Israeli retaliation against Jordan both posed a direct threat to Israeli security and placed arms purchases from Britain in jeopardy.

A certain warming in Israel's attitude toward Britain in 1951 has prompted one researcher to claim that this "was the beginning of a military under-standing between Britain and Israel culminating in the Anglo-Israeli joint operation in the Sinai in 1956."[17] In truth, Anglo-Israeli cooperation over the Suez crisis was "episodic." True, in 1952 Ben-Gurion hoped that the return to power of the Conservatives might effect a change in Israel's relations with Britain.[18] In addition, the possibility of Israeli involvement in a Middle East defense alliance under Anglo-American aegis came up again at the end of 1952,[19] and documents in the Israeli State Archives show that the issue of a strategic link specifically with Britain resurfaced briefly in 1954. However, the partnership of late 1956 hardly flowed from a strategic understanding. Anglo-Israeli relations deteriorated considerably prior to cooperation in late 1956, and the main thrust of Israeli policy toward Britain during the four years be-fore the Sinai campaign was, as noted, the procurement of arms.

There was some interest in London in accommodating Israel as well as stabilizing the Arabs into a pro-Western alignment.[20] However, Britain had signed the Tripartite Declaration in May 1950, the most important aspect of which was the arms clause, in which Britain figured centrally.[21] On that score, Israel had cause for worry. Britain had sold jets to Egypt even before the sign-ing of the declaration, making that country the only state in the Middle East to possess jet aircraft. The exigencies of the Korean War brought a tempo-rary halt to the delivery of jets, and in fact, the Egyptians received only 35 of 105 ordered,[22] but when in December 1950 the British turned down an Israeli request for jets, the Israelis felt that London was supplying "everyone except Israel."[23] In truth, the British had halted sales of both jets and tanks to all countries in the region. By mid-1952, however, Britain could once again contemplate diverting jet fighters for sale in the Middle East.[24]

THE ARMS RACE

Toward the end of 1952, it became clear to Israel that a dangerous arms race was developing in the region and that Britain was the primary source. In October of that year, the British decided to resume the sale of jets to the Middle East, a move prompted primarily by their desire to forge a closer re-lationship with the new regime in Egypt[25] but also by the urgent need to develop foreign arms markets.[26] The British offered Egypt, Lebanon, Syria, and Israel fourteen Meteor fighters each, and Iraq was to receive fourteen (roughly equivalent) Vampire fighter jets.[27] Britain did not offer Jordan jets because it was clear that Amman could not afford to purchase and maintain these aircraft and because in the British view, Jordan would in any case rely upon its treaty with Britain.[28] In November 1952, the Foreign Office informed Israel that delivery of the jets could begin before April 1953.[29]

British policy presented the Israelis with a dilemma. It became apparent that for purposes of a military balance, Britain viewed each of the Arab states as a separate unit to be weighed against Israel, whereas the Israelis held the position that the Arab states must be considered a single unit.[30] The Israelis realized that they could not maintain a quantitative balance—Israeli intelligence calculated that by the beginning of 1954 the combined Arab air forces would comprise 360 fighters, 120 of them jets[31]—so they resolved to create a qualitative edge.[32] The supply of Meteors would stymie this effort. The Meteor was no longer a state-of-the-art plane, and the Israeli Air Force (IAF) intended to delay the purchase of jets until it could obtain a more advanced model.[33] The sale of Meteors to the Arab states would force an economically hard-pressed Israel to invest in an inferior jet[34] and at the same time tilt the strategic balance in the region against it.[35]

It was for these reasons that the Israeli government delayed authorization of the purchase of Meteors until 25 November 1952.[36] Israel's policy makers had little hope of staying Britain's decision. However, Israel's unsuccessful remonstrations in London pointed up the difficulty involved in its attempts to forestall sales to the Arabs.[37] First, Israel attempted to justify a balance more favorable to it by stating its willingness to deploy arms provided it in a Western defense scheme. Second, the Israelis demanded that no arms be sold to the Arab states until those countries were willing to sign peace agreements with Israel. Third, claimed Israel, the internal instability of the Arab regimes made the sale of arms to those countries a highly dubious proposition.[38] Fourth, the Israelis expressed the fear that although the Arab arsenals lacked bombers, jet fighters Britain provided could be used to drop bombs on Israel. Finally, Israel emphasized its preference of a complete embargo of arms to the Middle East to a Western policy of balancing each Arab state separately against Israel.[39]

In response, the British Foreign Office made clear that an embargo would violate both Britain's obligations regarding the arms clause of the Tripartite Declaration and British obligations toward those countries with which Britain had treaties.[40] William Strang, permanent undersecretary at the Foreign Office, bluntly told Israeli ambassador Eliahu Elath that Britain's treaties with Arab states were no business of Israel's.[41] However, not all British officials were oblivious of Britain's interest in soothing Israel's fears. In October, the British embassy in Tel Aviv wrote, "They [the Israelis] are not pulling a fast one. I realize how essential it is for us to get on good terms with the Egyptians if we are to hold on to our Canal base. . . . But if in the end we are unable to come to terms . . . we shall need help in this part of the world that only the Israelis could provide."[42]

This evaluation notwithstanding, Foreign Secretary Anthony Eden in late January 1953 strongly protested the public relations campaign the Israelis had been conducting in Britain and in the United States against British arming of the Arabs. In Eden's view, the Anglo-Israeli dialogue on arms sales was to deal only with the "nuts and bolts" of the sales themselves. The Foreign Office would take a dim view of further Israeli démarches against Britain's policies in the region, including the sale of arms to Egypt, through which the British intended to prepare the ground for negotiations over the Suez Canal with the Neguib regime.[43]

Israeli insistence that the supply of Meteors had sparked an arms race prompted Eden's aide memoire stating, "It should not be assumed that the decision to release these aircraft necessarily heralds or provides precedent for further releases of jet aircraft to Mideastern states."[44] As we will observe, the opposite was true. The Meteor deal provided the catalyst for a sharp increase in the arms procurement efforts of the Middle East states. The immediate effect was apparent in the purchase requests of Israel and Syria, which had clashed sharply over their border in mid-1951,[45] but by late 1954, a more serious arms race developed between Israel and Egypt.

As Sharett had already made clear, the Israelis would demand jets in order first to close the gap with Egypt and then to create a more favorable balance vis-à-vis all of the Arab states in view of the Meteor deal.[46] Accordingly, on 23 December 1952, Israel requested an additional fifteen Meteors.[47] The Israeli armament effort was not limited to aircraft, however, and in June 1953 the Israeli government put in a request with Vickers Armstrongs manufacturers for thirty Centurion tanks.[48]

Israel's potential as a market meant that initially British policy toward it was favorable. At a Defense Committee discussion of 6 May 1953, the Foreign Office decided that it would be United Kingdom policy to help Israel build up its armed forces. The British Ministry of Supply was eager to sell Centurions in order to maintain volume of production, and in pressing their case for selling these tanks to Israel, the ministry noted that the Israelis considered the Centurions (a medium tank far superior to either the British Churchill or the American Sherman) a test case of the West's good intentions toward Israel.[49] The Foreign Office felt at this point that twenty to thirty Centurion tanks would not give Israel an undue advantage;[50] it was supposed that Syria and Iraq would quickly close the gap,[51] and there was small chance that Jordan would ever be able to keep abreast of Israel in expensive modern weapons.[52] The British had also become aware through meetings of the NEACC that the Israelis were considering purchase of the French AMX-13 light tank.[53] The Ministries of Supply and Defense were concerned lest refusing Israel Centurions lose the Israeli arms market for Britain.[54]

The Foreign Office raised a number of points that militated against granting the Israeli request for tanks. Both the Americans and the French, in the framework of the NEACC, objected to the sale, even when Britain proposed reducing the number to ten.[55] Furthermore, the British War Office became increasingly anxious lest the sale seriously damage relations with Jordan and Iraq.[56] When in September 1953 the Syrians backed out of a Centurion deal with Britain because they could not afford the tanks,[57] the British felt that this removed justification for supply to Israel.

The British also began to express concern at Israeli demands of "alarming proportions."[58] In mid-1953 Israel possessed some 315 artillery pieces, compared with 567 for the Arab states as a whole. Already, in the British estimation, Israel had about twice the artillery of any one Arab country, and compliance with the combined Israeli requests from the United States, Britain, and France would allow Israel a total of 479 artillery pieces. Because Israel had an advantage in handling these weapons, this would afford the Israelis a marked superiority over any or all of the Arab states.[59] The Foreign Office viewed Israeli orders for tanks in this light, and in what was in effect a reversal of a previous willingness to augment Israel's armored capability noted that the only point in favor of supplying the tanks to Israel was the need for foreign orders.[60] Thus of a total of 38 tanks on order by Israel, the Foreign Office recommended the release of only 8 Centaur light tanks.[61]

THE KIBYE RAID

Britain's decision to curtail arms to Israel preceded Israel's Kibye raid against Jordan of 14 October 1953, but the operation provided the Foreign Office with a convenient pretext.[62] On 2 December 1953, the Foreign Office authorized the sale to Israel of 6 Meteors and 20 Mosquitos, as this was part of a previous agreement and was accompanied by the sale to Syria of an additional 12 Meteors,[63] but it turned down a new Israeli request on 24 November 1953 for the purchase of 50 Sherman tanks.[64] This boded ill for Israeli procurement in Britain. By mid-1954, Israel's three-year armament plan called for the acquisition of 150 fully armed Shermans,[65] but the British were willing to sell Shermans only if they were scrap hulks and would release no more than 10 operable units.[66] The Foreign Office knew that the Israelis would turn increasingly to Paris for procurement but felt that "this risk must be accepted in view of the paramount importance of preventing the undue strengthening of Israel relative to its neighbors."[67]

The fallout from the Kibye operation was not limited to arms supply. In Ambassador Elath's estimation, the British would exploit the tension in order to press the Jordanians into accepting an increase in British troop strength, a move designed to find new stations for British troops that would evacuate the Suez Canal once an agreement was signed with Egypt.[68] He noted that the Foreign Office had in the past approached him about such an increase, seeking Israeli assent and presenting it as a boon to Israeli security. But increased British strength in Jordan as a result of an incident such as the Kibye raid had dangerous implications for Israel. Selwyn Lloyd, British minister of state, warned of the possible consequences should Jordan again challenge Britain to fulfill its treaty obligations. In Elath's words, "Even if the treaty is not invoked, even if it does not come to open war, it can still spell calamity for a small country like Israel to find itself at odds with Britain (and inevitably also with other great powers), who have no need of war to do us incalculable injury."[69] The Anglo-Jordanian Treaty was not originally meant to be used as a stick against Israel.[70] But following the Kibye operation and with the steady deterioration of the situation on the Israeli-Jordanian border, this was not to be the case in the future.

THE ANGLO-EGYPTIAN AGREEMENT OF 1954

In July 1954 Britain's reaching an agreement with Egypt that stipulated the final withdrawal of all British forces from that country by June 1956 heightened Israel's fears. The Anglo-Egyptian Agreement provided for the removal of a buffer vital to Israeli security[71] and kept alive the possibility that the United States and Britain might eventually be successful in drawing Egypt into a regional defense pact.[72] Several weeks before the signing of the agreement on 19 October 1954, the British lifted their partial arms embargo on Egypt[73] in effect since October 1951, when Cairo had denounced the 1936 treaty with Britain.[74] Coupled with the end of the embargo was what Israel believed to be the opportunity given Egypt to purchase equipment at the large base at Suez, including radar facilities.[75]

When Elath confronted the Foreign Office with the gravity of this prospect, the British responded that as yet, there had been no "formal" Egyptian request for purchase of this material.[76] But to the Israelis there was no distinction between arms "handed over" and those sold. The Egyptians had in the negotiations for the treaty acquired the right of first refusal at the auction sales, and as the British embassy in Tel Aviv put it, "there is in fact likely to be a very large quantity of weapons, ammunition and vehicles."[77]

THE QUESTION OF BRITISH BASES IN ISRAEL

The Israelis considered turning the British withdrawal from Egypt to advantage by offering Britain bases in Israel as an alternative. This idea had Sharett's support,[78] and in April 1954, the Israelis conveyed to the Foreign Office their disappointment that the British had not followed up on the military mission sent to Israel in 1952.[79] Although he was not in the government at the time, Ben-Gurion's disapproval took the matter off the Israeli agenda.[80] However, the Israeli Foreign Ministry discussed it again toward the end of 1954, and the concurrent correspondences that took place within the British Foreign Office and the Israeli Foreign Ministry are instructive for three reasons. The first is the attitude toward the British that guided Sharett as opposed to Ben-Gurion. The second is the extent to which British documents corroborate Ben-Gurion's fears. The third is the manner in which the subject of bases in Israel placed in bold relief the fact that Israel's border with Jordan was the most problematic aspect of Anglo-Israeli relations and how that in turn affected British arms policy toward Israel.

The Israeli approach to the British prompted a thorough Foreign Office review of the possibility of Anglo-Israeli cooperation. The office concluded that Britain's inability to fund attendant projects suggested by Israel (transit facilities, oil storage, and the repair and manufacture of equipment in Israel for British forces) as well the complete Arab refusal to accept any Israeli role in a common regional defense made cooperation unfeasible.[81] When in November 1954 Sharett and Elath again discussed the possibility of proposing British bases in Israel, their main consideration against such an approach to London was their opinion that Britain would be forced to choose between Israel and the Arab countries, resulting in bases in the latter.[82] Sharett, citing a speech on the Middle East by Eden in Parliament at the beginning of November 1954, also entertained the idea that Britain might guarantee Israel's security in the same way it did Jordan's.[83] However, Ben-Gurion told Sharett that this was an erroneous interpretation of Eden's intent,[84] and the Foreign Office divested the Israeli embassy in London of such hopes.[85] The Foreign Office view was that although the Israelis would not propose bases,[86] British troops in Israel, should the Israelis agree to it, might have a "stabilizing effect" on the Arab-Israeli conflict.[87] Nevertheless, the British rejected the idea of bases in Israel not because they objected to the tangential benefits that might accrue to Israel but because British troops there would be numerically inferior to the Israeli Defense Forces and it would be "most improbable that they could intervene effectively to prevent an Israeli attack on Jordan."[88] The Foreign Office concluded, "We should have to send a brigade of troops if they were not in effect to be hostages in Israeli hands . . . we could not find more than one regiment or battalion at the most for the purpose in mind, and so small a force would be completely swamped by the Israelis."[89]

BRITAIN'S VIEW OF THE ARMS BALANCE

During 1954 the Israelis tried to mitigate tensions with Jordan. Thus in mid-February, the Foreign Ministry approached the British with a request that London use its influence in Amman to bring the Jordanians to comply with the armistice agreement.[90] On 17 March terrorists operating from Jordan ambushed an Israeli bus at Scorpion's Pass in the Negev, killing eleven Israelis and wounding two.[91] When the United Nations Security Council failed to condemn Jordan, Israel withdrew from the Israeli-Jordanian Mixed Armistice Commission (MAC).[92] However, the Israelis continued to press for bilateral Israeli-Jordanian talks,[93] and in August the British Foreign Office suggested that London coordinate secret, high-level discussions between Jerusalem and Amman.[94]

Yet one month later, the Foreign Office rebuffed an Israeli attempt to pursue the matter.[95] The British claimed that these talks were too dangerous for the Jordanians.[96] The Israeli view was that the British had taken upon themselves to block anything of a higher-level nature than local commanders' talks, believing that London prefered a level of tension that might cause Jordan to request an increase in British troop strength.[97] Anglo-Israeli relations cooled considerably from this point on. A speech in the Knesset by Sharett in which he took British policy in the region severely to task prompted a sharp response from Eden.[98] The Arabs, noted the British foreign secretary, were too chary of direct contact with Israel for British mediation to have been of avail.[99]

By mid-1954, the deterioration along the Israeli-Jordanian border had altered the British view of the arms balance. The Foreign Office acknowledged that the general intention of the NEACC was a balance between Israel and the Arab states as a whole but nevertheless moved closer to the War Office view that Israeli military strength should be equal only to the Jordanian Arab Legion.[100] Furthermore, when in late December 1954 the Israelis again requested release of the Centurions, Britain's negative answer included the observation that the Israelis had little to complain about, as they were to receive Mystère-2s from France.[101]

It may have seemed to the Israelis that the Mystères should have had no connection with their request for the release of Centurion tanks.[102] But the British felt that swept-wing jets in Israeli hands would upset the entire Middle East military balance.[103] The supply to Israel of the Mystère-2 would make all other aircraft in the region obsolete (the difference in speed between the Mystère-2 and the Meteor was some two hundred miles per hour) and have a serious effect on Jordan.[104] Yet in British eyes, the most serious aspect of French supply to Israel of these jets was that the Royal Air Force itself had no equivalent aircraft in the Middle East,[105] and the available Israeli documents give no indication that the Israelis were aware of the extent to which this troubled the British.

THE TRICKLE POLICY

By early 1955, British policy would allow Israel a "trickle" of arms,[106] with the British Middle East Office (BMEO) recommending that even this amount be inferior in quality.[107] In fact, British arms sales to Israel had become negligible. On 28 February 1955, the Foreign Office authorized the release to Israel of six Centurion tanks,[108] but that same night Israel launched the Gaza raid against Egypt and the Foreign Office canceled the authorization. London's joining of the Baghdad Pact in early 1955 along with the arms restrictions it placed upon Israel seemed to lend credence to Defense Minister David Ben-Gurion's perception of Britain as a hostile power. Ben-Gurion gave vent to this feeling in his Independence Day speech at the Ramat Gan stadium on 27 April 1955, launching a personal diatribe against Anthony Eden, who had become prime minister on 6 April.[109]

Ben-Gurion's speech heightened the tense atmosphere in Anglo-Israeli relations,[110] but throughout most of 1955 the volatile Israeli-Jordanian border remained relatively quiet.[111] The "litmus test" of Britain's policy toward Israel that year shifted to the arms race between Israel and Egypt, the evidence of which points to Britain as the catalyst. In February 1955, the Israelis learned that Britain intended to fill Egyptian orders outstanding since 1949.[112] The British had yet another reason for supplying Egypt, which ran counter to London's previous assurances to Jerusalem regarding the consequences for Israel of the Anglo-Egyptian Agreement: the pressure exerted by the British Ministry of Defense to unload surplus equipment from the Suez Canal zone within a very rigid timetable.[113] Heavy French competition for the Egyptian arms market as well as Britain's desire to gain influence in Cairo exacerbated Israel's situation. In May 1955, Assistant Undersecretary of State Evelyn Shuckburgh openly told the Israelis that there was no type of weapon Britain was unwilling to sell Egypt.[114]

The British attempt to increase their influence in Cairo highlighted Britain's continued pivotal role in the formation of Western policy in the region. American refusal to sell the Israelis arms meant that arms from Britain took on a greater importance not only from a strictly military point of view but also as a test of Western intentions toward Israel.[115] Thus although the Israelis were unaware of the existence of Alpha, which returned Egypt to center stage in Western planning, Shuckburgh noted on 30 June 1955 that they were "afraid (rightly) that if we have a hand in it [negotiations] we shall suggest concessions by Israel."[116] Furthermore, the British were, in fact, searching for a way to link their arms policy to the progress of the joint Anglo-American plan.[117]

The Israelis themselves seemed to afford London an opportunity to influence Jerusalem's policies through arms supply in mid-1955, when Ben-Gurion had Shimon Peres make another attempt to obtain release of the Centurions.[118] In early June 1955, the Israelis suggested high-level talks with Egypt in an attempt to defuse the explosive border at Gaza[119] and later that month wished to exploit what they felt was the consequently better atmosphere in Anglo-Israeli relations.[120] Peres's mission was not limited to the issue of the tanks. The director general of the Israeli Defense Ministry told John Nicholls, Britain's ambassador in Israel, that the Israelis were worried about the piecemeal nature of their arms purchases from varied sources and wished to pursue a "rational purchasing program" in the United Kingdom.[121] Peres was aware that the British were conducting a review of their Middle East arms policy but attempted to convince the Foreign Office that his approach was on the military and economic planes alone.[122] The Israeli shopping list was extensive, including fourteen more Meteors (Peres claimed that Israel had committed itself to British types and must continue buying them), thirty Centurions (essential because Egypt had received thirty of the sixty they had ordered),[123] two hundred half-tracks, and an unspecified number of helicopters.[124]

The British Ministry of Defense was loathe to miss an opportunity to re-establish dominance of the Israeli market,[125] especially as Israel had not yet received any Mystères.[126] An additional British consideration was the opportunity to influence Israeli policy by strengthening the moderates while Sharett was still prime minister, a move Nicholls urged upon the Foreign Office.[127] However, Nicholls also warned the Israelis that arms they were receiving from France, of which the British were having trouble keeping track,[128] would influence London's view of the arms balance,[129] and in fact, Peres's mission achieved no more than a Foreign Office note that Britain might at some point authorize the sale of six Centurion tanks to Israel as a quid pro quo for "good behavior."[130]

During all of 1955, the only arms in any major category that Britain sold Israel were two Z-class destroyers (delivered in July and authorized because of what Britain perceived as Israel's weakness at sea),[131] nine Meteors, and twenty disarmed scrap Sherman tanks.[132] And although the Israelis had spent most of that year attempting to convince the Foreign Office to balance its arms sales to Egypt with parallel sales to them,[133] the British refused to deliver even six of the tanks Israel had requested more than two years earlier.[134]

Moreover, while Israel pressed for a balance in arms between itself and Egypt, the overriding British consideration was still the Israeli threat to Jordan. In this respect, the futility of Israel's attempt to acquire the Centurions seemed already to have come full circle when Elath and Peres met with Selwyn Lloyd (at that time minister of defense) in early July 1955. Lloyd ignored Israel's protests of Britain's sale of Centurion tanks to Egypt and cited the British army chiefs' objections to the sale to Israel on the grounds of the effect upon Jordan.[135]

BRITISH POLICY AFTER THE CZECH ARMS DEAL

In the view of the Israelis, the Soviet-sponsored Czech arms deal with Egypt in late September 1955 tilted the arms balance drastically against them. But in late November, the British claimed that the sale of arms to Israel would not only agitate the Jordanians but also undermine the British position by effecting a sharp increase in Nasserist influence in Amman.[136] By then, Israel's arms procurement was operating under the shadow of Soviet arms to the Nasser regime, and its efforts in London, as in Paris and Washington, had taken on a new urgency.

On 26 October 1955, Sharett met in Paris with Britain's foreign secretary, Harold Macmillan, as part of his effort to gain a commitment of arms from all three Western powers. The Israelis had met the previous day with Prime Minister Edgar Faure of France, who agreed to supply them with many of the arms they requested. However, the encounter with Macmillan pointed up the impasse in Anglo-Israeli relations. Earlier that day, Elath briefed Sharett on "the twists in British policy and our turns with them."[137] Anthony Eden had become extremely eager to bring Jordan into the Baghdad Pact; in fact, Britain's commitments to Jordan were so comprehensive that toward the end of 1955 the chiefs of staff were instructed to prepare plans for military action against Israel, including seaborne invasion, if Israel attacked Jordan.[138] The Israeli Foreign Ministry was aware of these contingencies and concluded that it might be better for Israel if Jordan joined the Baghdad Pact. That way, reasoned the Israelis, the split in the Arab world would be an accomplished fact, while Jordan's adherence to the pact would increase the chances that the United States would grant Israel a security guarantee.[139]

The subject of Jordan did not arise in Sharett's talk with Macmillan. But the Baghdad Pact was to blame, Sharett told the foreign secretary, for the Czech arms deal.[140] Israel must have arms, said Sharett, and a security guarantee "would help." Macmillan responded that there would be no security guarantee and Britain would not be responsible for a balance in arms between Egypt and Israel,[141] but there *would* be peace, which would result from concessions. This prompted Sharett to demand, "What concessions are you going to demand of the Arabs?" Macmillan, wrote Sharett, grew "wide-eyed." Shuckburgh, who accompanied Macmillan, interjected, "They make your lives difficult. They will stop doing so." Sharett fell upon Shuckburgh (whom the Israelis considered hostile): "Is that a concession? We also make their lives difficult. Abstaining from hostile acts comes in any case of making peace." Sharett wrote with bitter satisfaction that he had made a laughing-stock of Shuckburgh but that the result of the discussion was a disappointing note in Anglo-Israeli relations.[142]

British intentions regarding Israeli concessions became clear in Anthony Eden's Guildhall speech of 9 November 1955, in which the prime minister called for a truncation of the Negev. Eden's speech lent credence to reports the Israeli Foreign Ministry had received that the British wanted a base in Gaza that would facilitate a link from Cyprus through the Negev to Aqaba.[143] As the Israelis understood, the British military was willing to make do with Israeli authorization of passage through the Negev, but the Foreign Office insisted upon an Israeli territorial concession to the Egyptians, who would then allow both a British base in Gaza as well as transport rights through the Negev to Aqaba.[144] Ben-Gurion noted bitterly that "the British government amuses itself with the idea that if not for Israel, Britain would be able to reach accommodation with the Arabs." He also reminded American ambassador Lawson that seven months earlier, he had warned that Britain would be able to extract territorial concessions only by force, and if necessary, Israel would fight the British.[145]

FROM THE KINNERET RAID TO THE KALKILYA OPERATION

The poor state of Anglo-Israeli relations caused an even dimmer view in Israel of Britain's role than of the American or French part in the Western arms embargo on Israel, which followed the 11 December 1955 Kinneret raid against Syria. Indeed, by January 1956 the moderate Sharett was echoing Ben-Gurion's attitude toward Britain and its policies, instructing Elath to warn London "away from the illusion that Israel, in mortal danger and without modern arms for defense, was prepared to make concessions in order to save herself . . . they must weigh thoroughly their responsibility and beware of another failure."[146]

In truth, the British had in November 1955 agreed in principle to the supply of twelve Meteors, three Mosquitos, two hundred half-tracks, and forty twenty-five-pounder guns.[147] However, notice that the British gave the Israelis after the Kinneret operation that these arms would not be forthcoming was accompanied by the troubling realization that Britain was also trying to block French arms sales to Israel.[148] The British claimed they were doing so out of fear of the Arab reaction to the fact that Britain had allowed French Ouragan jets headed for Israel to land in Cyprus. There was no admission that it was because of Britain's fear of swept-wing aircraft in Israeli hands.[149]

In fact, the British had been attempting to forestall the sale of French Mystère jets to Israel since late 1954.[150] The Israelis were aware of this and temporarily shifted their efforts in Britain from procurement, which would in the best case yield a "trickle," to an insistence upon British noninterference with Israel's arms acquisitions from other countries, mainly France.[151] The Foreign Office objected to all but a few of the thirty AMX tanks, eight 155-mm howitzers and twelve Mystère-4As for which the French requested sales permits at the NEACC meeting of 28 February 1956[152] and made more frequent reference to the term "trickle" to emphasize that Britain was, in fact, providing arms to Israel. Yet despite the end of the temporary embargo of arms on Israel in early March 1956 and the turn in British and American policy toward Nasser at the same time,[153] the British still refused to authorize either Centurion tanks[154] or Canberra bombers, which Israel was now also requesting as an answer to the Ilyushin bombers in Egyptian hands.[155]

The United States and Britain added to the change in their policies toward Egypt a decision to augment the power of the Baghdad regime.[156] Thus in November 1955, Iraq acquired twelve Centurion tanks.[157] The supply of Centurions to Iraq became a tangible threat in Israeli eyes with the ejection of John Glubb, the British-born chief of staff of the Arab Legion, from Jordan on 1 March 1956, which accelerated the precipitous rise in influence of the pro-Nasser elements in that country.[158] In a meeting with Ivone Kirkpatrick, undersecretary of state for foreign affairs, Elath invoked the specter of radicalization in Jordan and the attendant dangers for Israel in order to press an unprecedented Israeli request for fifty Centurions. Kirkpatrick answered with a long diatribe about the "artificiality" of the Hashemite rule in Amman. Accordingly, Elath reported to the Foreign Ministry that the British were "cooking up" an Iraqi annexation of Jordan.[159] This would bring the IDF face to face with an Iraqi army equipped with a tank to which Israel had no answer.[160]

Radicalization in Jordan, increasing provocations from that country, and Israel's reactions created the potential for a clash with Britain in mid- to late 1956. For despite his dismissal of Glubb, Hussein was interested in restoring Anglo-Jordanian amity,[161] and Jordanian invocation of the treaty with Britain was a very real possibility should the king feel that large-scale Israeli reprisals threatened his regime. Bar-On documents in detail the deterioration along the Israeli-Jordanian border, the rise in activism following Sharett's June 1956 departure from the government, and the Israeli retaliatory raids against the Arab Legion.[162] The British Foreign Office believed that the rise in intensity of Israeli reprisals was directly connected to the flow of French arms to

Israel in the summer of 1956. By July 1956, the British felt that the twenty-four Mystère-4As and other weapons in Israeli hands might cause the Israelis to believe they were at "peak strength" and bring about a decision to launch a war against Jordan.[163]

In fact, Israel's view of its inferiority in armor meant that procurement of British arms remained a salient and even pressing goal, and as a result, Israelis found particularly disturbing Foreign Secretary Selwyn Lloyd's statement in the House of Commons on 2 July 1956 that the arms balance still favored Israel.[164] On 9 July, Peres presented a renewed request for Centurions, emphasizing that these were vital to Israeli security and that Britain was the only possible source.[165] As Kirkpatrick noted, Israel did not consider even the supply of sixty AMX light tanks from France sufficient.[166]

It was for this reason that Ben-Gurion's willingness to agree to certain conditions in exchange for the tanks made a considerable impression upon the British. If granted Centurions, said the prime minister, Israel would obligate itself not to employ them against Britain's Jordanian or Iraqi allies.[167] London was unwilling to sell Israel Centurions but anxious to impress upon the Israelis Britain's desire to maintain its policy of a "trickle" of arms. Thus the British authorized two hundred half-tracks and other items but told the Israelis that they would reconsider Centurions only in two months' time.[168] In response to continued Israeli pleas as well as to references to Israel's and Britain's shared hostility to Nasser, an exasperated Kirkpatrick promised Elath that if the situation became "grave," the British would pull Centurions from their units in Germany for Israel's use.[169] He did not say how Britain would define such a "grave" situation.

A British "deal" with Israel over the Centurions might have forestalled Israel's retaliatory operation against the Jordanian police fortress at Kalkilya on 11 October 1956. At any rate, the British as a result of this operation notified Israel that within three days, an Iraqi division would cross the Jordanian border in order to bolster the regime in Amman.[170] The British made clear that as far as they were concerned, the entry of Iraqi troops into Jordan was a move Israel should prefer to the alternative: the entry of Egyptian forces into that country.[171]

Britain sanctioned Baghdad's move despite previous statements from Israel that it would react to an Iraqi entry into Jordan with force.[172] In truth, on 1 October 1956 Ben-Gurion assured the American ambassador that Israel would not move if the Iraqis remained on the east bank of the Jordan River.[173] On 7 October, however, Iraqi prime minister Nuri Said called for a Middle

East settlement based on Israeli territorial concessions, which the British government publicly supported. Two days later, Foreign Minister Golda Meir informed Ambassador Lawson that until receipt of clarification from Britain on this matter, Israel considered its acquiescence to an Iraqi presence in Jordan in abeyance.[174] The British dilemma regarding Israel, Jordan, and the situation vis-à-vis Egypt may be summed up as follows: Negotiations toward the Suez campaign were already in progress, and Britain had, through France, made initial contacts with Israel on joint action against Egypt. Foreign Minister Meir thus reacted to the British position on Nuri's proposal by asking rhetorically whether it was still possible to wonder at Ben-Gurion's deep suspicion of Great Britain.[175]

Yet the documents in Israeli archives indicate that Britain took pains to reassure Israel regarding the entry of Iraqi troops into Jordan. Four days after Nuri's proposal and on the morrow of Kalkilya, Kirkpatrick, whom Elath suspected was the driving force in the Foreign Office behind the Iraqi move,[176] assured the Israeli ambassador that Britain would do nothing to violate Israel's sovereignty or territorial integrity.[177] On 15 October 1956, Kirkpatrick informed Elath that "the Iraqi Government assured H.M.G. that Iraqi forces will only be used (except of course in case of aggression by Israel) east of the river Jordan and away from the frontier. . . . They will not be used in case of border incidents." [178]

In Ambassador Nicholls's opinion, there was "an element of truth" in the Israeli assertion that the Iraqi entry into Jordan had radically altered Israel's strategic situation.[179] It was on the basis of this radical change that Israel made another attempt after Kalkilya to obtain Centurion tanks.[180] As long as Israel did not get the Centurions, Elath had told Golda Meir in August 1956, there was no change in Britain's "trickle policy." [181] The Foreign Office, however, remained adamant, Israel did not get the tanks, and in fact, the British withheld items of considerably less military value. Thus on 22 October 1956, with the Suez-Sinai campaign one week away, the British Air Ministry refused to supply K-type parachutes on the grounds that this was "offensive-type" equipment.[182] On 1 November, the Commonwealth Relations Office noted that (even with the outbreak of hostilities) Britain had delivered no tanks or bombers to Israel; the only items the British sent were three Meteor fighters and two Mosquitos.[183] Only in 1958 did Britain open its arms stores to the Israelis.

The British Foreign Office consistently weighed the Middle East arms balance in light of the overall supply of arms to the region, including French arms to Israel. Whatever perfidy the Israelis perceived in Britain's attempts to buy influence with arms in Arab capitals (especially Cairo) and whatever inconsistencies in British policies may be pointed to in historical perspective, the British believed they had operated fairly. This is in direct contrast to the Israeli view, which held that London's arms policies were in total disregard of the overall arms balance.

London's refusal to deliver the Centurion tank, the military item Israel most wanted to purchase from Britain, meant that in Israeli eyes, Britain had failed the litmus test of willingness to ensure the security of the Jewish state. Furthermore, British and Israeli interests and policies had so recently clashed over Jordan that David Ben-Gurion went to the "conference of collusion" at Sèvres with his deep mistrust of the British in general and of Prime Minister Anthony Eden in particular further heightened.[184] In Ben-Gurion's view, Britain's policy on arms was in stark contrast to that of France, which, having so augmented Israel's military power, had earned the appellation "ally."[185]

CONCLUSION

Anglo-Israeli tensions notwithstanding, Israel would not go to war in 1956 without British participation in the campaign. On 27 September 1956, Ben-Gurion recorded in his diary his insistence that Paris press London to agree that British participation include a defense of Israel against an Iraqi or Jordanian attack. Israel, for its part, would undertake not to attack Jordan or Syria.[186] The British were highly reluctant to cooperate militarily with Israel and assented only as a result of the relentless pressure applied by the French.[187] Indeed, at the conference at Sèvres on 22 October 1956, Selwyn Lloyd proposed a British plan that the Israelis found unacceptable: that Israel attack Egypt alone, whereupon Britain and France would intervene to safeguard the Suez Canal and stop the fighting. Only through the efforts of the French was a formula acceptable to all three parties reached. The Sèvres Protocol recorded that Israel would launch a "full-scale attack" on Egypt on 29 October 1956. The next day, Britain and France would demand that Egypt and Israel cease fire and withdraw ten miles either side of the canal, while Anglo-French forces established a "temporary occupation of the key positions on the Canal."[188]

Therefore, it was a great ambivalence, and not a developing strategic co-operation, that most characterized the Anglo-Israel relationship up to the eve of the Suez campaign. Moreover, as we will shall see, Britain's reticence at supplying anything more than very modest quantities of arms to Israel did not change after the Suez Crisis. Israel continued to view British policies with great suspicion, and a considerable change in this relationship took place only in the wake of the events of 1958.

3 FRENCH-ISRAELI STRATEGIC RELATIONS

1952–1956

Mutual antipathy toward Nasser brought France to provide Israel with the arms needed to counter the Czech-Egyptian arms deal of September 1955 and also facilitated French-Israeli military cooperation in October 1956. Yet the historical record shows that the Israelis pursued ties with France with great reluctance and because they had no choice. In truth, the Israelis never considered France a long-term alternative to the close relationship with the United States that they hoped eventually to achieve. The Israelis viewed the relationship with France as a means to procure the arms the United States would not provide and Britain sold in insufficient quantity and quality. In Israeli eyes, even a France which fulfilled Israel's main defense needs could not constitute an alternative to a close relationship with the United States.[1] Prime Minister Ben-Gurion saw inherent dangers in reliance upon France, which in his view pursued only its own narrow regional interests.[2] Although during the period 1954–56 the Israeli and French defense establishments forged close ties, recently released Israeli documents show that the Israelis viewed France's Middle East policies as ultimately incompatible with their own.[3]

QUAI D'ORSAY POLICY TOWARD ISRAEL

The urgency of obtaining arms led Israel to circumvent obstacles that the French Foreign Ministry (the Quai d'Orsay) raised.[4] The Quai favored selling Israel only a very limited quantity of arms, so as not to prejudice France's relations with the Arab states, especially Syria. The political instability and bureaucratic infighting of the French Fourth Republic made possible the circumvention of the policies of the Quai d'Orsay. Pro-Israel members of the French defense establishment with whom the Israelis cultivated close ties facilitated limited arms transactions beginning in 1953 and the large arms deal of June 1956, a phenomenon Sylvie Crosbie terms "unorthodox diplomacy."[5]

Ben-Gurion feared that this unorthodox diplomacy was a temporary state of affairs and knew that such diplomacy would undermine Israel's long-term relations with the French foreign-policy-making establishment.[6] Israel made clear its reluctance to rely upon France as an arms supplier as well as its mistrust of French Middle East policies well before the 1956 crisis. The Israeli Foreign Ministry consistently reported the warnings of senior officials of the Quai d'Orsay that a French backlash against a temporarily pro-Israel policy was inevitable.[7] Before the Suez-Sinai campaign, it was the Israeli Foreign Ministry that was most outspoken with regard to the hazards of reliance upon France. Yet Ben-Gurion also expressed misgivings regarding the connection. He expected a rapid French return to "orthodox diplomacy" during the period following the Suez-Sinai campaign and voiced his grave concern over the fact that France was Israel's sole source of arms.

Crosbie claims that Israeli-French ties suffered because of the "predilections of Israel's timorous and tradition-bound Foreign Ministry," and she attributes to the Foreign Ministry an "Anglo-Saxon" orientation that militated against cooperation with Paris.[8] True, the Israeli Foreign and Defense Ministries at times differed over approach, such as the degree of pressure it was wise to apply to one or another French ministry at a given point, but the two ministries never differed over the importance of procuring arms from any source possible. The success of the Israeli Defense Ministry in acquiring arms from France through unorthodox means was due to extenuating circumstances in that country, not to shortcomings or lack of effort on the part of the Foreign Ministry.[9]

Both Shimon Peres and Moshe Dayan have contributed to a myth about Israel's arms procurements that attributes to Moshe Sharett and the Israeli Foreign Ministry a great reticence at approaching the French for arms.[10] Yet Israeli documents clearly demonstrate that although the staff of the Foreign Ministry were outspoken about the risks of a close relationship with France, they spared no effort to obtain arms from that country.[11] It is important to note that whereas the French Foreign Ministry and the Defense Ministry pursued different policies toward Israel, the Israeli Foreign Ministry and Defense Ministry pursued the same goal with regard to France: augmentation of Israel's security through the procurement of arms from France, despite doubts about French reliability.

At the beginning of the 1950s, France's interests in the Middle East were a steady supply of oil from the region, unimpeded lines of communication to French Indochina, and quiet in French North Africa.[12] The French ascribed to themselves an influential role in the Middle East. Their strategic interests and the view in both Paris and Algiers that France was a "Muslim power" dictated the maintenance of the best possible relations with the Arab countries of the region. France, therefore, had little interest in close ties with Israel, and in fact, Moshe Sharett described France's attitude toward Israel at that time as "cold and calculating."[13]

France accorded Israel de jure recognition only on 21 May 1949, more than one year after its establishment.[14] A major reason for this delay was the opposition of the French colonial authorities in North Africa to recognition of the Jewish state,[15] an opposition based on deference to Muslim sensitivity on this issue.[16] When France extended Israel de jure recognition, Paris justified the move by noting that the Arab states had least tacitly, if indirectly, recognized Israel's existence by signing the armistice agreements.[17]

Yet in Israel's view, France was no longer a regional power but a "broken reed,"[18] and its claim to be a factor in Western defense of the region was, the Israelis felt, tenuous.[19] As we will see, this perception of France's position remained consistent throughout the period covered here. The United States and Britain consulted France on the proposed Middle East Defense Organization in 1952 but excluded it from their planning with regard to defense of the Northern Tier.[20] From the viewpoint of Israel, France's only avenue of influence in the region was Syria, and even this influence was severely circumscribed.[21] In early 1955 Shmuel Ben-Dor, the counselor at the Israeli embassy in Paris, wrote that it was incumbent upon Israel to proceed with "an awareness of France's limitations . . . the United States and Britain are the masters of this region."[22] The Israeli Foreign Ministry also warned that over-reliance on France was dangerous because of the incompatibility of French and Israeli regional goals. Israel and Syria clashed on repeated occasions, and these confrontations placed Israel in conflict not only with the Quai but also, eventually, with the pro-Israel French army and Defense Ministry.

FRENCH MIDDLE EAST ARMS POLICY

Some general background regarding French arms policy in the Middle East is in order. France's signature on the Tripartite Declaration of 25 May 1950 lent it, at least on paper, a status in the Middle East equal to that of the United States and Britain.[23] But U.S. Secretary of State Acheson and British Foreign Secretary Bevin included the French mainly because they "were supplying arms to Syria and this loophole should be plugged."[24] The French were less concerned than the United States and Britain about the political consequences of renewed conflict between the Arabs and Israel, anxious to break into the predominantly British arms market and thus willing to take a much more flexible stance toward the limitations prescribed by the Tripartite Declaration.[25]

In fact, the Tripartite Declaration did not plug the Syrian "loophole." The French refused to disclose to the Americans and the British the scope of their arms sales to Damascus,[26] and in late 1951 the British embassy there could report only that "all we know is that French arms are pouring into Syria."[27] The French justified arms to Damascus by claiming that the Syrians "of course needed arms. They had to defend themselves against the Jews. Few understood as well as the Syrians what aggressive intentions the Israelis harbored, and the French thought it only fair not to deny the Syrian army the means to defend itself should the necessity arise."[28]

But in December 1953, the British military attaché in Damascus obtained a detailed list of French weapons sales to the Shishakli regime between 1949 and 1952. According to this document, the French estimate of the total value of their arms sales to Syria during these years was 10 billion francs (about $2.8 million),[29] making France Syria's main arms supplier at this time. During the same period, Damascus' second largest supplier, the United States, sold Syria arms worth less than $450,000.[30] The main item France sold Syria during this period, over British and American objections,[31] was a consignment of fifty-two Sherman tanks.[32]

Despite their support of Syria, the French sold arms to Israel as well, including sixty Mosquito bombers (vintage 1941) in 1950[33] and one hundred Sherman tanks in 1951 (over the objections of the United States and Britain),[34] because they wanted a larger share of the Middle East arms market.[35] From January 1953 to December 1954 alone, Britain sold $3.2 million worth of arms to Egypt and $4.3 million to Israel. France lost its dominance of the Syrian arms market to Britain at the end of 1952 with the British sale to Damascus of Meteor jets, and its total share of the Israeli arms market from 1949 to 1954 was only some $5 million.[36] The French defense establishment, eager to promote arms sales as a means of supporting France's military industries, signed a contract with Israel in June 1952 for the sale of three Nord-2500 transport planes and twenty-five Ouragan jet fighters.[37] However, officials of the Africa and Levant Department of the Quai d'Orsay blocked the sale because they did not wish to prejudice the remaining French influence in Syria.[38]

Israel hoped the French Defense Ministry would overcome the Quai's opposition, so that Israel would be able to purchase the Mystère-2 jet.[39] But when in October 1952 Britain decided to sell fourteen jets each to Egypt, Iraq, Syria, Lebanon, and Israel,[40] Israel felt constrained to purchase the Meteors Britain offered.[41] The French, meanwhile, protested that Britain had agreed that Syria and Lebanon were to be France's clients and claimed that they had made no effort to impinge upon Britain's lucrative Egyptian market.[42] France's attempt to prevent British domination of the Syrian and Lebanese aircraft markets by offering those countries Ouragan jet fighters failed,[43] and in fact, by early 1953 the Syrians had also requested of the United Kingdom Centurion tanks and Daimler armored cars.[44] The French Foreign Ministry continued throughout 1953 to attempt to persuade Damascus to buy French rather than British jets and used the framework of the NEACC to object (unsuccessfully) to the planned British sale of an additional twelve Meteors to Syria.[45]

Because the rise in tension on their border with Jordan made it less likely that Britain would consent to sell them certain types of arms they had requested, especially the Centurion tank,[46] the Israelis approached France in late 1952 with a request for thirty AMX-13 tanks, twenty-six 155-mm howitzers, and twenty 75-mm guns.[47] At the same time, loss of the Syrian arms market apparently lent greater force to the French Defense Ministry's arguments in favor of selling arms to Israel. Thus in June 1953, the French requested NEACC authorization for the sale of twenty 155-mm howitzers to Israel.[48]

The United States objected to this proposed sale on the grounds that it would tilt the arms balance in Israel's favor,[49] and the Quai d'Orsay used the objections as an excuse to withhold arms. At a meeting of the NEACC in September 1953, the French expressed agreement with the American position and reaffirmed their intention to refuse Israel tanks. But at the same meeting, the French representative admitted that "someone in the French Ministry of Defense" had already committed France to the supply of twenty-six 155-mm guns to Israel.[50] The Israelis had secured a contract for the howitzers through the personal intervention of Deputy Prime Minister Paul Reynaud.[51] Indeed Pierre Gilbert, France's openly pro-Israel ambassador in Tel Aviv, actively encouraged the Israeli Defense Ministry to cultivate closer ties with its French counterpart and with individuals in the French government sympathetic to Israel.[52]

THE EFFECT OF KIBYE ON FRENCH-ISRAELI RELATIONS

The Israeli operation in the Jordanian village of Kibye on 14 October 1953 prevented the Israelis from making progress with regard to procuring the AMX tanks. Ya'akov Tsur, the Israeli ambassador to France, broached the subject of the tanks in a meeting with Alexandre Parodi of the French Foreign Ministry in early November. Parodi replied that Israel should not expect a prize for the Kibye raid.[53] The French saw in the raid an ominous portent for Israeli-Syrian relations. The Quai d'Orsay was willing to have Israel place AMX tanks in the Negev but did not want them "climbing the Syrian heights."[54] French ambassador Gilbert also expressed concern lest Israel prejudice France's interests in Syria or undermine the Syrian regime.[55] In a lecture in Israel on French foreign policy on 20 December 1953, Gilbert acknowledged that France had attempted to press the Syrians to reach accommodation with Israel and failed. Nevertheless, warned Gilbert, France was not willing to countenance an "Israel on the warpath."[56] As we will observe, Israel's relations with Syria would come between Israel and France in late 1955, when Israel already had a French commitment to supply a large quantity of arms.

Ambassador Gilbert made the "natural connection" between the rebellion against France in Algeria and Israel's deepening conflict with Egypt.[57] By 1954, it was clear that Egypt under Nasser was aiding the Algerian rebels.[58] Gilbert helped Shimon Peres, director general of the Israeli Ministry of Defense, arrange a trip to France for Chief-of-Staff Moshe Dayan in early August 1954. Gilbert entertained vague notions about creating a joint French-Israeli front against Nasser and saw this as the main purpose of Dayan's visit.[59] In fact, Dayan saw the purpose of his trip as arms procurement; in his view, intelligence sharing was a French, not an Israeli interest.[60] Nevertheless, Dayan had Deputy Chief of Military Intelligence Yehoshafat Harkabi meet with Robert Lacoste, a key figure in the French colonial government (who in February 1956 became resident minister in Algeria). Israel's intelligence services were well informed on events regarding Algeria and in 1954 began to work closely with French intelligence.[61] In reality, Harkabi greatly exaggerated the information Israel had on Nasser's involvement with the Front de Liberation Nationale (FLN) in Algeria, his purpose to convince the French defense establishment of the wisdom of providing arms to Israel.[62]

During Dayan's visit, the Israelis secured the agreement in principle of the French defense establishment to supply the Ouragan jets and the AMX tanks that the Quai had blocked as well as Mystère-2 jets, radar equipment, and SS-10 antitank missiles. French defense officials also expressed a willingness to consider the sale of twelve Mystère-4s (a jet far superior to the Mystère-2).[63] However, the Quai d'Orsay used the Israeli threat to France's interests in Syria as reason to continue to hold up arms shipments to Israel.[64] Thus despite the fact that the Quai emphasized that Dayan was not a guest of the French government,[65] Dayan met with Parodi of the French Foreign Ministry, who suggested that Israel was about to attack Syria. Dayan assured him that Israel had no such intention; both France and Israel were "bastions of the West in the region and had identical interests."[66] Pro-Israeli French defense minister Pierre Koenig also warned Dayan that France did not want to see a war between Israel and Syria. Although Dayan answered that Israel was close to reaching a modus vivendi with Syria,[67] the Quai was not impressed and reduced the number of Mystère-2s the Israelis would receive from the thirty they had requested to a mere six.[68]

On 9 August 1954, the French Foreign Ministry informed the British that they intended to proceed with the sale of these six jets to Israel.[69] The British vehemently opposed the sale on the grounds that it would place a weapon in Israeli hands for which even the Royal Air Force (RAF) in the Middle East had no answer.[70] The French Foreign Ministry attempted to justify the sale by claiming that it would strengthen the hand of Prime Minister Moshe Sharett and the moderate camp in Israel.[71] In the British view, the French were using the specter of Mystères to Israel to force Britain to abandon its plans to sell additional Meteors to Syria.[72] The French claim that the sale would help Israeli moderates was disingenuous, because in September 1954 the Quai informed the Israeli embassy in Paris of its intention to sell Egypt arms once the Anglo-Egyptian Agreement was signed.[73] The French Foreign Ministry wished to supply no fewer than twenty-five Mystère-2s, which Egypt had earlier requested and which France had hitherto refrained from selling them.[74]

The supply of twenty-five Mystères to Egypt could hardly have strengthened Sharett's hand. But the Quai wished to "compensate" Egypt for the Mystère sale to Israel and to demonstrate to the Arabs that they were showing the Israelis no favoritism.[75] The French Foreign Ministry told the Israelis that they, too, could widen the scope of their arms purchases in France. But in fact, the French were referring to surplus items of which the Israelis had little need and not to the tanks, planes, and artillery pieces in which Israel was most interested.[76]

ISRAEL'S FOREIGN MINISTRY AND RELATIONS WITH FRANCE

During the months following Dayan's visit in August 1954, Shimon Peres and Yosef Nahmias of the Israeli Defense Ministry[77] began to forge clandestine ties with a large number of high-ranking officials in government ministries in France with a view to procuring arms.[78] These efforts did not remain secret, and they heightened the desire of the Quai d'Orsay to undo the damage done France's relations in the Arab world by publicity given to its ties with Israel.[79] The Israeli embassy in Paris continued its efforts to convince the French Foreign Ministry to release the items promised Israel and resented the Israeli Defense Ministry's demand that even more pressure be applied the Quai. Ben-Dor complained that Shimon Peres "cannot appear suddenly and demand that the embassy staff approach the secretary-general of the Quai d'Orsay just because someone has the feeling that the embassy is not operating with the proper enthusiasm on arms procurement."[80]

At the same time, the Israeli Foreign Ministry demonstrated that it was no less concerned with weapons purchases than its defense counterpart. In October 1954, Prime Minister Sharett met with Edouard Depreux, former French minister of the interior and an influential supporter of Israel. The Western Europe Section of the Israeli Foreign Ministry prepared a list of arguments in support of arms to Israel that the prime minister was to present his guest and reminded Sharett that he should express no doubts regarding French-Israeli friendship.[81] Nevertheless, the Foreign Ministry view was that "closer relations with France should be approached with caution. It is doubtful whether France would be willing to concentrate upon Israel and abandon the Arab states." [82]

In early 1955, the signing of a defense agreement between Turkey and Iraq and the attendant danger to Israel brought Sharett to consider an approach to all three Western powers for guarantees of Israel's security.[83] The Israelis in fact actively pursued the goal of a security guarantee only from the United States. The idea of a guarantee from France aroused considerable opposition in the Israeli Foreign Ministry, best expressed by Ben-Dor:

> If there are those with ruminations about our ties with France, I am one of them. . . . If I may be allowed to use military terminology, I would say that from the point of view of our long-term diplomatic strategy, we should be wary of an over-identification or too close an association with France. We must for the moment exploit the existence of mutual interests. In this case too, we must act carefully lest our "partner" disappoint us at a critical moment, either because of domestic weaknesses or vacillating diplomatic considerations.[84]

In fact, the Israeli government did not make such an approach.[85] The French claimed that cooperation could in any case only take place in the framework of opposition to the Baghdad Pact and would have to include the Arab states.[86] Nevertheless, the head of the Western Europe Section noted that Israel's position dictated behaving toward the French *as if* Israel saw them as loyal partners,[87] because arms procurement prospects in France appeared more promising than those in either the United States or Britain.[88]

The Israelis hoped that French objections to the Anglo-American arming of Iraq might prompt the French to release arms to Israel.[89] However, the claim that Ben-Gurion's return to the government as minister of defense in February 1955 brought about a decision to equip the IDF solely with French arms is unfounded.[90] One of the few documents that reveal details regarding the arms procurement policies of the Israeli Defense Ministry clearly demonstrates that the Israelis had no intention of allowing France to become their exclusive source of arms.[91] Thus, for instance, the Israeli air force preferred to delay the purchase of jets until France released Mystères for sale. But the Israelis would judge arms from various sources upon their merits, and under no circumstances would the Israeli Ministry of Defense agree to limitations regarding procurement options,[92] as Israel attempted to obtain arms from France while concurrently making every effort to obtain arms from the United States and Britain.

FRENCH ARMS TRANSFERS TO ISRAEL IN 1955

Few French arms reached Israel in 1955. British records of the NEACC reveal that during that year France delivered only five of thirty AMX-13 tanks for which Israel had a contract in late 1954.[93] The only tanks Israel obtained from France in 1955 were fifty-five Shermans, transferred as scrap hulks from Britain to Cherbourg in France and refitted (without prior knowledge of the Quai d'Orsay) with 75-mm guns.[94] In late 1954, the French transferred eighteen of the twenty-six 155-mm howitzers that the Israelis had requested in late 1952. Yet continued efforts by both the Israeli Defense Ministry and the embassy in Paris failed to secure the last eight guns,[95] and Paris authorized their delivery only in February 1956.[96] During the same period, the French sold Egypt twenty AMX-13 tanks, four 155-mm howitzers,[97] and according to the *Arms Trade Registers*, probably also twenty AMX 105-mm howitzers.[98]

Israeli efforts during 1955 to secure either the Mystère-2 or the Mystère-4 also came to naught.[99] At the end of March 1955, Nahmias of the Israeli Defense Ministry was convinced that the French failure to authorize Mystères was due only to delays in production that France would overcome within two to three months.[100] By July 1955, twelve Israeli pilots were training on Mystère-2s in France,[101] and by the end of August, Israel had secured a commitment for the sale of fifteen of these jets.[102] The French promised that the Mystère-2s would be released during the second half of September 1955,[103] and early that month the Israelis approached the British Air Ministry with a request for staging rights for the first five jets through Nicosia in Cyprus.[104]

But in early October 1955, the French informed the NEACC of their decision to supply Israel with twelve Ouragans instead of fifteen Mystères. The Quai d'Orsay told the British that Ouragans would suit Israel's purpose while not presenting a problem to the RAF,[105] basing its decision less on a perceived need to placate British anxieties than on a desire to moderate Egyptian hostility toward France's North African policy.[106] In Israeli eyes, however, the

French decision also expressed the Quai's displeasure at Israel's vigorous protests at the French arming of Egypt and Syria[107] as well as the campaign aimed at convincing the Jews of North Africa to immigrate to Israel.[108]

FAURE PROMISES ARMS: OCTOBER 1955

The Czech-Egyptian arms deal of September 1955 forced the Israelis to heighten their efforts to obtain arms from France.[109] To the staff of the Israeli Foreign Ministry, this was a distasteful task. In their view, the aid that had thus far been extended by French defense officials came only because of hostility to Egypt and was thus "out of hatred of Haman rather than love of Mordechai."[110] Yet as Gazit points out, the Foreign Ministry never called into question the necessity of doing everything possible to obtain arms.[111] On 22 October 1955, Sharett met with Peres, Harkabi, and General Haim Laskov, and the four discussed which items to request in an approach to Faure. Sharett thought there was little chance of obtaining arms from France, especially a weapon such as the Mystère-4.[112] The government of Edgar Faure was unstable and expected soon to fall, and in this situation it seemed unlikely that the Israelis could circumvent the Quai.[113] Furthermore, the staff of the Israeli Foreign Ministry harbored a sense of foreboding with regard to the future of relations with France should they succeed in "cuckolding" the Quai.[114]

Sharett met with Faure on 25 October 1955, and the latter agreed to supply everything the Israelis requested, including the Mystère-4.[115] Sharett was amazed at the alacrity with which the French prime minister assented but also suspicious. Did such haste not demonstrate irresponsibility and recklessness?[116] On 10 November, Peres secured a contract from the French Defense Ministry. The list of arms to be supplied was extensive, and although it did not include Mystère-4 jets (because of American control of off-shore procurement),[117] this contract infuriated the Quai d'Orsay. Foreign Minister Antoine Pinay took Tsur severely to task over this break with diplomatic protocol and affront to the authority of the Quai.[118] Yet Ambassador Tsur wrote that although "the arms matter will stand between us for a long time to come, on this we can under no circumstances retreat."[119]

THE KINNERET RAID AND THE ARMS EMBARGO

Israel's attack on Syrian positions on the northeastern shore of Lake Kinneret during the night of 11 December 1955 provided the French Foreign Ministry with a new reason to block the supply of arms to Israel.[120] Bar-On claims that the French attitude toward this large-scale retaliatory operation was one of ambivalence. He notes Peres's impression that "the French did not care all that much about the shooting around the Kinneret" as well as Tsur's observation on 20 December that "the reaction was less forceful than I had feared."[121] However, as Tsur's diary clearly indicates, the Israelis made these comments when they still thought that France intended to deliver arms in accordance with the recently signed contract.[122] Instead, the Kinneret operation was damaging to Israeli-French relations, because its effect was a serious blow to a Syrian regime the stability of which most of official Paris considered vital to France.

Following the Kinneret operation, France joined the United States and Britain in an arms embargo on Israel until February 1956.[123] In his diary entry of 1 January 1956, Sharett referred to Ben-Gurion's depression over this embargo and to Peres, who in Sharett's words had "realized that he is not such an eminent authority, with everything obtainable in France through string-pulling and underhandedness."[124]

Sharett's references to the dismay of Ben-Gurion and Peres were less an expression of schadenfreude at their discomfort over the results of the Kinneret operation than of the foreign minister's feeling that the raid was "a stab in the back" of procurement.[125] Sharett's diary account of his 16 December 1955 meeting with Foreign Minister Pinay includes only the laconic observation that Pinay met his request for arms with a vague response.[126] But Pinay's account reveals that Sharett staunchly defended Israel's action against Syria and queried the French foreign minister as to when Israel could expect to receive *sixty* Mystère-4A jets. Pinay's response also demonstrated to Sharett how disparate were the Israeli and French views of the Israel-Syria conflict. The French foreign minister gave no answer with regard to the jets but ended the meeting by deploring the gratuitous attack on Syria, as that country had not menaced Israel.[127]

Less than one month before the Kinneret raid Tsur had warned that the French Foreign Ministry was in a "panic" at the thought that Israel might, through conflict with Damascus, "push Syria into Iraqi arms." The ambassador reminded Foreign Ministry director general Walter Eytan that "strengthening Syria against a possible Iraqi attack is the policy of both ardent supporters of Israel and her opponents. Military circles struggling against arms to Egypt are unwilling to lift a finger to withhold arms from Syria. The French do not see Syria as a danger to Israel."[128]

On 9 January 1956, the Western Europe Section of the Israeli Foreign Ministry informed Sharett that during the month following the Kinneret raid the internal situation in Syria had deteriorated considerably. The French had had to employ their influence in Damascus in order to discourage a Syrian operation against Israel, fearing that the failure of such an operation would bring about a pro-Iraqi coup in the Syrian capital.[129] Anger at Israel over this fact had grown not only in the Quai d'Orsay but also at French army headquarters.[130] This anger, noted the head of the Western Europe Section, had "done more damage than expected and is at the center of their interpretation of the Kinneret incident."[131]

At the beginning of February 1956, Guy Mollet formed a new socialist-led government in France. Christian Pineau became foreign minister, the pro-Israeli Radical Maurice Bourgès-Maunoury defense minister, and Abel Thomas, a close associate of Bourgès-Maunoury and sympathetic to Israel, became director general of the French Defense Ministry. When these men took office, the French were negotiating with Syria for the sale to that country of fifty AMX tanks, twenty 105-mm self-propelled guns, ten 105-mm Howitzers, and ten to fifteen 155-mm guns.[132] The Western arms embargo upon Israel in reaction to the Kinneret raid had made the Israelis chary of renewed conflict with Syria,[133] and in mid-February 1956 Israel decided to halt work on its Jordan River project on the Syrian border.[134] On 10 February 1956, Pineau told Tsur that France would now honor outstanding arms contracts with Egypt.[135] France's representatives at the NEACC had in November 1955 requested authorization to sell Egypt an additional thirty AMX-13 tanks and thirty 155-mm Howitzers[136] and on 10 January 1956 informed the NEACC that they intended to proceed with the sale.[137]

The sharp French reaction to the Kinneret raid, the French desire to further arm Syria, and Pineau's policy of rapprochement with Egypt reinforced the Israeli view that France was intent upon pursuing a Middle East policy completely at odds with Israel's interests. When Tsur protested this policy to Pierre Maillard of the Levant desk, Maillard replied that in the final analysis, among the Arab states it would be Egypt that would make peace with Israel. By contrast, said Maillard, Israeli accommodation with Iraq could not be envisioned even in the long term.[138]

The French foreign minister resisted his own staff's urgings that France keep arms out of Israeli hands.[139] On 2 February 1956, Pineau decided to end France's part in the embargo and to release the arms for which Israel already had a contract.[140] The most important item for the Israelis was the Mystère-4A; Peres's and Nahmias's contacts with Bourgès-Maunoury and Thomas helped secure French agreement by the end of February to supply twelve of these jets.[141] On 28 February 1956, the French requested that the NEACC approve the sale of these Mystères as well as all of the items for which the Israelis had contracted in November 1955. This was not yet the "big arms deal," but it included hundreds of parachutes and fifty napalm petroleum drop tanks, to which the British objected completely.[142] As we will see, the much larger arms deal two months later prompted the Quai to attempt to salvage its position in the Arab world by trying to use the NEACC to obstruct transfers to Israel that the French cabinet had decided to carry out. At this point, however, the Quai told the British that the sale of twelve Mystère-4s was justified in light of the Soviet sale of MiGs to Egypt.[143] On 11 April 1956, the first three of the initial dozen Mystère-4s which the Israelis were to receive arrived in Israel.

CIRCUMVENTING THE QUAI D'ORSAY

Bourgès-Maunoury brought Faure and Pineau to agree that Egyptian hostility and the rapid deterioration of France's position in Algeria justified accelerated arms sales to Israel.[144] Rapidly growing hostility to France in Syria, fueled by Damascus' close ties with Cairo and Soviet arms transfers,[145] also made it more difficult for the Quai to present the relationship with Syria as reason to withhold arms from Israel.[146] The three French leaders agreed that large-scale arms sales to Israel were feasible only if the normal channels of the French Foreign Ministry were circumvented, because the Quai would oppose the sales.[147]

On 17 April 1956, Guy Mollet also demanded that the Israeli embassy in Paris desist from all contact with the French Defense Ministry. This demand was based not on concern that Tsur and his staff would interfere with an arms deal but rather on the French prime minister's desire that only he and Pineau make decisions, which they would then pass on for execution to the French Defense Ministry. Mollet the socialist did not want Bourgès-Maunoury, a Radical, to carry on simultaneous discussions with the Israeli embassy, as it might create the impression that Bourgès-Maunoury was doing more for Israel than was Mollet.[148] Paris authorized an additional twelve Mystères at the end of April 1956 without the involvement of either the French or Israeli Foreign Ministries.[149] The parallel exclusions of both foreign ministries from involvement in the arms deal was thus limited to a bureaucratic similitude and did not correspond to an affinity in policy between the Israeli Foreign Ministry and the Quai d'Orsay.

The reaction of Sharett and the staff of the Israeli Foreign Ministry was of slight at having been removed from the procurement effort in which they had been all along involved.[150] At a meeting on 3 April 1956 that included Ben-Gurion, Sharett, Peres, and Dayan, the chief-of-staff noted what he claimed were the achievements of Peres alone with regard to procurement in France. Dayan demanded an end to the involvement of the embassy in Paris in arms matters, and Ben-Gurion supported this demand. Sharett wrote angrily in his diary that it was as if "Tsur had not lifted a finger and as if the whole great episode had not commenced with my meeting with Faure at the end of October [1955]."[151]

On 18 March 1956 the prime minister had warned that "war within a few months could not be avoided unless Israel got the arms needed to counter Egypt's weapons."[152] Ben-Gurion attributed what he claimed was Sharett's failure to secure the large arms deal with France to the foreign minister's disagreement with Ben-Gurion's view that a clash with Egypt was inevitable.[153] Put simply, the prime minister later implied that Sharett did not pursue a large deal with France with the requisite enthusiasm because he feared that such a level of armament would allow Ben-Gurion to attack Egypt.[154]

Thus the April 1956 meeting foreshadowed Sharett's resignation, which Ben-Gurion forced, on 18 June 1956. By way of comparison, the reaction of the French Foreign Ministry was one of frustration at being flanked by a French Defense Ministry that through arms sales to Israel undermined the entire basis of what the Quai viewed as correct French Middle East policy. In mid-March 1956, Maillard of the Levant desk of the Quai told Ben-Dor that French-Israeli arms deals were an aberration beyond which there was no basis for cooperation between the two countries. Ben-Dor paid lip service to the ostensible common interests of both countries in the Middle East: opposition to the Baghdad Pact, status quo regarding Syria, and a partnership against Egypt.[155] But the attitude of the Quai as well as the ongoing interoffice struggle in Paris made the Israelis leery of future vicissitudes in relations with France even as modern French arms arrived in Israel. As Tsur wrote in late

May 1956, "Despite our achievements—and they are by no means insignificant—I do not predict a rosy future for procurement in France. The Algerian struggle has put a card in our hand and aroused a wave of admiration for Israel among wide circles in France. Yet in truth, this is admiration born of desperation. . . . Sympathy for Israel and honest concern for its fate are diluted by the fear of a chasm between France and the Arab world." [156]

THE ARMS DEAL OF JUNE 1956

On 23 June 1956 Peres, Dayan, and Harkabi met near Paris with French defense officials and signed a deal for a large quantity of modern arms for which Israel agreed to pay $80 million.[157] This was the principal arms transaction with France in 1956, the French providing Israel with 72 Mystère-4 jets, 120 AMX-13 tanks, 40 Super-Sherman tanks, artillery pieces, ammunition, and spare parts.[158] In Ben-Gurion's eyes, the opportunity to obtain a large quantity of modern arms dictated agreeing to the close ties that the French defense establishment now pressed upon Israel. French officials, noted Harkabi, hoped for a much closer intelligence relationship with the Israelis, especially in light of what they thought Israel knew about rebel activities in Algeria.[159]

Ben-Gurion exclaimed that "with an ally like France, Israel is willing to go all the way." [160] Yet Peres later wrote, "Ben-Gurion began to appreciate the relations between our two nations [Israel and France] only with great reluctance," [161] and Bar-On points out that the Israelis were not eager to participate in "unnecessary adventures." [162] In truth Bourgès-Maunoury, who urged upon his government a closer relationship with Israel, did not think Israel had much to offer France beyond intelligence sharing. The French defense minister saw in a well-armed Israel France's most effective deterrent against Egypt,[163] although even Nasser's 26 July 1956 nationalization of the Suez Canal did not immediately bring French leaders to contemplate military action.[164] In August 1956, France and Britain began contingency planning for a joint operation against Egypt, but initially there was no intention of including Israel.[165]

The French Foreign Ministry was still determined to stymie the close ties the French Defense Ministry was building with Israel and to bridge the growing gap between France and the Arab countries.[166] And because it was clear to the Israelis that the French defense establishment's ascendancy in the determination of French foreign policy was temporary, the Quai d'Orsay's efforts were an ominous portent for the future of French-Israeli relations. At the end of June 1956, the Quai authorized the sale of 155-mm howitzers to Egypt.[167]

In the Israeli view, the French Defense Ministry was not selling heavy arms to Egypt behind the back of Foreign Minister Pineau; instead, the sale reflected Pineau's own remaining ambivalence regarding ties with Israel and the scale of weaponry France was selling Israel.[168] Only in early July 1956 was Tsur able to report to Israel's new foreign minister, Golda Meir, a promise by Pineau to halt all arms sales to Arab countries.[169]

THE QUAI ATTEMPTS TO BLOCK ARMS TRANSFERS

The Quai d'Orsay's representatives at the NEACC defended France's decision to sell Israel an initial consignment of twelve Mystère-4s, but when Mollet, Pineau, and Bourgès-Maunoury decided to sell Israel a total of seventy-two Mystères, the bureaucracy of the Quai resisted and the Quai's representatives at the NEACC attempted to maneuver their British and American colleagues into blocking these sales.[170] As the British initially thought that this was "another attempt at French trickery,"[171] the counselor at the French embassy in Washington felt constrained to take into his confidence the first secretary at the British embassy, who reported that

> the French government was under very strong pressure by pro-Israeli elements to supply all orders, and it is difficult for them, for political reasons, to resist without some outside help . . . they are trying to get us to state reasoned objections which could be used in Paris in defense of a decision to cut down the orders . . . de Laboulaye went on to say that he knew there was a majority of Ministers in the French Cabinet in favor of supplying the whole of the Israeli requests. What was needed (presumably by the Quai d'Orsay) was help for the minority.[172]

In fact, such efforts by the Quai through the NEACC were useless, because France's disregard of American and British objections to these large-scale arms sales meant that the NEACC had in effect ceased to function as a regulatory agency. In the opinion of one British official, the NEACC had become a committee for the rearming of Israel.[173] Nevertheless, the French Foreign Ministry set as its goal a radical change in France's arms policy toward Israel at the first opportunity. Maillard apprised the Israeli embassy in Paris of the deep anti-Israel sentiment among high officials of the Quai: French-Israeli friendship was based "solely on the blood spilled in North Africa and bound to change at any moment."[174]

During the summer of 1956 France and Israel broadened considerably the scope of their intelligence sharing on Egypt. The French defense establishment's interest in Egypt's military deployment increased following the nationalization of the Suez Canal, and Ben-Gurion personally instructed the IDF to supply such intelligence as Defense Minister Bourgès-Maunoury requested. In early August 1956, the French chief-of-staff requested that the Israelis carry out aerial photography of Egyptian military installations and provide information regarding the capacity of Israel's ports and airfields. Dayan was interested only in arms and was unwilling to take any initiative with regard to the cooperation that the French intelligence chiefs had in mind,[175] but Ben-Gurion told his reluctant chief-of-staff, "We must relate to them as brothers. The aid which they are providing and our partnership with them is vital to us; we must cooperate with all our heart."[176]

During September 1956 the French initiated discussions with Israel on the possibility of Israeli participation in an Anglo-French operation against Egypt.[177] Ben-Gurion had become convinced that the Israeli alternative to such participation was a campaign in which Israel would stand alone against Egypt.[178] On 30 September, Meir, Dayan, and Peres met in France with Pineau, Bourgès-Maunoury, and Thomas, Meir enumerating the conditions Ben-Gurion had set down as essential for Israeli participation. The first was French recognition of Israel's limitations with regard to armor and aerial capability; the tanks Israel had received from France would be fully integrated into the IDF only at the beginning of January 1957, and the jets on 1 March. The second condition was British cooperation in and American prior knowledge of the operation. The third condition was Israeli control of the coast off the Strait of Tiran.[179]

The assurances the French gave the Israelis with regard to British cooperation and American tacit consent were vague,[180] for France had secured British participation only at a secret conference at Sèvres on 22 October 1956,[181] and both France and Britain withheld knowledge of Operation Musketeer (the Suez campaign) from the Americans. Israel's part in the campaign strained its relations with the United States. Moreover, military cooperation in late 1956 did not result later in British arms to Israel. France, however, agreed at the end of September 1956 to augment the arms deal of June with another large-scale transaction in October, and this had a great effect on Ben-Gurion's willingness to consider a military partnership. In this second arms deal the most important items, sent to Israel several days before the Sinai campaign opened on 29 October 1956, were an additional one hundred Super-Sherman tanks, two hundred armored personnel carriers, three hundred six-by-six trucks and twenty tank transporters.[182]

At the beginning of October 1956, Ben-Gurion wrote of his apprehensions regarding a military undertaking against Egypt. Although Israel had an interest in striking a blow at Nasser, he feared that Egypt's Soviet-made bombers would destroy large sections of Israel's cities or that "volunteers" from Russia would rush to Egypt's aid. Also of concern was that Israel would have only France to rely on in a campaign against Egypt; in Ben-Gurion's eyes, this was insufficient protection.[183] Although ties forged between the two defense establishments as well as among the leaders of the two countries from June to October 1956 contributed greatly to the confidence necessary for an Israeli decision to participate in a joint military operation, the Israelis harbored deep reservations about this type of cooperation with the French. Yet the military aid France provided Israel was not a matter of philanthropy, and French urgings that Israel participate in such an operation, Ben-Gurion knew, could not be brushed aside.[184] We shall see that Israel would prosecute its Sinai campaign in accordance with the agreement at Sèvres.

CONCLUSION

The common ground that France and Israel found in enmity to Nasser was the basis for military cooperation between the two states from mid-1956. For the Israelis, however, France's willingness to continue to provide arms on a large scale was a major factor in Israel's agreement to launch a joint military venture. Ben-Gurion was convinced that refusal of the proposal would jeopardize his country's arms relationship with France.[185] The decision to accept this cooperation bore out what an Israeli diplomat told the French ambassador to Israel at the beginning of 1956: "Only the country which supplied arms in amounts worthy of that term would have the privilege and opportunity to find a listening ear among Israel's leaders."[186]

Immediately after the Sinai campaign, French support for Israel became, in the public arena, the French government's official policy. The Israeli press, writes Crosbie, "in a state of euphoria optimistically hailed its new champion."[187] In fact, we will see that such cooperation with France was a temporary state of affairs. As the Israelis continued to pursue a strategic relationship with the United States, whatever euphoria existed among Israel's leaders over relations with France dissipated shortly after the Suez campaign of 1956. In Israeli eyes, the French continued to provoke the grave doubts regarding dependence upon France as a source of arms that had throughout marked Israel's view of that relationship.

4 SUEZ AND SINAI, 1956: 29 OCTOBER TO 6 NOVEMBER

The agreement that Britain, France, and Israel reached at Sèvres on 22 and 23 October 1956 created a temporary military alliance among the three countries. The "scenario" agreed upon required that Israel subordinate its strategy to the diplomatic exigencies that the plan entailed. Thus Israel prosecuted its campaign against the Egyptians in accordance with the protocol of those meetings with the French and the British, and the Israeli Defense Forces carried out two distinct types of military operations: those Israel undertook in the service of its French and British partners and those that advanced Israel's strategic goals.[1] Yet Israel also achieved its strategic objectives in the Gaza Strip and the Sinai Peninsula independently of and despite a delay in operations by the two European powers.

During the week of 22–29 October 1956, French aircraft arrived in Israel in order to aid in the defense of Israeli air space in case of either an Egyptian or a Soviet air attack. Prime Minister David Ben-Gurion feared that Egypt might respond to the Israeli assault in the Sinai with air raids on Israel's cities. Indeed, during this campaign, French forces in the region and the IDF maintained a high level of coordination. The British, on the other hand, were reticent to deal so closely with the Israelis, going so far as to protest the presence of two senior IDF officers at French admiral Barjot's command post in Cyprus. French naval vessels patroled Israel's coast, but at France's behest IDF chief-of-staff Moshe Dayan tendered a written request for this protection, because to do otherwise might have raised the ire of a British command that discouraged all but the most limited contact with and obligation to the Israelis.

The main strategic objective of Israel's military campaign was the capture of Sharm el-Sheikh at the southern tip of the Sinai Peninsula on the Strait of Tiran, which would ensure Israel's freedom of navigation through that waterway.[2] Israel's objectives also included removal of both the military threat from an Egypt in possession of modern Soviet arms and the fedayeen, who operated against Israel from the Gaza Strip. In order to minimize both American pressure and the possibility of Soviet involvement, Israel's leaders wanted the campaign to be of the shortest possible duration.[3]

Israel's operation, designated Kadesh, began on the afternoon of 29 October 1956 with a parachute drop at the Mitla Pass in the Sinai Peninsula. On the afternoon of 30 October, Britain and France served Egypt and Israel with an ultimatum: Both belligerents were to cease hostilities immediately and allow British and French forces to deploy along the Suez Canal in order to ensure free navigation of the waterway. Britain and France had coordinated this move with Israel, and the Israeli attack served the British and French by providing the pretext for intervention. The Egyptians rejected the ultimatum, as the British, French, and Israelis had anticipated, and Israel now expected its Sèvres partners to fulfill their part of the agreement by commencing bombing of Egyptian positions.[4]

The British and French, however, were slow in initiating Operation Musketeer, the Anglo-French Suez campaign that was to have begun at dawn on 31 October with an aerial assault upon targets in Egypt. The delay of approximately eight hours elicited the great concern of Ben-Gurion, who was anxious lest the allies' failure to launch Musketeer both expose Israel's cities to air attack and jeopardize the position of the Israeli paratroopers already deep in the Sinai Peninsula. In fact, on 31 October Ben-Gurion demanded of his commanders that they withdraw the Israeli paratroopers who had been dropped at the Mitla Pass only two days earlier, as those troops might become engaged in encounters with the Egyptians, extrication from which might be difficult. Only Chief-of-Staff Moshe Dayan's insistence that Israel could achieve its objectives even without the Anglo-French bombing convinced Ben-Gurion to allow the troops to remain in the Sinai Peninsula.[5]

The immediate reason for the allied delay was greater Egyptian resistance than the Royal Air Force had expected. But Israel had altered its original battle plan in accordance with the Sèvres protocol and had agreed not to move to secure its most important objective, the Strait of Tiran, until Britain and France took action. Israeli Defense Ministry director general Shimon Peres protested to France, which placed pressure on Britain to dispatch the bombers and thus allow the French, too, to begin the attack upon targets in Egypt.[6]

On 1 November 1956, on the initiative of the United States, the United Nations General Assembly voted to demand that Israel withdraw its forces to the armistice lines and that Britain and France cease immediately their aerial attack on Egypt. Israel would be forced to comply but was determined to complete its conquest of the Sinai Peninsula before a cease-fire arrangement could take effect. After the initial paratrooper drop at the Mitla Pass, Israeli forces launched a three-pronged attack in the Sinai Peninsula. On 31 October, Israeli armored units won battles at Abu Agheila, the Kuafa Dam, Bir Hassna, Jebel Livni, and Bir Hama.[7] By 2 November, Israel had completed its capture of the Gaza Strip and the IDF had reached a line ten miles east of the Suez Canal, beyond which the Sèvres agreement stipulated Israeli forces not advance. By 3 November, Israel had defeated the Egyptian army in the Sinai Peninsula. The only strategic objectives the Israelis had not yet achieved were the securing of Sharm el-Sheikh at the southern tip of the Sinai peninsula and the opening of the Strait of Tiran to Israeli shipping. Thus on 3 November Israel announced that it would accept a cease-fire on condition that Egypt agree as well. The Israelis correctly calculated that their forces would take Sharm el-Sheikh by the time the Egyptians gave their assent.[8] On 4 November, Israeli troops occupied the Egyptian outposts at Ras Nasrani on the Strait of Tiran, and on 5 November the Israelis captured Sharm el-Sheikh.[9]

Britain and France, however, were not yet ready to commence the next phase of Operation Musketeer and prevailed upon the Israelis to delay their acceptance of a cease-fire. Whereas the United Nations attempted to obtain agreement to a cease-fire that would prevent an Anglo-French troop landing,

Israel wished to have British and French troops on the ground before a cease-fire went into effect. It was for that reason that Prime Minister Ben-Gurion was willing at least to consider an Israeli operation on the eastern bank of the Suez Canal and an attack upon the Egyptians at Kantara, about which he was not enthusiastic. Such an assault by Israel in the service of the British and French would provide cover for the allied paratroopers, who were to attack Egyptian positions even before a joint Anglo-French amphibious operation landed troops along the Egyptian coastline. However, the British, whose reluctance to expose their paratroopers to Egyptian armor had brought the French to propose the IDF operation across the canal, refused to consider an Israeli move beyond the lines determined at Sèvres. In truth, Ben-Gurion greeted news of Britain's refusal to consider an Israeli attack across the Suez Canal with relief: the prime minister had no wish to have Israel involved in "the international morass of the canal."[10]

France maintained pressure on its British ally to assent to an earlier attack, and on 5 November paratroopers of both armies landed in the vicinity of Port Said and Port Fuad in Egypt, preparing the way for the landing of additional allied troops at these two sites the next day.[11] This, however, was the end of the Anglo-French military campaign. Britain and France did not prosecute Operation Musketeer beyond 6 November 1956 and achieved neither control of the Suez Canal nor the overthrow of Egyptian president Nasser, the two most important goals of Operation Musketeer. The United States placed severe economic pressure upon Britain, including an American failure to support the faltering British pound sterling and a refusal to furnish either Britain or France with emergency oil supplies.[12] Moreover, the Soviet Union was by 6 November less preoccupied with the uprising in Hungary, and Soviet prime minister Bulganin cabled the governments of Britain, France, and Israel an implied threat to employ missiles against them should they not assent forthwith to the UN's demand for a cease-fire.[13]

Israel regarded the Soviet threat with the utmost gravity, but the Bulganin cable arrived twelve hours after completion of a military campaign in which Israel both attained its main strategic goals and discharged its obligations toward its (temporary) allies.[14] Yet we will see that neither France nor Britain could ensure that Israel receive consideration of its security concerns before withdrawing from territory it occupied in the course of the 1956 conflict. Only the United States, which demanded unconditional Israeli withdrawal, could provide the guarantees the Israeli government considered vital to its security. Moreover, the following chapters will demonstrate that even after the Suez-Sinai campaign, Israeli leaders continued to view with suspicion Britain's goals in the Middle East and with trepidation the uncertain duration of France's supply of arms to and support of the Jewish state.

5 SEEKING A STRATEGIC RELATIONSHIP WITH THE UNITED STATES

1957–1960

Let us turn now to Israel's attempt after the Suez-Sinai campaign to establish a strategic relationship with the United States and to obtain American arms. What we shall see is that obtaining arms from the United States remained the most important goal in Israel's foreign policy, that arms constituted the primary reason for Israeli interest in a strategic relationship with the United States (which was in fact not achieved), and that while Israel pursued a strategic relationship with the United States it regarded the prospect of binding ties with great ambivalence.

Ben-Gurion's conviction that Israel must refrain from binding ties was a lodestar in his conduct of Israeli foreign and defense policy. There was a degree of ambivalence in his approach, and the researcher must take this into account when examining Israel's relationship with the United States during this period. Ben-Gurion gave his blessing to efforts to achieve military cooperation with the United States as well as ties with the U.S. defense establishment through a connection with NATO. These attempts, conducted primarily by the embassy in Washington and by Reuven Shiloah of the Foreign Ministry, brought the prime minister, who cited the examples of the biblical kings David and Solomon, both of whom formed successful alliances,[1] to defend the *idea* of a formal treaty with the United States.

On the other hand, Ben-Gurion emphasized the advantage of Israel's independence of such ties. No European country, he noted, was as free as Israel, with the exception of Switzerland. There were, he pointed out, no foreign bases on Israel's soil, no control over its army, and no political dependence. Outside the Soviet bloc, Israel was the country whose military size, deployment, and organization was most secret. Despite the fact, stressed Ben-Gurion, that "there were those who would have been happy to have entered into a defense treaty with the country which could ensure our security and whose guarantee has global value."[2] The prime minister thus pressed his subordinates to obtain arms and an American guarantee of Israel's security but to leave a formal defense treaty with the United States for some undefined point in the future.

STRAINED RELATIONS WITH THE UNITED STATES

Ben-Gurion's immediate concern was security through the acquisition of arms. During the months following the Suez-Sinai campaign it became clear that the United States would continue its refusal to sell Israel arms, and Israel intensified procurement efforts in Europe. Yet Israel's success in arms procurement in France and later in Britain and Germany in no way diminished the importance of its relationship with the United States. Less than three weeks after the end of the Sinai campaign, Ben-Gurion stressed that improvement of relations with the United States was imperative.[3]

Israel's collaboration with Britain and France and the attack on Egypt in late 1956 strained relations with the United States.[4] Two immediate obstacles stood before Israeli efforts to mend its relationship with the Eisenhower administration: the violation of trust President Eisenhower felt Israel had committed by the invasion of Sinai[5] and Israel's continued refusal to withdraw completely from all territory occupied during the fighting until it obtained adequate assurances of its security.

On 13 January 1957, Israel made clear that it would not withdraw from the Strait of Tiran until its freedom of navigation was assured. The Israelis demanded concrete guarantees of their right to transit the Suez Canal, announced that they would continue to occupy the Gaza Strip, objected to the presence of a UN force there, and demanded that the United Nations declare at least the eastern part of the Sinai Peninsula a demilitarized zone.[6] Israel sought to delay final withdrawal from these areas in order to explain its actions and obtain greater support from the American public for their demands. Thus the Israeli embassy in Washington lobbied with bureaucrats, politicians, congressmen, prominent Republicans, elite leaders, and the American Jewish community and succeeded by February 1957 in creating a previously nonexistent sympathy for their position.[7]

Ben-Gurion's diary and a book by Mossad chief Isser Harel reveal that both men were even more concerned over the deterioration of relations with the Central Intelligence Agency (CIA) than with the State Department and the White House. During the Suez-Sinai campaign and the diplomatic crisis that ensued, the CIA and the Mossad conducted much of the important communication between the United States and Israel.[8] It was thus with consternation that the prime minister and his secret services chief regarded CIA head Allen Dulles's anger at Harel for "not telling him the truth" about plans to attack Egypt.[9] Harel's desire to repair this relationship prompted him to request permission to divulge "secret information" to the Americans,[10] perhaps, as Ben-Gurion's diary suggests, intelligence regarding the Soviet-supplied buildup of the Egyptian and Syrian air forces, intelligence of a nature the Israelis did not normally transmit to the Americans.[11] Ben-Gurion's diary also reveals that he had two motives for divulging such information to the United States. The first was the prime minister's hope that the United States might respond by selling jets to Israel, and the second was his desire to provide intelligence that might forestall what he feared would be an American policy of rapprochement with Nasser.[12]

ISRAEL'S VIEW OF THE SOVIET THREAT

Israel also feared that an American rapprochement with Nasser, coupled with Soviet penetration of the region, would further endanger Israel's security and claimed that withdrawal from Sinai would mean a buildup of Soviet war potential in "the Sinai area."[13] Reuven Shiloah requested that the State Department provide clarification of the American attitude toward "the question of the preservation of Israeli independence against possible aggression."[14]

Washington responded that although the United States viewed the Soviet arms buildup in the region as serious, this should not affect Israel's compliance with the UN resolution calling for a complete withdrawal from Egyptian territory.[15] The White House held that only withdrawal would allow the United States to draw friendly Arab regimes into a program to thwart communist influence in the Middle East.[16] For as long as the administration was in conflict with Senate leaders of both parties over the question of sanctions against Israel, Congress would not authorize the program.[17] On 20 February 1956, President Eisenhower addressed the American people and confronted the opposition to sanctions against Israel. Eisenhower's speech convinced Ben Gurion that Israel must bow to American pressure to complete its withdrawal,[18] and the Israeli pullback removed the main obstacle to the program that became known as the Eisenhower Doctrine.[19]

ISRAEL AND THE EISENHOWER DOCTRINE

The Eisenhower Doctrine, approved by Congress on 9 March 1957,[20] authorized economic as well as military assistance and the deployment of American troops should any country in the area request aid to thwart overt armed aggression from a state controlled by international communism.[21] Congressman James P. Richards, with the personal rank of ambassador, left for the Middle East on 12 March to head a special mission to explain the resolution to leaders in the region.[22]

On 24 March 1957, Foreign Minister Golda Meir informed the Foreign Affairs Committee of Mapai that Richards would arrive in Israel within a few weeks and that the government had to formulate its policy toward the Eisenhower Doctrine and its strategy in negotiations with the American representative.[23] Among the Israelis, three approaches emerged. The first was primarily (but not solely) that of the embassy in Washington, which recommended unqualified support of the doctrine. A second, more diffuse approach found expression among those members of Mapai whose attitude toward both the Eisenhower Doctrine and the United States was one of ambivalence. A third approach was that of Mapai's coalition partners, Mapam and Ahdut Ha'avoda, which called for a total rejection of any association with the Eisenhower Doctrine on ideological grounds.[24]

At the end of March 1957, Israeli minister in Washington Reuven Shiloah met with William Rountree of the Near East Affairs office. Rountree noted the diminished British presence in the region and the filling of the vacuum by the Soviet Union. When Rountree stated that the United States was going to "stop the Soviets," Shiloah observed that it was not clear to the Israelis what the United States expected of them.[25] Did the Americans have a specific task for Israel? Rountree replied that Richards would bring with him no military plans. The purpose of Richards's mission was to explain the program, to determine which countries were prepared to participate, and to discuss aid expenditures.[26]

Israel would not wish to forfeit the symbolic value of association with such an American plan, but "the hard part," Meir told Mapai's Foreign Affairs Committee, would be the requirement of a commitment on the part of the participating countries.[27] Israel's acceptance of the American program would entail Israeli identification with the principles of the doctrine. These principles were resistance to Soviet aggression and recognition of the right of the United States to operate against Soviet penetration of the region.[28] The dilemma this created for the Israelis will become clear below. Initially, however, Israel focused its attention upon using the doctrine to obtain economic assistance and possibly the military aid that the United States had hitherto refused to grant.

The Israelis knew that the total amount of money available for implementation of the Eisenhower Doctrine was $200 million. They also knew that this was not a special allocation but rather the amount of money left over from aid programs of fiscal year 1957, and that in no instance would any country receive more than $30 million.[29] It is not clear whether the Israelis were aware that given the bureaucratic complications involved, it was doubtful whether the Americans could spend a substantial portion of $200 million by the end of fiscal year 1957 (30 June).[30] In any case, Rountree warned that Israel could expect very little of the Richards mission financially, between $5 and $10 million at most.[31] But the Israelis were unsure of the scope of Richards's future authority. With the resumption of U.S. government aid (suspended when Israel invaded the Sinai),[32] the Israelis expected to receive $20–25 million in grant form for fiscal year 1957.[33] Finance Minister Levi Eshkol noted that the small sum Israel *might* receive through the Richards mission did not in itself justify adherence to the Eisenhower Doctrine. It was nevertheless difficult for the Israelis to contemplate rejecting the doctrine: the Americans might give out much larger sums in the future and, Meir added, the United States might decide to allocate all foreign aid in the region via the Richards mission.[34] Eshkol expressed the hope that Israel would be "left alone." Meir took this view one step further, stating that Israel should give no answer at all. However, Eshkol noted that Israel would have to come out firmly in favor of the

Eisenhower Doctrine if called upon to do so by the United States, because ideologically, "the world already knows who we are." [35]

Shortly after the announcement of the Eisenhower Doctrine, Israel's representatives in the United States began a campaign aimed at obtaining "Richards money" in addition to other forms of economic aid.[36] Israel apprised the United States of the danger to its economy posed by inflation, which had resulted, claimed the Israelis, from the absorption of large-scale immigration rather than expenditures on the Suez-Sinai campaign.[37] This was an effort to stress to the Americans that Israel would not construe aid accorded in the framework of the Eisenhower Doctrine as U.S. support for its recent military venture.[38] The effort proved futile, as one week later the State Department informed Israel not only that it would receive none of the $200 million earmarked for the doctrine[39] but also that the United States would dole out additional aid only in the context of the fight against communism.[40]

On 7 April 1957, the Americans made clear that they expected Israel to give Richards a definite answer. Ben-Gurion told Meir and Yaakov Herzog, head of the United States section of the Foreign Ministry, that Israel would not be able to adhere to the Eisenhower Doctrine; to do so would endanger current immigration of Jews from Poland as well as the three million Jews remaining in the Soviet Union.[41] Yet a number of considerations precluded what might have been a precipitately negative response to the American proposal. In the first place, Israel wished to exploit a warming in American-Israeli relations that had been brought about by developments in the region. In the second place, Israel feared that by remaining outside of the Eisenhower Doctrine it would afford the Arabs an advantage, worsening its own position in the region while doing nothing to gain protection from the more remote but greater Soviet threat.[42] In the third place, the Israelis realized that despite the danger to the Jews under Soviet rule, a compromise formula allowing an affirmative Israeli response to Richards might, after all, be possible.

The Americans made clear that their greatest concern in the Middle East at this point was the future of Jordan: the United States wished to bring Amman into the sphere of the Eisenhower Doctrine.[43] Donald Bergus of the State Department noted half-jokingly that Jerusalem's job was to make King Hussein understand that his main ally in the region was Israel.[44] In mid-April, with unrest in Amman growing, Iraqi forces entered Jordan. Meir warned U.S. ambassador Edward Lawson that Israel would not remain passive if, as a result, there were incidents on the Israeli-Jordanian border.[45] Lawson pointed out that the Iraqi move had American support but also noted that the United

States and Israel had a mutual interest in maintaining the status quo in Jordan. The Israeli-Jordanian border remained quiet. At the end of May 1957, the embassy in Washington reported that Israeli restraint had done "much to restore U.S. trust in Israel."[46] The Near East Affairs office made a point of informing the Israelis that the United States had pared a "fantastic" Jordanian request for arms to the minimum necessary for Amman's domestic security.[47]

In Ambassador Abba Eban's view, it was untenable that Israel forego exploiting the change in the climate of American-Israeli relations by saying no to Richards while Jordan and other Arab countries reaped the benefits of the Eisenhower Doctrine.[48] Israel could not afford to miss the opportunity to exploit whatever deterrent potential the doctrine might provide. If the Israelis refused to adhere to the doctrine, they would be in the anomalous position of protesting their isolation while contributing to it.[49]

On 2 May 1957, Richards arrived in Israel for a twenty-four-hour visit. The differences between the American and Israeli positions came to the fore during Richards's meeting with Meir on 3 May. Meir reminded Richards of Israel's firm opposition to communism and stated Israel's interest in the doctrine as a security guarantee in the event of an attack by an Arab state "influenced" by international communism.[50] She referred specifically to Syria, but when the foreign minister demanded that Richards clarify what he meant by a communist-dominated state, the latter evasively replied that "we have no answer for that except the general statement that if you are in accord with the doctrine and were attacked by international communism or a communist-dominated state and asked for our help, we would help."[51]

Israel's publicly stated position presented a problem to the Americans. The Israelis did not tell Richards that they wanted a nonbinding joint statement so as not to foment a crisis with the left-wing members of the government coalition.[52] Instead, they told Richards of their fears regarding Soviet Jewry and asked whether the United States would accept as Israeli adherence to the doctrine a joint statement along the lines of that of Afghanistan, which omitted reference to the communist threat. Richards answered that Washington hoped for "a more forthright stand" but agreed that the United States would state that only "technical reasons" prevented Israel from reaching a final decision on the doctrine at this time.[53]

In truth, the American response put the Israelis in a difficult position, and following the meeting, the prime minister and his foreign minister poured out their resentment of both Richards and the State Department to Herzog: The absence of any joint declaration at all, they claimed, created political difficulties, because both Mapai's coalition partners and the opposition would view this absence as a failure.[54] Richards (who in fact had objected to visiting Israel)[55] had remained only one day, and this, said Ben-Gurion and Meir, not Israel's own problem with the formulation of a statement, was to blame for the fact that no joint declaration had been issued. Furthermore, they complained, Israel had a *right* to a joint declaration. Other countries would interpret anything short of a joint declaration as discrimination against Israel on the part of the United States, exposing Israel to aggression from its neighbors.[56]

On 7 May 1957, the Foreign Affairs Committee of Mapai again debated the question of adherence to the Eisenhower Doctrine. Ehud Avriel claimed that of all of the countries approached, Israel had the greatest need of the doctrine.[57] It was essential that the Arabs not constitute the only influence upon the United States.[58] However, Meir Argov reminded the committee that one month earlier, its members had agreed that Israel should remain aloof of the doctrine if possible. Argov cast aspersions upon the American attitude toward Israel in general and in specific terms the unwillingness of the United States to stand up for Israel's right to transit the Suez Canal. Herzl Berger noted that Israel would have to declare in favor of the doctrine but pointed out that this was out of fear of a negative American reaction should the Israelis refuse to do so. Mordechai Namir supported Argov's opinion that "American policy regarding the Sinai campaign was hostile. [There were] Bulganin's threats on one hand, and those of the United States on the other."[59]

The anti-American tone of the discussion surprised Ben-Gurion. The prime minister reminded his colleagues that the United States supported Israel's right to freedom of navigation, whereas the Soviets called the Strait of Tiran "an Arab sea." Israel's interest, noted Ben-Gurion, was "the achievement of the greatest possible degree of cooperation with the United States."[60] This was also a reminder to members of the committee loath to foment a government crisis that Mapai would not allow Mapam and Ahdut Ha'avoda to dictate foreign policy. The Israeli embassy in Washington, for its part, was outspoken about the need to neutralize the anti-American position of the two left-wing parties and their desire to prevent Israel's adherence to the Eisenhower Doctrine. Eban urged that "the prime minister reach the most radical conclusions from the attempt to scuttle the matter."[61]

Nevertheless, the anticommunist nature of the program made a statement on the Eisenhower Doctrine a difficult proposition. On one hand, the Soviet Union's anti-Israel stance created a powerful argument in favor of casting aside inhibitions based on concern for the Jewish communities in eastern

Europe and the Soviet Union. Reuven Bareket observed that two days before the Mapai Foreign Affairs Committee's 7 May meeting, the Soviets had already prematurely broadcast Israel's adherence to the doctrine.[62] Avriel argued that although the welfare of Soviet Jewry would always be uppermost in Israel's consciousness, the fate of that community did not hinge upon the nature of an Israeli statement on the Eisenhower Doctrine. Aharon Remez added that there was in any case no perceivable "crack in the wall of Aliyah [Jewish immigration to Israel]" from the Soviet Union, and Dov Yosef agreed that little Israel did would make a difference in the eyes of the Soviets.[63]

On the other hand, Dov Yosef urged that Israel refrain from making an anticommunist pronouncement. If Israel did not adopt an openly anti-Soviet position, the Soviet Union would understand that Israel had withstood pressure from the United States to do so. Ben-Gurion pointed out that, in fact, the United States had not demanded an "anti-communist manifesto."[64] But when later the same day (7 May 1957) the Israelis presented another draft of a proposed joint statement, the Americans responded that "the language proposed falls short of its purpose and it would be preferable to have the Government of Israel issue a more forthright unilateral statement of which we could appropriately take note."[65]

On 18 May 1957, the Israelis reluctantly agreed to the American proposal of separate statements, and on 21 May the Israeli government issued an official communiqué. The Israeli statement did not mention communism at all but merely noted that Israel "opposed aggression against the territorial integrity and political independence of any country. It entertains no aggressive intent against any other people or nation anywhere."[66] The United States government issued an acknowledgment of the Israeli statement the same day.[67]

DIVERGENT VIEWS OF THE EISENHOWER DOCTRINE

The manner in which the Israelis lent their support to the Eisenhower Doctrine demonstrates that their reticence at joining an anti-Soviet defense pact had not disappeared. Yet once the Israelis issued a statement of adherence to the doctrine, they expected an American quid pro quo. We have noted that the initial Israeli goal with regard to the Richards mission was to get additional money and if possible arms, and that Israel adhered to the doctrine having received no promise of either. However, Israel assumed that it would receive the Exim Bank loan for which Dulles had in April 1957 approved a study mission. Apparently, the Israelis did not interpret what State Department officials told them during a 24 June meeting as a harbinger of future trouble over this loan. At that meeting, Dulles told Eshkol and Eban of his disquiet at providing additional funds in view of Israel's own immigration policy on one hand and the unsolved Palestinian refugee problem on the other. Dulles then asked about the communist tendencies of the Polish and Hungarian Jews. Eshkol answered that these immigrants had had enough of communism. The matter was dropped for the time being, and the embassy in Washington assumed that economic aid for fiscal year 1958, both in grant and Exim loan form, was secure. As we will observe, this was not the case.[68]

The Israelis then turned their attentions to the strategic aspects of the doctrine, but Washington quickly disabused them of certain assumptions. Israel did not anticipate a U.S. refusal to acknowledge that in the Israeli case there was "an inseparable link between international communism and the intra-area problem of relations with the Arab states."[69] The problem was that despite their watered-down statement supporting the Eisenhower Doctrine and despite having received no clear answer from the United States regarding their position should Israel come under attack,[70] the Israelis regarded the result of the Richards mission as a bilateral agreement that bound the United States to defend Israel in the event of an attack by either Egypt or Syria, countries "controlled or as good as controlled by international communism."[71]

In the summer of 1957, Syria became the focal point for great power rivalry and at the same time the focus of Egypt's struggle for regional primacy.[72] To the Israelis it appeared that a test case of the Eisenhower Doctrine was at hand with the rise in tension between Israel and Syria. The takeover of the Syrian army by an officer with "communist sympathies,"[73] the supply of arms from the Soviet Union,[74] and rumors to the effect that there were a large number of Soviet advisers in that country[75] increased Israeli fears that a border incident with Syria would involve the Soviets.[76] In early August, Eban asked Dulles for assurance that the United States would defend Israel in case of a Soviet-backed Syrian attack.[77] Dulles's evasive answer increased the feeling among the Israelis that the United States was unlikely to use force to back the Eisenhower Doctrine.[78] The prime minister's growing fear of a clash with the Soviets led him to confide to his diary that Israel must avoid conflict with Syria.[79]

In Israeli eyes, Western competition with the Soviet Union in supplying arms to the Arabs heightened the fecklessness of the doctrine,[80] and on 10 August 1957 the United States turned down an Israeli request for purchase of C-82 transport planes, half-tracks, machine guns, and ammunition.[81] Ben-

Gurion told Dulles in a message on 12 September 1957[82] that the Israelis also felt unease at American unwillingness to agree that tension between Israel and its Arab neighbors was primarily the product of Soviet penetration of the region rather than of factors endemic to the Arab-Israeli conflict.[83] The absence of a response on the part of the secretary brought the Israelis to demand that the United States directly warn the Soviet Union against an attack on Israel.[84] Dulles gave a vague assurance of protection under the Eisenhower Doctrine[85] but refused to issue a warning that he felt would enhance the Soviet image in Arab eyes.[86]

THE U.S. AND ISRAELI APPROACHES TO NATO

Growing alarm over the Soviet threat[87] led to an attempt by the Israelis in late 1957 to ameliorate their security situation through a connection with NATO.[88] Researchers have misunderstood Israeli overtures to NATO and Ben-Gurion's attitude toward these approaches. The attempt to forge ties with NATO was not a struggle between American and European "orientations" in Israeli foreign policy. According to one version of this attempt, Reuven Shiloah's motive for seeking ties with NATO was his desire to ally Israel with the United States. Defense Ministry director general Shimon Peres opposed him with an initiative designed to bring Israel closer to western Europe (specifically, France), and it was up to the prime minister to decide between the two approaches.[89] In fact, Ben-Gurion's interest in the idea of ties with NATO waned, but only when it became clear that such a bond would attain for Israel neither arms nor a guarantee against Soviet aggression.

Indeed, Ben-Gurion's intentions were also misunderstood at the time. On 16 September 1957, Herzog told Moshe Sharett that Ben-Gurion was intent upon Israeli entry into NATO. Both Herzog and Sharett agreed that this was a "harebrained scheme," and Sharett wrote that "the tyrant [Ben-Gurion] is again scaling a slippery slope."[90] Neither Sharett nor Herzog mentioned Shiloah's role, although in fact it was Shiloah who convinced a reluctant Ben-Gurion of both the desirability and feasibility of ties with NATO.[91] Ben-Gurion made clear in his diary that he urged caution, whereas Shiloah advocated an "association" with NATO that had membership as its final goal.[92] Shiloah described his plans in a letter to Israeli ambassador to Italy Eliahu Sasson,[93] who replied that "the chances of either full or partial integration into NATO at this time appear not only slim but nonexistent, and it would be a mistake to request it."[94]

The disagreement between Ben-Gurion and Shiloah over the approach to be taken to NATO points up Ben-Gurion's ambivalence toward such ties: he wanted to secure the benefits such ties could proffer but shied away from the obligations a formal connection would entail.[95] The prime minister insisted that Israel's priorities remain the procurement of arms and an American warning to the Soviet Union regarding aggression against Israel.[96] Shiloah thought that Israel could obtain arms by working through NATO in order to forge ties with the American defense establishment.[97] Ben-Gurion, on the other hand, preferred to concentrate at this point upon France and Germany, on the correct assumption that the United States would continue its refusal to sell arms to Israel.

Nevertheless (as Shiloah wrote to Eban), Ben-Gurion was amenable to this "NATO approach" if it produced arms and a guarantee from the United States.[98] On 6 October 1957, Meir broached to the Americans the subject of strategic cooperation and the possibility of U.S. support of a greater role for NATO in the Middle East. Ben-Gurion had Meir tell the Americans that Israel wanted U.S. aid in expanding Israel's airfields and ports so that Israel could play a role in regional defense.[99] But Meir could get nowhere with this or any of the requests she submitted to Dulles during their meetings on 8 and 12 October. These requests were for arms, additional money for Israel to purchase arms, a direct warning to the Soviets regarding Israel, and a security guarantee to Israel along the lines of one that Turkey had recently received, to be accomplished by extending NATO's jurisdiction to the Middle East.[100] Israel received instead a stern warning from the United States not to allow points of contention on its border with Jordan to erupt into open conflict.[101] The Israelis were dismayed to learn that despite their adherence to the Eisenhower Doctrine, the view in Washington was still of Israel as the main *obstacle* to Western efforts to stem Soviet expansion.[102]

A visit to Israel by U.S. general Alfred Gruenther, former NATO chief, provided another opportunity for a petition to the Americans for strategic cooperation and arms. On 16 November 1957, Shiloah proposed to Gruenther Israeli coordination with the U.S. Sixth Fleet.[103] Gruenther was receptive in principle, but when Shiloah brought up the sale of submarines to Israel as an answer to those in Egyptian possession, the general told him that Israel would have to rely on the Sixth Fleet for protection.[104] Gruenther was also unenthusiastic about the idea of an Israeli association with NATO.[105]

On the same day Shiloah met with Gruenther, an interoffice meeting took place during which the Israelis decided upon policy regarding the NATO convention to take place in December 1957. Present at this meeting were Ben-Gurion, Mossad chief Isser Harel, and representatives of the Defense and Foreign Ministries. The Israelis decided to demand that the United States place before the convention a proposal that that organization declare that the independence and territorial integrity of *all* of the countries of the Middle East was a fundamental principle of its policy.[106] At this meeting Shiloah secured Ben-Gurion's agreement that Israel's approach to the United States over NATO include separate talks with the Americans on bilateral security and defense arrangements.[107]

In fact, Shiloah and the embassy in Washington also used these separate talks to attempt to greatly widen the scope of their plans for military and scientific cooperation with the United States. The framework for the cooperation they wished to achieve was the "Pool of Resources of the Free World," a concept referred to in NATO's Declaration of Common Purpose, which suggested that the Western nations pool their resources and establish ties between the existing defense alliance and other individual friendly governments.[108] On the military plane, Israel would ask the United States to explain to its NATO allies the need to arm the IDF with a view toward raising its technical and qualitative level to that of NATO's European armies.[109] Ben-Gurion viewed this as a convoluted way of procuring arms, and although he did not forbid the ambitious initiatives regarding the Pool of Resources, he made clear that he wanted concrete results on arms and an American warning to the Soviets well before the December 1957 NATO convention.[110]

But the United States had no intention of selling arms to Israel, issuing a guarantee of Israel's security, or encouraging the Europeans to receive Israel into NATO. The State Department decided to divert Eban's attention from these efforts with a protest against Israel's conduct in a dispute with the Jordanians over Mount Scopus in Jerusalem.[111] Moreover, the State Department called into question the economic aid Israel had assumed was secure.[112] By early January 1958, the State Department's delay of the Exim loan would force the Israelis to deal with the question of economic aid rather than with designs for a strategic relationship with the United States.

Yet the lack of encouragement from Washington did not deter Shiloah from pursuing fantastic plans for scientific cooperation with the United States. Shiloah may have thought that the vague wording of the Pool of Resources suggested by President Eisenhower and British prime minister Harold Macmillan created an opportunity to present the Americans with far-reaching proposals.[113] Although there was some cooperation between the Americans and both the Israeli Technion and Weizmann Institute (centers for the study and research of science), the State Department's political considerations severely circumscribed such cooperation,[114] and Shiloah proposed a dual approach in order to circumvent these obstacles.

First (proposed Shiloah), Eban would obtain the consent-in-principle of the State Department that Israel be included in the "pool." Once that was obtained, Israel could recruit American Jewish scientists to carry this cooperation much further than the State Department actually intended. These scientists, Shiloah pointed out, would wield considerable power in Washington through the expanding military industries of the United States, and their influence would facilitate a role for Israel in Western defense of the Middle East.[115] Second, Israel would send a delegation of ten of its leading scientists in order to make an impression on American Jewish scientists and aid in this recruitment.[116]

Ernst Bergmann, chairman of the Israeli Atomic Energy Commission, firmly opposed Shiloah's proposals, warning that the Israelis were deluding themselves in thinking that the United States had any interest in including Israel in the Pool of Resources. He pointed out that the cooperation to which Shiloah referred was in fact limited to the contracting of certain services by the U.S. Research and Development Command.[117] Thus, for example, the Israelis had succeeded in obtaining a $600,000 grant for completion of a number of scientific projects but had for political reasons been turned down by the Rockefeller Foundation.[118] The chairman of the Atomic Energy Commission also objected to Shiloah's idea of sending Israeli scientists to the United States for "propaganda purposes." [119] Finally, noted Bergmann, Israel was involved with France in both atomic and military research, and this precluded free interaction with the United States in these areas.[120]

Bergmann demanded that all contact with foreign countries on sensitive scientific matters be coordinated with Director General Shimon Peres of the Defense Ministry,[121] and it appears that on this matter Bergmann, not Shiloah, enjoyed the support of Ben-Gurion.[122] Shiloah, who admitted his own ignorance of scientific affairs,[123] may also have been ignorant of the most significant developments between Israel and France in the area of atomic energy. At any rate, this was the end of Shiloah's attempt at an independent initiative vis-à-vis the United States on scientific matters.[124]

The results of the NATO meeting of 30 December 1957 effectively ended Israeli hopes of association with that alliance as well as hopes that such ties would facilitate cooperation with the U.S. defense establishment.[125] During the days immediately following the NATO convention, Shiloah continued to urge upon Meir the very same policies that he had prior to the NATO meeting,[126] including the need to maintain pressure primarily on the United States rather than on Western Europe to supply arms. However, Israel had now shifted its arms initiative almost completely to western Europe. The Israeli Defense Ministry excluded Shiloah from procurement efforts in Western Europe, which Ben-Gurion termed "Peres' domain."[127] In early January 1958, the Foreign Ministry instructed Shiloah to focus arms procurement efforts in the United States upon enlisting American aid in facilitating purchases in Europe.[128]

DELAY OF THE EXIM LOAN

Since the Richards mission, the Israeli embassy in Washington had scarcely dealt with economic matters, demonstrating instead a clear preference for working toward strategic cooperation with the United States. Haggai Eshed claims that Israel shifted its efforts in Washington in early 1958 to an intensification of the attempt to gain American support for what became known as the alliance of the periphery.[129] In fact, when in January 1958 the staff of the United States Section of the Foreign Ministry enumerated the goals to be pursued in Washington, they placed economic aid at the head of the list.[130] The Israelis assumed that the mission of the Exim Bank to Israel in August 1957 had resulted in approval of the loan for which Israel had long been lobbying. During the first week of January 1958, the State Department informed Ambassador Abba Eban that it had delayed approval of the loan. This came as a shock to Eban, who protested to Dulles: "This position is incomprehensible in the light of the sympathy and encouragement which you have expressed on this matter since April 1956. . . . Continued delay will not only frustrate basic economic development projects . . . but will cripple water development in Israel, thus injuring the whole pattern of her economy. Moreover . . . this matter obviously has a deep impact on United States–Israel relations as a whole."[131]

The delay forced the staff of the embassy in Washington to channel nearly all of its energies into an all-out drive to obtain the Exim loan,[132] and Eban made abundantly clear his displeasure at having to resume this effort at the expense of security-related affairs.[133] Only on 20 February 1958 did the United States approve the loan.[134]

Once Israel had secured the loan, the Foreign Ministry instructed Eban to press not for U.S. support for the periphery plan but for arms, this time with the claim that the United States was obliged to balance Israel's military capability with that of the new Iraqi-Jordanian union.[135] The Americans responded to an Israeli request for 106-mm recoilless rifles by noting that they had no intention of selling Israel "anything that shoots."[136] The Israelis may have found it difficult to present their demands in the context of the Jordan-Iraq union when they knew that the United States was supplying almost no arms to Iraq.[137]

Shiloah insisted that even if arms were not forthcoming, Israel had nevertheless to continue to pursue a security guarantee.[138] He suggested that Israel work toward a secret defense pact with the United States in the framework of the Eisenhower Doctrine to be achieved with the help of Generals Gruenther and Walter Bedell-Smith,[139] and he pressed the prime minister to support yet another attempt at Israeli association with NATO.[140] Ben-Gurion's diary indicates that he was too involved with arms procurement in France and Germany to respond enthusiastically to Shiloah's exhortations.[141] Nevertheless, Shiloah continued to pursue his American contacts, prompting Ambassador Lawson's observation that his "free wheeling" was "outside regular lines of command," and that the Israeli Foreign Ministry was making a "red-faced effort to cover its ignorance of his activity."[142]

The Israeli Foreign Ministry felt that Shiloah was forcing the pace; the head of the United States section cabled Eban his wish that the Israeli embassy, not Shiloah, handle the matter of a security guarantee from the United States: "While everyone sees the matter of defense ties with the United States as important and most desirable, only a small minority believes that it can be achieved under the present conditions. The prime minister and foreign minister are not part of this small minority. *It is up to you, in Washington*, to decide upon the timing of a renewed initiative on this matter."[143]

The overflights of Israel that the United States requested in July 1958 for American and British aircraft in order to bolster the Jordanian regime presented an opportunity for such a renewed initiative. We have already noted these overflights in the context of Anglo-Israeli relations; however, it is important to note in the context of American-Israeli relations that Ben-Gurion was not engaged in "brinkmanship."[144] Israeli hesitation over allowing the overflights was not an attempt by Ben-Gurion to force the United States to grant Israel a security guarantee. Israeli documents clearly show that the Israelis hesitated before allowing the overflights precisely because a U.S. guarantee did not exist.[145] The Israelis, no more expecting that Washington would suddenly grant a formal security guarantee than they had in the previous months,[146] cooperated in the hope that a quid pro quo might be forthcoming at some time in the future. Ben-Gurion made clear in his diary that Israel desired to prove its ability to perform a "decisive service to the entire West."[147]

The documents of the Israeli Foreign Ministry amplify the impression that Ben-Gurion's halting of the overflights on 2 August 1958 could hardly have been a move calculated to pressure the Americans to grant arms and a security guarantee, for the embassy in Washington later protested vehemently the haste with which the Israeli government had halted the flights, claiming that it had in fact been on the verge of obtaining "virtually everything" (arms, a guarantee, and encouragement of Israeli ties with the Middle East periphery states) the prime minister had requested of Dulles.[148] Herzog of the embassy in Washington went as far as to suggest that the prime minister had impeded efforts to make headway on arms and a security guarantee by failing at least to consult the Americans before stopping the flights.[149] He also complained that whereas on one hand Israel demanded that the United States take drastic measures in order to deal with Nasserism and communism, on the other hand the Israelis quickly caved in before a Soviet protest and would have done better to have simply informed the United States of their displeasure at the flights.[150] Herzog claimed that Israel's conduct had severely compromised its image in American eyes.[151]

Nevertheless, Israel received its "reward" from the United States in the form of the sale of one hundred 106-mm recoilless rifles, authorized on 26 August 1957.[152] The Americans were also instrumental in facilitating Israel's Centurion tank deal with Britain. Even with this assistance, however, Ben-Gurion perceived the United States as more a hindrance than a help in arms procurement in Europe. While the Americans encouraged the British transfer of tanks to Israel, they objected to Britain's sale to Israel of submarines.[153] Washington also objected to the sale of jets to Israel by France and Italy, lest it appear that the United States was behind too many arms transfers to Israel.[154]

The Israeli ambassador to Washington took issue with the view that the United States was obstructing Israel's efforts to augment its security and at the beginning of October dispatched a circular memo in defense of U.S. policy toward Israel.[155] Eban cited the expansion of procurement opportunities in the United States since Dulles's August 1958 promise to "reassess" Israel's arms needs.[156] But the ambassador also pointed out that the United States had always insisted that Israel purchase arms in Western Europe. The Americans had been consistent on this matter, and the fact that this was not to the liking of the Israelis did not free them of the obligation to understand the reasons behind this policy, which, noted Eban, were based upon

the American calculation that the United States has for ten years carried the main burden and responsibility for Israel's sovereign status. The United States aided in obtaining recognition of the Jewish state, campaigned for its acceptance to the United Nations and provided the underpinnings of its economy: the development of its agriculture and industry, the strengthening of its scientific institutions, supply of a large proportion of its foodstuffs, support in terms of credit and the prevention of its economic collapse.[157]

Thus, observed Eban, the United States did not feel any obligation to augment massive economic aid with a commitment to fill the role of purveyor of arms to Israel.[158] The fact remained, however, that the United States had, from the establishment of the Jewish state until the end of 1958, granted Israel less than $900,000 in military aid. The combined total of U.S. military aid and sales to Saudi Arabia, Iraq, Jordan, and Lebanon during this period was $137.1 million. Israel's efforts to obtain military aid from the U.S. were "a sad story." [159] Ben-Gurion's decision at the end of 1958 to virtually abandon the attempt to obtain a security guarantee from the United States further underscores the poignancy of Israel's failure on this plane. The prime minister based this decision ostensibly on the reduced Soviet threat to Israel after the events in the region of summer 1958, but as Ben-Gurion made clear, the Israelis also made this decision in order to allow them to concentrate efforts upon acquiring arms from the United States rather than a security guarantee that would entail no arms.[160]

The sale of one hundred recoilless rifles was a turning point only in the sense that prior to this, the United States had refused to sell Israel "anything that shoots." Viewed in the proper perspective, these antitank rifles were purely defensive in nature, and the significance of the American decision to sell them to Israel should not be overstated.[161] When Ben-Gurion met Eisenhower in March 1960, the president promised to review Israel's arms requests,[162] and in late May 1960, the United States agreed to sell Israel $10 million in electronic (mainly radar) equipment.[163] Eisenhower nevertheless reiterated the American refusal to take on the role of principal arms supplier to the Middle East, affirming a policy toward Israel that remained consistent throughout his presidency.

The strategic relationship that some researchers have ascribed to this period did not in fact exist. That it did not was due at least in part to the same trepidations and reservations that characterized the policies of the governments of both countries throughout the 1950s. At the end of 1958, the Israelis again discussed among themselves the question of requesting free military aid from the United States. Israel based the decision to refrain from doing so upon the same considerations that had guided policy when the Israeli government had examined this possibility some years earlier: Israel did not want an American military mission "poking around" its defense facilities.[164] But even had the Israelis been willing to pay this price, the American answer would have been no. The State Department in mid-1959 instructed the new American ambassador to Israel to refrain from visits to IDF establishments and to "avoid as well any activity that can be interpreted as support or sympathetic interest in the IDF."[165]

The subject of the alliance of the periphery has not been dealt with in depth here. However, recently declassified documents in both Israel and the United States indicate that on this plane as well, the Israelis failed to secure American backing. The Israelis hoped that American involvement in such an alliance might create the basis for strategic cooperation between Israel and the United States. Indeed, it may be assumed that there was a certain degree of intelligence sharing between the United States and Israel regarding Israel's relations with the Middle East periphery states.[166] The United States "quietly expressed interest" in Israel's relations with Iran, Ethiopia, and Turkey, yet the Americans remained unreceptive to Israel's requests for tangible assistance for this "project."[167] Thus the Israelis failed to convince the United States to extend military aid to Israel on the basis of Israel's shared concern with Turkey over the threat from Nasser.[168]

The American and Israeli views of the Middle East drew closer after the events of mid-1958. Yet Israel's attempt to bring U.S. military aid to a level commensurate with American economic support of the Jewish state failed almost completely. For this reason, too, the ascription to this period of the term "strategic relationship" is in fact premature. Furthermore, the sale of one hundred recoilless rifles in 1958 was a "one-time deal," and the next American sale of arms to Israel did not take place until 1962, when President John F. Kennedy authorized the sale of Hawk antiaircraft missiles.[169] As we will see, Israel had no choice but to continue to concentrate intense arms procurement efforts in western Europe.

CONCLUSION

Failure to secure a strategic relationship notwithstanding, the centrality of the United States in Israel's foreign policy must again be emphasized. In late 1958, Ben-Gurion told Mapai's Central Committee that "the West is not monolithic, nor is Israel's attitude toward the Western countries." [170] Israel continued to purchase arms from any source available and, in practice, this meant western Europe. However, Ben-Gurion also noted that it was "the future of relations with the United States which will have the greatest bearing of all." [171] In one of his last letters to Dulles before the secretary's death in May 1959, Ben-Gurion reiterated in detail and at length Israel's value to America in the struggle between East and West. [172]

We have seen that Israeli-American ties during this period do not correspond with certain claims made with regard to this relationship. One such claim is that because Israel could fulfill its defense needs in France, the American refusal to sell arms was "not critical." [173] The final chapter of this book will demonstrate that, in fact, reliance upon France alone for arms was a source of great concern to Israel's leaders, and they made every attempt to ameliorate this dependence. In December 1957, Prime Minister Ben-Gurion told the Central Committee of Mapai that he put the United States "at the head of Israel's friends," an attempt to place relations with the United States in what Ben-Gurion considered the proper perspective. [174] The prime minister was aware of the bitterness among Israelis at the lack of American "political support," [175] that is, the American refusal either to provide arms or to explicitly guarantee Israel's security in light of greatly increased Soviet penetration of the region. Ben-Gurion pointed out that nevertheless, Israel's highest priority was a continued effort to obtain an arms supply from the United States commensurate with the level of American economic assistance to Israel. He warned that Israel was not likely to receive arms from the United States within the next three years (that is, before the end of the Eisenhower administration). [176] However, his emphasis on American arms refutes the claim that Israel viewed obtaining arms from the United States as anything less than urgent. During the months following Ben-Gurion's March 1960 meeting with Eisenhower, Israel continued to press its case for receipt of the Hawk missile.

Secretary of State Christian Herter conveyed the American refusal of Israel's request for these missiles in a personal letter to the Israeli prime minister on 4 August, 1960.[177]

Another claim regarding U.S.-Israeli relations in the late 1950s cites a "new American interest in Israel which during this period led to . . . the development of a strong entente between the two countries" and to a "gradually maturing" strategic relationship.[178] The strengthening of relations, which the United States initiated after the Israelis during the 1958 overflights of Jordan had demonstrated their ability to provide assistance in a crisis, was limited to economic and technical aid, hardly the strategic backing in the form of arms that the Israelis sought.[179]

Yet for Israel, the procurement of arms from the United States was imperative. The great reservations that the Israelis harbored regarding the durability of ties with France, their main supplier of arms at that time, was only one reason for this view. Israel's leaders believed that in the long term, only American arms could provide an answer to the growing volume of U.S. arms in the hands of the pro-Western Arab states and the Soviet-supplied arsenals of the USSR's Arab clients.[180] Even at the highwater mark of arms procurement in France, "Israel never abandoned the hope that the arms stores of the United States would not be closed to her forever." [181]

I should carefully note, too, the continued Israeli reservations regarding binding ties with *any* power. The argument that Israel's adherence to the Eisenhower Doctrine in 1957 meant the disappearance of Israeli reticence at openly joining an American-backed defense pact is unfounded,[182] as is the assertion that the Eisenhower Doctrine "symbolized a new era in relations between the two countries." [183] We have seen that both of these claims are inaccurate. The question of Israeli adherence to an American defense pact was not put to the test, because the United States did not offer Israel such a pact. And in fact, although the Israelis made clear both in private [184] and openly their commitment to the free world and opposition to communism,[185] they believed that in practice, Israel must remain uninvolved in great power rivalries while maintaining close ties with the West.[186]

6 IN PURSUIT OF ARMS FROM BRITAIN

1956–1959

  The dominant element in Israeli relations with Britain following the Suez-Sinai campaign remained the British role as an arms supplier to the Middle East. Britain's relations with the Arab states, its role with regard to the supply of oil, and its cooperation with the United States on plans for a peace settlement were the factors impeding an improvement in Anglo-Israeli relations. The first part of this chapter will deal with the poor state of Anglo-Israeli relations from the end of the Suez-Sinai campaign to the end of 1957, the steady improvement in relations that began in early 1958, and the strategic dimensions of that change. The second part of this chapter will analyze Anglo-Israeli cooperation on the British overflights of Israel in mid-1958 designed to keep King Hussein in power in Jordan. The overflights were a central factor in Britain's decision to sell Israel the item it most desired to purchase from that country, the Centurion tank.

On 2 November 1956, the United Nations General Assembly passed a resolution calling for a suspension of arms deliveries to Israel and Egypt.[1] The Israelis had several reasons to protest Britain's strict adherence to this resolution. First, they felt that Britain's continued arming of Jordan and Iraq while the Soviets were supplying Syria seriously undermined the Arab-Israeli arms balance.[2] Second, Britain held up delivery of items for which Israel had already paid, including three Meteors that although long obsolete as day fighters, Israel still needed urgently in order to complete a unit of night fighters.[3] Third was the United Kingdom's "discriminatory policy." The Israelis objected to the British claim that Israel had little need of additional arms because it had proven during the Suez-Sinai campaign what it could do with fewer arms than its adversaries.[4] The Israelis also objected to the line taken by the British that Israel's large store of captured arms and equipment obviated its need for arms purchases.[5]

The Foreign Office pointed out that neither Britain nor Israel could afford to be caught in breach of a United Nations resolution[6] and admonished the director general of the Israeli Defense Ministry, Shimon Peres, declaring that the British opposed "black market transactions."[7] The Israelis were unconvinced. Ambassador to Britain Eliahu Elath protested that the Foreign Office's policy of strict adherence to the UN prohibition on arms sales so soon after Israel and Britain had cooperated in Operation Musketeer was in fact part of London's "general political attitude" toward Jerusalem.[8] Indeed, the records of British Cabinet debates and the tone of British diplomatic communication with Israel indicate that London at the end of 1956 still thought in terms of the Alpha plan, which called for Israeli territorial concessions to the Arab states.[9] In Israeli eyes Britain again manifested this attitude when on 19 January 1957 it refused to join France in voting against a call in the United Nations for Israel's unconditional withdrawal from the Sinai Peninsula.[10]

In fact, British arms "caught" by the ban at the beginning of November 1956 were a small fraction of the total Israel was to receive from the West, mostly from France.[11] But in Israeli eyes Britain's arms policy, even if explicable in light of the UN sanction, was an extension of a hostile policy toward Israel, an accusation the Israelis leveled openly.[12] The point that most rankled the Israelis was Britain's refusal to release even spare parts for arms Israel already possessed.[13] The British gave the Israelis further cause to suspect them of duplicity when in early February 1957, Foreign Secretary Selwyn Lloyd reneged upon a promise the British had made one month earlier to provide spare parts in secret.[14]

In early 1957, the Israelis perceived an opportunity to improve relations with Britain and to effect some change in its arms policy. According to Ambassador Elath, Britain's cooperation with Jordan in ending the defense treaty between those two countries[15] removed the major obstacle in Anglo-Israeli relations.[16] At the same time, Israel was concerned about the disposal of arms and equipment at British bases in Jordan. The Foreign Office stated that the British would neither leave behind nor sell any equipment to the Jordanians.[17] However, the Israelis learned that the Jordanians had been stealing British arms, equipment, and ammunition from the large base at Zarka. Britain had entrusted security to the Jordanians when the British transfered troops from the base because of tension following the Suez campaign. The Jordanians took material worth some £3.5 million, including twenty twenty-five-pound artillery pieces and fourteen seventeen-pound guns.[18] The Israelis claimed that this, as well as tank sales to Jordan,[19] upset the balance and pressed the British to provide arms to Israel in secret.[20]

The Israeli attempt to balance the arms theft and sales to Jordan with releases to Israel failed. For Ben-Gurion, the test of Britain's policy toward Israel continued to be its willingness to provide arms. In a meeting with the British ambassador to Israel on 11 June 1957, Ben-Gurion "spent most of the time talking about the supply of arms to Israel in the context of the unfriendliness of British policy."[21] For the Israelis, spare parts for destroyers and the release of reconditioned Derwent engines for Meteors had become "a shibboleth."[22] Anglo-Israeli relations thus took a turn for the worse when Britain delivered neither arms nor spare parts, even after Israel's final withdrawal in March 1957 from territory occupied during the Suez-Sinai campaign.[23]

In fact, the Foreign Office recognized the need to balance Soviet arms to Syria with a supply to Israel[24] and by mid-March 1957 worked to bring the United States to agree to an end to the arms ban.[25] Although the British did not wish to supply either the Hunter jets[26] or the Centurion tanks the Israelis perennially requested,[27] London felt bound to at least honor outstanding obligations.[28] It was not until August 1957, however, that this became British policy, and in the meantime, the issue of oil supplies to Israel by British-based companies had become an additional and serious source of tension between Israel and Britain.

The Israeli economy had already come under serious hardship when, follow-ing the Suez-Sinai campaign and without warning, the Soviet Union cut off oil supplies to Israel.[29] This left Israel in a situation in which the United States supplied one-third of its oil, and Britain, primarily the Shell Oil Company, two-thirds.[30] By the middle of May 1957, the Israeli government had to deal with an imminent refusal of the British companies to ship oil of either Iranian or Far Eastern origin to Israel.[31] The possibility that at the June 1957 meeting of the Baghdad Pact Iraq would obtain a decision to prevent in any manner possible the flow of Iranian oil to Israel heightened Israeli fears.[32] In Israel's view, Great Britain, also a member of the Baghdad Pact, was perfectly will-ing to sacrifice Israel on the altar of its interests in Iraq,[33] and London's vague assurances to the contrary had little effect.[34]

The Israelis urged London to forestall the move by the oil companies, making clear to the British that this would place Israel's economy under severe stress in the areas of foreign currency, oil prices to consumers, and a loss of tax revenue.[35] Foreign Minister Golda Meir charged that by allowing the stoppage the British were, in effect, aiding the blockade of the Israeli port of Eilat[36] as well as abetting the Arab economic boycott of Israel.[37] On 14 July 1957, Meir informed the British ambassador, Francis Rundall, of Shell Oil's notice that it would stop supplying crude oil from Iran and of the termination of its operations in Israel. The danger, noted Meir, was that Shell might stop supplying Israel with oil from other sources as well,[38] such as Venezuela.[39]

The Israelis made a parallel effort in London to bring the British to stay the consortium's decision by presenting the British government's sharehold-ing in British Petroleum, one of the major companies involved, as evidence of Britain's ability to influence the decision.[40] Elath accused the British of having known of the decision in advance and of having done nothing to pre-vent it. Furthermore, claimed Elath, the decision was a political one, part of Britain's overall policy since the Suez-Sinai campaign of appeasing the Arabs and discriminating against Israel in every area, especially arms sales.[41]

The Israelis dealt with the problem of a supply of crude oil by purchasing Iranian oil "under the counter" through Switzerland and the Standard Oil Company of Ohio, albeit at higher prices.[42] The British continued to insist that their decision was an economic one taken strictly by the companies in-volved, not a political one by the British government,[43] and that in any case it was a decision not to the liking of the Foreign Office.[44] However, for the

Israelis the Shell affair was a serious test of Anglo-Israeli relations that Britain had failed. In the British view, the effect of Shell's decision was "foreseeable and inevitable," and the Foreign Office realized that the affair was, in Israeli eyes, further evidence of Britain's ill will toward the Jewish state.[45]

RENEWED ISRAELI SUSPICIONS OF THE GUILDHALL PLAN

In August 1957, Britain decided to release spare parts and maintenance items[46] without clearance of the NEACC in order to avoid U.S. objections.[47] In this case, Britain decided it would circumvent Washington lest the Shell affair along with its position on arms lose for Britain "all influence over Israeli policy."[48] Britain wished to at least partially mollify the Israelis, and this created a dilemma for London, especially in view of its relations with Iraq. Although the value to Britain of these arms transactions with Israel was marginal, and the political risk, especially with regard to Iraq, was great,[49] the Syrian and Egyptian threats to Amman and the internal convulsions in Jordan made quiet on King Hussein's western border imperative.[50] A conflict between Israel and Jordan, feared London, would give either Damascus or Cairo an excuse to send forces into Jordan.[51] One way of achieving quiet on the Israeli-Jordanian border was a limited release of arms to Israel, despite the widely held view in the Foreign Office that

> the Israelis are trying to get us onto a slippery slope. . . . Next we shall be told that the Israelis cannot keep their aircraft in the air without the supply of trainers, and that in order to maintain the status quo it is our duty to supply them with further aircraft, and so on and so on. In the end the Arabs are bound to find out. Indeed the Israelis may well tell them just for the pleasure of getting us into trouble with the Arabs . . . the effect on the weak Iraqi Government might be disastrous.[52]

For the Israelis, it seemed unreasonable that Hussein's troubles earn him the ten Centurion tanks and modern jets that London was, in September 1957, rumored to be about to send to Jordan.[53] Indeed, the Israelis were well aware that should *they* again press for the Centurions they had been waiting for since 1953, the British response would be negative.[54] Israel expected some quid pro quo for its concern over Hussein's fate.[55] Thus when Golda Meir assured the British that Israel would keep things quiet on the Jordanian border and "take a back seat"[56] to Western initiatives, it was in exchange for spare parts to Israel from Britain.[57]

Israel's deep mistrust of Britain resurfaced when by early November 1957 no progress had been made on the delivery of any military hardware beyond spare parts. British failure to release the three Meteors, any Centurions, and guns for torpedo boats heightened Israeli suspicion.[58] Israel's patience was wearing thin because the delays seemed unreasonable when the Soviets were (according to Israel) planning to construct naval bases in Egypt and in Syria.[59] Elath expressed Israel's lack of faith in Britain in rather extreme fashion when he met Foreign Secretary Selwyn Lloyd on 10 December 1957. The ambassador opened with a warning that a British attempt to force a peace settlement based on Anthony Eden's November 1955 Guildhall speech would require force.[60] Elath then brought up the additional complaints Israel harbored regarding United Kingdom policy: arms supplies, acquiescence to Nasser's actions regarding Suez and the Gulf of Eilat prior to the Sinai war, Lloyd's pressure on Israel to withdraw from Sinai even before the United Nations pursued the matter, and the Shell affair. The Foreign Office regarded this as a dredging-up of old grudges, but of the grievances Elath presented, the British found the Guildhall matter most disturbing,[61] because Elath's conclusion was that as long as the Guildhall plan was part of British policy even in theory, Israel would view every British move with suspicion.[62] Lloyd resented "having the meaning of the Guildhall speech twisted by the Israelis in order to have a grouse."[63]

Actually, the fear that the United States and Britain would again press them to cede territory had never ceased to worry the Israelis.[64] What the Foreign Office called the latest spate of "Guildhallitis" was the very real Israeli fear that the United States and Britain were about to renew their attempts to apply the secret Alpha plan.[65] The Foreign Office attributed Elath's "outburst" to inaccurate information that Israel's borders would be one of the main questions discussed at the upcoming NATO conference (in December 1957).[66] The Israelis had learned that the other parties to the conference opposed any initiative on the matter,[67] and the British denied that they had attempted to place the matter on the agenda of the NATO conference.[68] However, the important factor in mitigating Israeli fears was the realization in Jerusalem that the United States was unwilling to pursue such an initiative.[69] By late December 1957, "the obsession with the chimera of British plans to impose territorial concessions on Israel had spent most of its force."[70]

The end of this latest round over Guildhall was followed by Britain's release on 1 January 1958 of the jets and artillery pieces Israel had long been demanding.[71] There is no clear indication that the British timed this release in order to stem what they termed the "appreciable deterioration [in Anglo-Israeli relations] of the last few months," and in any case, the reaction in Israel was mixed, because the British release of arms was too little, too late.[72] The Israeli Defense Ministry now considered the Meteors too outdated even as night fighters,[73] and regardless, three of them would make little difference to the Israeli Air Force.[74] In April 1957, the embassy in London applied to the Foreign Office for one hundred half-tracks,[75] but by June the Israeli Defense Ministry had decided that it would direct its procurement efforts in London toward obtaining only one item—the Centurion tank. Besides the attempt to acquire the Centurion, Israel's focus on British arms policy would be primarily in order to pressure Britain to limit its arms shipments to Arab countries.[76]

Despite the limited utility to Israel of this arms release, the effect was a slight improvement in Anglo-Israeli relations. The 14 February 1958 Arab Union between Iraq and Jordan put these relations further to the test.[77] The union created a potentially explosive situation between Israel and Jordan, yet the Israelis made considerable effort to remain aloof of conflict.[78] At the end of January 1958, the British ambassador reported to Lloyd that "there is a growing body of evidence of some change in Israel; of increasing evidence to seek progress by quiet diplomacy towards easing some of the problems which go to make up the Arab/Israel conflict. . . . There is no doubt that Ben-Gurion's government are resolutely intent to keep 'all quiet' on all borders if they possibly can."[79]

With the establishment of the Iraq-Jordan Arab Union, Israel evinced a growing willingness to cooperate with Britain in order to defuse tension with Jordan. London served increasingly as a channel of communication between Jerusalem on one hand and Amman and Baghdad on the other. Two weeks after the establishment of the union, the Foreign Office passed the Israelis the message that King Faisal of Iraq was interested in maintaining quiet with Israel.[80] Britain had a keen interest in keeping the Israeli-Jordanian border peaceful, and the Foreign Office regularly showed the Israeli ambassador to London telegrams sent by Britain's ambassadors in Jordan and Iraq.[81] The Israelis attempted to secure Iraqi adherence to the armistice agreement to which Baghdad's Jordanian partners-in-union were signatory.[82] The Iraqis refused, but Ambassador Francis Rundall of Britain noted that "the Israel government have decided that it is wiser to keep their conciliatory powder dry."[83] In mid-June 1958, the Israeli embassy in London reported that the British now recognized "Israel's [potentially] positive role in the Western defense system and in preventing Nasser's expansion."[84] At that point, the circumspect Israeli appraisal was that it was too early to determine whether the change in Britain's attitude toward Israel portended a practical change.[85] In one month's time, the opportunity for actual Anglo-Israeli cooperation arrived,[86] and as we shall see, Israel used this cooperation primarily to acquire arms.

BRITISH OVERFLIGHTS OF ISRAEL

On 14 July 1958, Prime Minister Nuri Said was overthrown in a coup in Iraq. On 15 July King Hussein, faced with an uprising in Jordan, appealed to the Western powers for assistance.[87] The British requested the same day that Israel allow the Royal Air Force to overfly Israel for the purpose of furnishing military assistance to Jordan.[88] The Israelis took advantage of the permission they granted Britain to obtain arms and guarantees of its borders but not an alliance.[89] In fact, Israel received arms from Britain as a later reward for its cooperation, not through the employment of "brinkmanship."[90] Two scholarly contentions regarding subsequent events may be challenged: First, that neither the United States nor Britain had considered an Israeli role in such an eventuality as the Jordan crisis and second, that Ben-Gurion feared that the overflights, termed Operation Fortitude by the United States and Britain, might complicate Israeli plans for an invasion of the West Bank.[91]

In fact, both American and British contingency planning took into account the possibility of an approach to Israel in the event of a crisis in Jordan. In April 1957, a State Department memorandum titled "Emergency Overflight Clearance for U.S. Aircraft" recorded that the State Department requested of the Israelis "advance clearance in principle for a small number of U.S. aircraft to overfly Israel en route to Jordan. When and if the flight became necessary, we would make an emergency request through the normal channels."[92] The British were also aware of the need to carefully coordinate any entry into Israeli air space with Jerusalem as well as of Israel's extreme sensitivity to unauthorized incursions.[93] An incident in February 1958 in which a British Canberra bomber entered Israeli air space without prior notice drove home to London the fact that the RAF would have to obtain Israeli permission for any overflight of the Israeli Control Area.[94] The British ambassador warned that "for obvious reasons the Israeli Air Force is very quick on the trigger. . . . There is a real risk of trouble. Apart from this however, there are bound to be political repercussions from what they will regard as a deliberate flouting of their rules."[95]

The fact that the British requested permission for overflights on 15 July 1958, even before the Jordanians asked for help,[96] is additional proof that they had considered this eventuality beforehand. Predictably, Israel was offended when the RAF carried out its first flights before Israel had granted its official consent.[97] When Prime Minister Macmillan apologized, he drew upon the improvement in Anglo-Israeli relations of the past few months, noting that Britain and Israel "were at one in recognizing the need to preserve the independence of Jordan."[98]

As for Israel's view of Jordan, there too previous accounts of these events need adjustment. When Israel granted official permission for the overflights, Ben-Gurion confided to his diary that "the deployment of the British army in Jordan is not to our advantage."[99] Israel wished to remain aloof of conflict and demanded that British troops flown to Jordan not take part in any clashes that might occur on the Israeli-Jordanian border,[100] a condition to which the British agreed.[101] Israel's demand does not mean that it feared a British occupation of Jordan that would thwart Israeli hopes of territorial aggrandizement. Indeed, noted Ben-Gurion, "the time when Britain could take over a foreign country has passed."[102] Rather, Israeli contingency plans for conquering the West Bank were to be employed in case the Allies *failed* to save the Jordanian monarch.[103] At a meeting of the Knesset's Foreign Affairs and Security Committee on 16 July 1958, several members did in fact propose an invasion of Jordan.[104] The activist Ahdut Ha'avoda party advocated grabbing the West Bank whether the British stayed in Jordan or not.[105] However, Landau, of the right-wing Herut party, suggested that such a move be made only if Nasser succeeded in taking control of Jordan. Ben-Gurion rejected Ahdut Ha'avoda's demand and agreed with Landau, adding that Israel would invade Jordan only if the IDF had the necessary arms and the Soviets did not support Nasser.[106]

The British themselves, although ever suspicious of Israel's aggressive intentions, considered it unlikely that the Israelis would seize the West Bank. Thus, according to Rundall, "the prime minister is well aware that Israel's first interest is to keep Nasser's hands off the Arab Union. He must, therefore, also realize that the lesser risks have to be accepted to this end."[107] The Americans concurred, doubting that the Israelis would risk wrecking any "partnership or closer collaboration with the West, as long as they were badly in need of arms and clearly scouring the world for them. Aggressive action on her part might close all the doors except the French."[108]

Ben-Gurion used the term "partnership" when he demanded, with commencement of the overflights, close consultation with Britain on political, military, and intelligence matters.[109] The British understood well that Ben-Gurion was not proposing an alliance.[110] They also understood that his request for arms was not "brinkmanship" but the "psychological moment to extract his long-term price [and] all he thinks the traffic will bear." The British ambassador to Israel emphasized that it would be "a mistake to dismiss Ben-Gurion's proposal as blackmail."[111] When Rundall met with Ben-Gurion on 19 July 1958, the prime minister noted, "Either we can be partners . . ." Rundall, prompting him to finish the sentence, continued, "Or . . ." Ben-Gurion then said that there was no "or"; Israel would not be "unfriendly" if the British turned down the Israeli proposal.[112]

The Israelis made clear to Whitehall that what they wanted most was arms, not a formal guarantee and not a strategic alliance.[113] They were requesting an *informal* guarantee, and the best one to be had was through the provision of arms.[114] Israel had requested a "steep bill," which included several squadrons of Hunter jet fighters, three squadrons of bombers, one hundred Centurion tanks, and two submarines.[115] The list was far more extensive than any Israel had previously submitted, but there is no evidence that the intent was to force Britain's hand. Foreign Office documents give no indication that the British felt this bill had to be paid promptly and in full in order to ensure continued Israeli agreement to the overflights. With the rapid unfolding of events in Iraq, the Foreign Office had already decided that in principle Britain would pursue a closer relationship with Israel, although there was no sense of urgency: "Our preliminary reaction is that we must avoid giving it [Ben-Gurion's approach] a discouraging reply. Much will depend on our future relations with Iraq, but we doubt whether we can in future maintain our 'stand-off policy' towards Israel merely to please the Iraqis."[116]

Moreover, Rundall's opinion was that although "it would keep the atmosphere sweet" if the British showed a willingness to discuss Israel's arms requests,[117] Britain did not have to take the actual figures in the requests presented by the Israelis seriously.[118] The Foreign Office knew that "the Centurions are really the touchstone of our intentions as far as the Israelis are concerned."[119] The Israeli Foreign Ministry noted that the British were preparing a new long-term policy in the region and warned that it was incumbent upon Israel to avoid presenting the West with rigid demands during the crisis.[120] Thus, although Israel received only the vaguest assurances regarding either arms or guarantees, Ben-Gurion agreed to a continuation of the overflights and even a five-day intensified airlift, beginning 27 July 1958.[121]

THE SOVIET NOTE TO ISRAEL

On 2 August 1958, the Soviet Union sent Israel a note containing a denunciation of Israel's assent to the overflights.[122] Ben-Gurion regarded this as a grave development,[123] and he informed Rundall the same day that the overflights must cease immediately.[124] Meanwhile, neither the United States nor Britain met Ben-Gurion's demands for explicit guarantees, while the outrage the Americans expressed at what they perceived as an Israeli cave-in to Soviet pressure weakened Israel's position vis-à-vis the West.[125] On 4 August, the British made clear to Ben-Gurion that Israel had enough of a guarantee under the terms of the Eisenhower Doctrine.[126] On 6 August, the Israelis allowed a partial resumption of American flights in exchange for only a vague American promise to give "careful consideration to Israeli defense requirements" and British agreement to receive Foreign Minister Meir in London for "high-level strategic talks." [127]

Indeed, it had been apparent enough to London all along that the Israelis were "clearly playing for arms or a border guarantee as a quid pro quo." [128] But although Israel demanded an explicit Western guarantee in exchange for a continuation of the overflights after the Soviet warning, Ben-Gurion did not use the Soviet threat in order to pressure Britain into providing arms. When Israel agreed to the intensification of the flights on 27 July 1958, Operation Fortitude had been in full swing for ten days. It was on the basis of these ten days that the Israelis hoped to receive their reward. Shimon Peres arrived in London on 31 July for a one-day survey of the chances of acquiring British arms.[129] The British gave no indication that they thought Israel was "blackmailing them." The Foreign Office view was that Ben-Gurion would in fact have liked to have continued the overflights but after the 2 August warning could not bring the matter of a full renewal of British flights before his reluctant and even "frightened" cabinet.[130]

Israel used the situation in Jordan, not the Soviet note, to pressure the British into granting arms. On 6 August 1958 Ambassador Elath told Macmillan that "Israel would feel stronger in not getting involved militarily in Jordan if it was itself in a better military position" [131] and hinted in unsubtle fashion that there was no need to expand upon this point.[132] It is not clear upon whose instructions Elath was acting, as there is no evidence of such an initiative in Ben-Gurion's diary or elsewhere. In any case, the British considered this "carpet-dealer's stuff," [133] especially as Golda Meir had stated the day before that even if trouble arose in Jordan, Israel would not invade.[134] Rather than enhance Israel's chances in London of establishing a long-term arms relationship, Elath's move encouraged the Foreign Office to promise the Israelis nothing for the future but to buy them off with a one-time, limited arms shipment in order "to be done with them." [135]

The fact that London did not choose to provide arms at this juncture was, ironically, to Israel's benefit. The Foreign Office later noted that arms were "*not* the price which Israel exacted for permitting us to overfly Israel to come to Jordan's rescue." [136] Rather, Britain intended to both reward the Israelis and provide them with an incentive for good behavior in the future by providing the military item Israel most desired. Thus, noted the Foreign Office, "we have to remember that the government of Israel was privately extremely cooperative in the matter of the overflights . . . they have been friendly about what might happen in a new emergency, and the plain fact is that it is extremely important in the interests of King Hussein that Israel remain cooperative." [137]

The Israeli Foreign Ministry noted the change in Britain's policy toward Israel but warned against expecting a "revolution." [138] When Golda Meir met Selwyn Lloyd in London on 11 August 1958, Lloyd's stated objective was "to establish relations of confidence with Israel" and to "consult the Israelis fully on everything." [139] The two agreed upon cooperation that marked achievement of the consultation Ben-Gurion had demanded at the beginning of the crisis. Within a short time, contact with the British included Persian Gulf, Afro-Asian, and NATO affairs, and most important to Jerusalem, Britain agreed to sell Israel the Centurion tank.[140]

BRITAIN SELLS THE CENTURION TO ISRAEL

The Centurion sale, along with a steady increase in intelligence sharing, ushered in a "honeymoon period" in Anglo-Israeli relations that the Israelis were eager to place on a long-term basis.[141] Ben-Gurion, perennially suspicious of the British, admitted to his diary in early November 1958 that there was "some movement" in the British attitude toward Israel.[142] But not all of the Israelis were so circumspect. Shimon Peres, feeling that a new day had dawned, "held forth about the beauties of some kind of commonwealth relationship and the use of bases in Israel for the Royal Navy."[143] The British warned against such unrealistic expectations; the pace in developing relations could not be forced.[144] Nevertheless, relations between the two countries improved considerably. At the end of 1958, the Israeli Foreign Ministry noted (not without bitterness toward the Americans) that contact with the Foreign Office was far more "encouraging and enlightening" than that which Israel had ever enjoyed with the State Department.[145]

For Israel, another welcome outcome of its cooperation with Britain on the overflights was London's official disavowal of the Guildhall plan.[146] However, as noted above, the British had in effect already abandoned this plan in late 1957, when it became clear that it would not enjoy American support. In truth, the Israelis realized that Britain was now carefully coordinating virtually all of its policies in the Middle East, including arms sales, with the United States.[147] Indeed, the Foreign Office told the Israelis that "the question of tanks is one which we should like to handle on the basis of an agreed Anglo-American policy."[148] American approval allowed Britain to complete the initial Centurion deal (fifty-five tanks, enough for one regiment) with Israel at the end of October 1958.[149] The correspondence of the British Foreign Office reveals that the British fully intended to continue to sell Israel arms on this scale.[150]

With the purchase of the Centurion, the Israelis had achieved their primary aim with regard to Britain. On 27 August 1958, Peres informed the British that Israel would not be interested in purchasing aircraft from the United Kingdom.[151] Precisely why Israel withdrew its application for these jets is not clear, although it is possible it was because the British wished to supply only Meteors, not Hunters. Israel in any case would probably have been unable to pay for jets in addition to the Centurions, which placed an extraordinary burden upon the Israeli budget.[152] At any rate, the immediate Israeli goal in the field of armor was the acquisition of a total of 165 heavy tanks; 55 of these were the Centurions from Britain and the remaining 110 were to be American M-47s, of which Peres hoped France and Italy would each supply 55.[153] These 165 heavy tanks were to be balanced against a total of some 400 heavy tanks already in the Arab arsenals,[154] but in fact Israel was at that point unable even to finance all of the Centurion tanks and had later to hold the British to an agreement to supply the rest when it was able to pay.[155]

The Centurion, which had been the object of Israel's procurement efforts in Britain since early 1953 and in Israeli eyes the litmus test of British intentions toward the Jewish state, became the main armor of the IDF until at least the late 1960s. By 1966, Israel had acquired some 250 Centurions from Britain.[156] Only in 1970, with purchase of the M-60 (Patton) tank from the United States, did Israel acquire a fighting vehicle superior to the Centurion.[157]

CONCLUSION

As we shall see in the next chapter, Britain was unwilling to supply the intermediate-range surface-to-surface missiles Israel requested of the United Kingdom in 1959. Nevertheless, the British supply of tanks meant that Israel had at least partly succeeded in alleviating the situation whereby France was its sole supplier of arms. Whereas the United States still refused to sell the Israelis almost any arms and objected to other European arm sales to Israel, Washington's approval facilitated Britain's supply of these tanks.

Israel did not seek, as has been claimed, to use the overflights as an opportunity to obtain a strategic alliance with Britain. For Prime Minister David Ben-Gurion, the time when Israel might have sought a strategic alliance with Britain had long passed. In his view, there was no point in such an alliance, because Britain's position in the region had been so diminished.[158]

In the area of arms sales, however, there were four reasons why Britain remained a salient factor in Israeli considerations. First, Ben-Gurion feared that France, Israel's primary source of arms from mid-1956, would abruptly halt sales to Israel.[159] Second, this fear, coupled with American unwillingness to sell Israel arms, heightened the importance of all other possible sources of arms, including Britain. Third, the gradual reemergence of close Anglo-American coordination of policy in the region following the Suez-Sinai campaign, which included arms supply to the Middle East, meant that the United States encouraged Israel to seek arms in western Europe, and that the United States would supply only spare parts and only in cases in which the particular item was unavailable elsewhere.[160] And fourth, Israel desired to acquire a heavy tank, unavailable in France, to counterbalance those in Arab possession.

The Israeli perception of Britain after the Suez-Sinai campaign was of a power in decline attempting to hold on to influence in the region through appeasement of the Arabs. The Israelis viewed a further lessening of British influence as inevitable, but it seemed to them that Britain might well damage vital Israeli interests in the process of that decline.[161] Indeed, a certain euphoria in Israel over cooperation with the British during the 1956 campaign quickly dissipated when it became clear that Britain was a "broken reed."[162]

British prime minister Anthony Eden made clear that Britain demanded an Israeli withdrawal from the Gaza Strip and the Sinai Peninsula, a policy dictated largely by fear of a Kuwaiti oil stoppage.[163] The Israelis realized that the British could do further damage by upsetting the Arab-Israeli arms balance through a considerable augmenting of the arsenals of their Arab clients, primarily Jordan and Iraq.

Yet the British had an interest in maintaining a modicum of influence upon Israel as well as upon their Arab clients. The limited modus vivendi between Britain and Israel reached by mid-1958 grew out of basic agreement on the desirability of the maintenance of the status quo in Jordan[164] and included intelligence sharing on Middle East affairs. An improvement in Anglo-Israeli relations was also possible because by the end of 1957 both sides understood, albeit tacitly, that there would be no settlement along the lines of Guildhall[165] and because there was a gradual change in Britain's arms policy toward Israel, which included the release in early 1958 of arms the British had withheld since the Suez-Sinai campaign.

Finally, by late 1958 the Israelis had less reason to fear that despite its decline in the region Britain might yet do great harm to Israel through the sale of arms to Arab states. Following the 1958 coup, Iraq, a lucrative arms market for Britain, turned almost exclusively to the Soviet Union for weapons.[166] Thus the fact that the United Kingdom was left with the much smaller Jordanian and Kuwaiti markets also marked a British decline in the region, and Israeli protests in London against Britain's arming of the Arabs ceased to be a major stumbling block in Anglo-Israeli relations.

7 THE QUESTION OF A FRENCH ORIENTATION

1957–1960

Following the Suez-Sinai campaign, did Israel consider pursuing a foreign policy based on a French "orientation"? Scholars dealing with this period have suggested that the Israelis weighed their relationship with the United States, found it wanting, and decided to cast their lot with France and other western European powers, such as the Federal Republic of Germany. One researcher claims that in 1958 "Israel was guided by France in . . . the decision to opt for a European orientation in foreign affairs."[1] Yet no such decision was ever made. Another scholar asserts that in cultivating the Israeli Defense Ministry's relations with France, Shimon Peres "laid the foundations for the theory of a 'European' policy and thus preempted the Foreign Ministry by several years."[2] Neither explanation of the "theory" of this "European policy" nor the reason why the Foreign Ministry finally had the good sense to adopt it is forthcoming.

In fact, recently declassified documents demonstrate that the Israelis harbored serious reservations regarding ties with France, even after cooperation between the two countries in the war of 1956. Israel never perceived France as a long-term, viable alternative to the achievement of a close strategic relationship with the United States. Furthermore, the Israelis considered close ties with Germany to be more important as a possible alternative than complement to relations with France. As noted in a previous chapter, Israel viewed Bonn as a possible "back door" toward the acquisition of arms from Washington because of American-German ties in the framework of NATO. Yet in Israeli eyes, neither France nor Germany, the two main components of what some scholars have termed the "European orientation," could constitute a long-term alternative to a strategic relationship with the United States.

FRANCE PRESSURES ISRAEL TO WITHDRAW FROM GAZA

At the end of February 1957, French Prime Minister Mollet and his foreign minister, Christian Pineau, arrived in Washington to attempt to repair relations with the United States.[3] Israel was one of the topics on their agenda. Pineau and Secretary of State Dulles reached a formula that would avoid the need for UN sanctions in order to force an Israeli withdrawal from the Gaza Strip. The French at this time wished to rebuild bridges to the Arab world and were also under pressure from NATO and other European countries to help facilitate the resumption of a full flow of oil from the Middle East. Thus on 27 February 1958 Pineau proposed that the Israelis withdraw on their own initiative. The Israelis would do so, suggested Pineau, with the understanding that Egyptian forces would not return to Gaza, even though it must have been apparent to the sides involved that there was no assurance that the Egyptians would refrain from doing so.[4]

FRANCE AS ISRAEL'S SOLE SOURCE OF ARMS

Crosbie quotes Pineau as saying that "France did not exert the least pressure on Israel."[5] In Israeli eyes, however, the French role was not so benign. One of the reasons Israel agreed to the proposal was, as Prime Minister Ben-Gurion told Chief-of-Staff Moshe Dayan, the fear that France "would desert, leaving Israel completely alone and without arms."[6] Dayan answered that Israel had arms enough for the next year. Ben-Gurion pointed out that this would not suffice if Israel rejected the American-French proposal, in which case there would be sanctions.[7] At a meeting of Mapai's Central Committee on 3 March 1957, the prime minister warned of the danger in not submitting to the French proposal.[8] At that meeting, Foreign Minister Golda Meir denied that the French had actually threatened to "abandon" Israel if it did not respond favorably to the proposal,[9] but less than two weeks later, Ben-Gurion reminded the committee that whatever misgivings the Israelis had about relations with France,[10] Paris was, in the meantime, Israel's only source of arms.[11]

Israeli fears seem exaggerated in light of the figures on French arms transfers to Israel from 1956 to 1959. At the beginning of 1957, three of the four Israeli front-line air squadrons were equipped solely with French jets, whereas only one was made up of the older British Meteors.[12] Israeli tank units were now equipped mainly with French seventy-five-millimeter guns in either old Shermans or new French AMX tanks, and all of Israel's artillery, French-supplied, was of recent manufacture.[13] By June 1958, Israel's arsenal of French jets included twenty Ouragan fighters, fifty-seven Mystère 4A fighters, and fifteen Vautour-2 light bombers.[14] Israel had to pay the full commercial price for each item,[15] but France was amenable to extending credit (albeit very limited) for these purchases. Thus, by the end of 1959, Israel had a total of twenty-four Vautours,[16] bought through a credit arrangement whereby the Israelis paid $11 million in 1958 and the balance, another $11 million, in 1959.[17] In July 1958, the French agreed to sell Israel twenty-four Super-Mystère B-2 fighters (the answer to Egypt's Soviet MiG-19s) on credit over three-years, interest-free.[18]

ISRAEL FEARS A FRENCH-ARAB RAPPROCHEMENT

Bar-Zohar notes that Israel's doubts regarding the durability of the French-Israeli relationship were based upon the instability of the French political system.[19] In fact, doubts about Israel's relationship with France were far more profound than mere misgivings regarding French politics. The fall of the Mollet government in May 1957 heightened Israeli anxieties, but they were to some extent allayed when in that same month, the French urged the Israelis to submit an arms procurement plan for the next few years. This, noted Ben-Gurion, would reduce Israeli vulnerability to the political vicissitudes of the French Fourth Republic.[20] However, the relationship with France came under increasing criticism in Mapai Party forums during early and mid-1957. In January 1957, Mapai's Central Committee noted that French-Israeli friendship notwithstanding, this was the same socialist government that a few months earlier had courted Nasser in the hope of convincing the Egyptian president to desist from aiding the Algerian rebels.[21]

Indeed, to the Israelis it was obvious that their relationship with France was based on little more than mutual animosity toward Nasser. Even their close relationship with the French defense establishment, they feared, would disappear once France solved its Algerian problem. The question was not whether French-Israeli friendship would survive a French-Arab rapprochement (the consensus was that it would not) but how long it would take France to conclude its Algerian difficulties. In May 1957, Mapai secretary general Giora Yoseftal warned that Israel had already placed too many hopes upon ties with France. The French were bound to move toward a compromise with the Arabs of Algeria, and Israel, he said, should abandon the line of "brotherhood" with France in foreign policy.[22] When Zalman Aran disagreed and expressed the view that the relationship with France would be of long duration, the only reason he cited was his opinion that the French would be unable to give up Algeria.[23]

The demise of the Mollet government in May 1957 increased the freedom with which the Quai d'Orsay pursued a rapprochement with the Arabs. Support for Israel was confined to ineffectual pro-Israeli pressure groups, such as the Alliance France-Israël.[24] The Israelis maintained close ties with the French army and Defense Ministry. Yet while Ben-Gurion wrote of a French promise to grant arms in an emergency upon ten days' notice and to lend Israel French army equipment upon notice of twenty days,[25] the French emphatically denied that they would help Israel militarily in the event of a new round of hostilities.[26]

BEN GURION AND FRENCH VERSUS AMERICAN GOALS

A coalition headed by the Radical Maurice Bourgès-Maunoury replaced the Mollet government, which the year before had helped pave the way for French arms sales to Israel. When this coalition fell in late September 1957, Ben-Gurion again confided to his diary his deep concern over the future of French-Israeli relations.[27] However, as long as Israel depended upon France for arms, public pronouncements criticizing relations with that country had to be curbed. When Mapai member of Knesset David Hacohen, for example, made disparaging remarks to the press about the relationship with France in late 1957, Ben-Gurion reprimanded him.[28] But in the more restricted Foreign Affairs Committee of Mapai (the usual number of participants there was twelve), Ben-Gurion warned against harboring "illusions" regarding the relationship with France. The prime minister drew a comparison of Israeli relations with France on one hand and the United States on the other and left no doubt as to where Israel's long-term interests lay. In Ben-Gurion's eyes, the French were pursuing regional goals entirely different from those of the United States.[29] An alliance with the United States was possible because the Americans, as leaders of the free world, had interests that "transcended oil matters in Saudi Arabia."[30] The French, he continued, would never be either willing or able to "stand by Israel against the entire world,"[31] and thus the duration of Israel's relationship with France would necessarily be limited to "a few short years."[32]

Ben-Gurion's view that the French did not share the broader concerns of the free world with regard to the Middle East was reinforced by the attitude of the French government toward the events of mid-1958. In July 1958, the prime minister told the French ambassador that he was surprised that France had not joined the United States and Britain in sending troops to Lebanon.[33] There was a fundamental difference between the Israeli and the French approaches to the upheavals in Lebanon, Iraq, and Jordan.[34] The Israelis wished to see Western containment of Nasserism; President Charles de Gaulle, on the other hand, called for a multilateral approach to the problems of the Middle East, including Soviet participation,[35] which was anathema to Israel. Thus in early September 1958, Meir explained to de Gaulle that Israel had allowed American and British overflights of its territory because it saw a weakening of Nasser's influence in Jordan to be in its interest.[36]

RELATIONS WITH GERMANY AS AN INSURANCE POLICY

Uncertainty regarding the relationship with France also played a major role in Israel's development of close ties with West Germany. In late December 1957, Bourgès-Maunoury (at that time minister of the interior) told the Israelis that France, West Germany, and Italy had decided to organize a secret pool for arms research, and he advised Shimon Peres to forge closer ties with West Germany so that Israel could participate.[37] In fact, the Israelis knew of the pool and were already cultivating closer ties with Bonn for this reason.[38] There was, however, a more important motive behind Israel's efforts to achieve a closer relationship with West Germany: Israel's perception of ties with Bonn as "insurance," especially in the area of defense procurement, should France at some point prove reluctant to continue to supply arms. This calculation became even more salient when de Gaulle became president of the Fifth Republic in May 1958, because this signaled the beginning of the end of Israel's "unorthodox relationship" with France.[39]

In early 1958, Ben-Gurion told the Foreign Affairs Committee of Mapai that "the future of Israel's relations with France depends upon relations with Germany."[40] The need to find money for arms purchases from France provided an immediate reason for the turn to Germany. The French were willing to extend limited credit for arms purchases but could not finance Israeli arms procurement in France. Israel needed large sums of money for arms, and this prompted Ben-Gurion to note that "unless economic aid for arms purchases could be secured elsewhere [read Germany], assistance from France would come to an end."[41] It is possible that the French themselves encouraged the Israelis to regard Germany as a potential financier, as the French received financial backing from the Federal Republic when the United States disapproved of their nuclear research program.[42]

THE INCIPIENT ARMS CONNECTION WITH GERMANY

The French continued to supply arms to Israel even after de Gaulle became president in May 1958. Despite this, Ben-Gurion saw greater long-term potential in ties with Germany. He believed it was incumbent upon Israel to develop closer relations with the Federal Republic because West Germany was already the foremost economic and industrial power in Europe.[43] It was to Bonn, said Ben-Gurion, that Israel should turn for capital investment in major development projects.[44] The prime minister made specific mention of such areas as the chemical industry and development of Israel's ports, areas in which France could help "only a little," whereas countries such as Holland, Italy, and Belgium would follow West Germany's lead with regard to similar aid to Israel.[45]

The Israelis also sought closer relations with West Germany because they feared that the benefits in the area of defense that might accrue them as a result of closer French-German relations would not materialize if the Paris-Bonn relationship deteriorated.[46] For example, Ben-Gurion recorded in his diary Israel's interest in a French-German plan to develop a medium tank that was supposed to be operational in 1961.[47] However, in late 1957 Ben-Gurion also noted that it was essential that Israel forge bilateral ties with West Germany in order to obtain weapons "not available anywhere else."[48] As we shall see, he was probably referring to missiles.

Israel's leaders thus viewed arms from West Germany as the most important aspect of the pursuit of closer ties with the Federal Republic.[49] By early 1957, they had begun to explore the possibility of developing defense ties with West Germany that would be completely independent of ties with France. As Ben-Gurion noted, this was in keeping with the policy of achieving security through the acquisition of arms from any possible source regardless of the nature of the regime involved.[50] The government's authority to approach any country for this purpose was defined in Article 36 of the 1955 coalition agreement between Mapai and Ahdut Ha'avoda and Mapam.

In Ben-Gurion's view, defense ties with the Federal Republic had two additional advantages over those with France. First, of all of the countries of Western Europe, West Germany had the most influence with the United States, and this influence, Ben-Gurion told the Central Committee of Mapai, was particularly salient with regard to NATO affairs.[51] Second, Ben-Gurion observed that Chancellor Konrad Adenauer felt a strong sense of German moral obligation toward Israel, and this could translate into a long-term commitment to aid Israel in arms development and procurement. When in late December 1957 Peres met the defense minister of the Federal Republic, Franz Josef Strauss, the latter spoke of a specific German obligation to augment Israeli security as a step toward eliminating the "terrible abyss between the German and the Jewish people."[52]

Unlike in the arms relationship with France, there existed in German-Israeli relations a moral dimension that could be turned to advantage, even if only in secret. Israeli representatives met with officials of the West German Defense Ministry as early as May 1957 in an attempt to secure a supply of ammunition from the Federal Republic.[53] As in the case of French-Israeli relations, Ben-Gurion placed all matters related to arms procurement from the Federal Republic in the hands of the Israeli Defense Ministry[54] and on a covert basis, largely because the West German Foreign Ministry, like its French counterpart, was sensitive to the Arab reaction to German ties with Israel. The Federal Republic feared that Arab states would retaliate against overt defense support for Israel by granting diplomatic recognition to the Pankow (East German) regime.[55] The West German government repeatedly denied that any arms deals with Israel were afoot, expressed surprise that the Israelis thought that the Federal Republic could offer any type of arms not available elsewhere, and declared that it would do its best to prevent the supply of arms to a part of the world where tension was already high.[56]

Nevertheless, as Ben-Gurion noted in his diary, Strauss was willing to provide the Israelis with two refurbished World War II submarines as well as training for the crews.[57] It is possible that Ben-Gurion meant submarines when he refered to arms that could not be obtained elsewhere.[58] It is more likely, however, that he was, as the British assumed, refering to missiles.[59] Indeed, by 1957, Ben-Gurion hoped to secure German help both in setting up a heavy arms industry in Israel and in obtaining guided missiles.[60] If this is so, then it was probably the purpose of Peres's trip to Bonn in December 1957.[61]

THE COALITION CRISIS OF DECEMBER 1957

The importance Ben-Gurion attached to the arms connection with West Germany is evident in his reaction to the breach of secrecy surrounding these ties committed by one of Mapai's coalition partners, Ahdut Ha'avoda, on 17 December 1957. On 15 December, the Cabinet voted by a majority of one to send a high-ranking official mission to West Germany led by Peres and Dayan.[62] Ahdut Ha'avoda may have feared that the government was attempting to lay the groundwork for the establishment of diplomatic relations with Germany. The party's disclosure two days later in its newspaper (*Lamerchav*) of the government's intention to dispatch the mission resulted in two separate condemnations in the Cabinet, the first taking Ahdut Ha'avoda to task for undermining the security of the state by compromising the possibility of obtaining arms from any available source and the second censuring the left-wing party for having violated the coalition agreement.[63]

Ben-Gurion declared that security had been prejudiced in a manner that precluded the possibility of sending the mission to West Germany,[64] but he demonstrated his determination to nevertheless forge a defense link with the Federal Republic when, despite this declaration, he sent General Haim Laskov, Dayan's designated successor as chief-of-staff,[65] with Peres to Bonn during the last week of December 1957.[66] The prime minister also emphasized the urgency of obtaining arms from West Germany by calling for the adoption of a number of clauses that both Ahdut Ha'avoda and Mapam would have to accept if they wished to remain in the government. One of these was the passing of a law obligating all members of the government to maintain the secrecy of the protocols of Cabinet meetings. When the two left-wing parties refused an ultimatum to accept Mapai's conditions by 31 December

1957, Ben-Gurion tendered his resignation. Six days later, the two parties accepted most of these conditions and the government was reconstituted with the same membership.[67] Contacts with the Federal Republic toward the procurement of arms proceeded apace.

FRANCE, GERMANY, AND GUIDED MISSILES

The term "guided missile" warrants clarification, as frequent references to such missiles are made in both archival documents and secondary sources without proper elucidation. Israel eventually acquired four types of guided missiles, the least sophisticated of which was the wire-guided antitank missile. (Israel received two hundred Nord SS-10 antitank missiles, with a range of one and a half kilometers, from France in 1956.)[68] Air-to-air (AAM, which constitute the main armament on jet interceptors) and surface-to-air (SAM) missiles are far more sophisticated. The United States granted final authorization to the sale of 288 Raytheon Hawk SAMs with a range of thirty-five kilometers to Israel in 1963, and it was only in 1966 that Israel acquired the French Matra R.530 AAM, with a range of eighteen kilometers for mounting on Mirage jets.[69] Ben-Gurion noted in his diary as early as 1954 that Israel had to acquire a fourth type of missile, which he termed the "V-2" (the designation given by the Nazis to the weapon they used against Britain during the latter part of World War II), an intermediate-range surface-to-surface missile (SSM).[70]

Researchers who have studied the question of whether Israel has an atomic bomb suggest that the Israelis were interested in a surface-to-surface missile as a means of delivery[71] for a military nuclear capability developed with French assistance. Although it cannot be determined whether Israel in fact ever developed such a capability, it appears that the uncertainty and doubts that existed regarding conventional arms and the future of the relationship with France also existed in the area of nuclear development. Plainly stated, it is entirely possible that the Israelis wished to acquire from France both the means to produce an atomic bomb and the missiles to deliver such a bomb before a change in relations with France could preclude such cooperation. Thus on 3 October 1957, France and Israel signed an agreement whereby France would provide the blueprints, technical assistance, and materials necessary for the building of a twenty-four megawatt reactor at Dimona in the Negev desert.[72] The French Foreign Ministry objected to the arrangement and insisted that the Israelis commit themselves to consultation with France on every matter related to the construction of this reactor.[73] Shimon Peres, the key Israeli figure in these negotiations, promised that Israel would use the reactor only for peaceful purposes.[74]

At the end of December 1957, Ben-Gurion told Mapai's Central Committee that the development of nuclear power for military purposes was not an option for Israel.[75] Nevertheless, certain researchers present a strong case for the assumption that the Israelis, and especially Ben-Gurion, did in fact have in mind a military nuclear option. Frank Barnaby claims that "at least from the time of the Suez War and possibly before that, Israel was determined to assemble the means to build nuclear weapons,"[76] adding that Israel began to acquire the technology and personnel to produce nuclear materials for weapons almost immediately after the establishment of the state in 1948.[77] Shlomo Aronson notes that in early 1958, a number of leading scientists resigned from the Israeli Atomic Energy Commission in protest at Ben-Gurion's intention to develop such an option.[78]

There is strong evidence that despite the French Foreign Ministry's opposition, key figures in France conspired to pass on to the Israelis technology necessary for the creation of a military nuclear capability. Crosbie claims that the government of Bourgès-Maunoury, which signed the agreement providing Israel with the twenty-four megawatt reactor, fully intended to afford the Israelis a military nuclear option.[79] Barnaby offers further support for this claim, citing a 1986 interview with Professor Francis Perrin, French high commissioner for Atomic Energy from 1951 to 1970, in which Perrin admitted that the French secretly gave Israel details of nuclear weapons technology.[80]

According to Aronson, the French-German-Italian agreement of 1957 (the Pool of Resources discussed in an earlier chapter) included cooperation in the nuclear field, and this was another reason for Israel's heightened interest in ties with Bonn in addition to those with Paris.[81] This interest may also have included a desire to benefit from the fruits of French-German joint development of missiles that the Israelis assumed would (eventually) provide a delivery system for nuclear warheads.[82] But the "clandestine" and haphazard manner in which Israel had secured France's agreement to provide the reactor[83] probably served to increase the feeling among the Israelis that they should assure themselves an option besides that of the French with regard to the development of guided missiles. It is this uncertainty that suggests that Israel viewed the connection with Bonn as a way to gain access to research in areas such as missile development, even if Paris proved unwilling to share this technology once it was developed.

Studies suggesting that Israel sought guided missiles from West Germany provide little or no documentary evidence to support their claim. However, recently released documents provide clear evidence that Israel sought the technology with which to develop SSMs, capable of carrying nuclear warheads, from the United States and Britain. The possibility that the Israelis sought this technology with the intention of sharing it with West Germany and France cannot be discounted completely, but it is more likely that Israeli mistrust of French intentions, especially after the rise of de Gaulle in May 1958, increased the Israeli desire to avoid depending upon Paris to provide a means of delivery.[84] The latter possibility is especially salient in view of de Gaulle's instruction to Perrin in 1959 to halt French nuclear cooperation with Israel[85] and his decision to do the same with regard to Germany.[86]

In August 1957, Peres told Ben-Gurion that within two or three years, the French would be manufacturing sophisticated guided missiles,[87] but by mid-1959 France had yet to produce such a missile.[88] This fact, as well lack of faith in French intentions,[89] led the Israelis to seek the technology and materials for the production of guided missiles from both Washington and London.

ISRAEL ATTEMPTS TO OBTAIN U.S. AND BRITISH MISSILES, 1958–1959

Israel apparently began its efforts toward acquiring the know-how to manufacture missiles within weeks of de Gaulle's assumption of power. In the summer of 1958 the Israelis applied to Washington for Nike surface-to-surface missiles, but the Americans firmly turned down the request.[90] In early 1959, the Israelis approached London with a request for samples of liquid rocket propellant to be used by Israeli research scientists.[91] The British refused the request, but the Israelis told the Foreign Office that they would in any case develop such a missile by obtaining the fuel "elsewhere."[92]

In the British estimate, the Israelis were planning to produce surface-to-surface missiles with a range of one hundred to two hundred miles. Such missiles would not only be able to carry a nuclear warhead but, according to the Foreign Office, they would be useless without them.[93] Consultation between the British Foreign Office and Defense Ministry from February to April 1959 indicates that although the British were unaware of the progress Israel may already have made in the field of nuclear development, they strongly suspected that the Israelis were attempting to create a military nuclear option. Thus this correspondence includes the observation that "we must assume that the Israelis realize that a nuclear warhead is involved. They surely cannot conceive that one of the nuclear powers would be prepared to supply this, or that they have the resources to develop one themselves."[94]

On 10 April 1959, the British embassy in Tel Aviv wrote to the Foreign Office that it had neglected to report a speech Shimon Peres had made at Israel's Weizmann Institute (where Israel carried out atomic research) in which the Defense Ministry director general refered to a "secret weapon" Israel was attempting to obtain. Peres's address aided in corroborating British (and American) suspicions, although, as the embassy staff pointed out, "the veil of secrecy which was immediately pulled over this speech prevented us from finding out to which weapon Peres refered. We deduced that it was probably a guided missile or something atomic."[95] The embassy also reported that in early April, Meir Weisgal, director of the Weizmann Institute, had during a dinner with the British ambassador shed a little more light on the subject:

> He told the ambassador that there had for some time been a heated argument within the Ministry of Defense as to whether Israel should try to acquire the atomic bomb. Brigadier [Dan] Tolkowsky, who was moved last year from heading the Air Force to be a "planner" in the ministry, had apparently been set to carry out a review of Israel's atomic policy. He concluded that it would be foolish for Israel to try to get an atomic bomb, both because of the expense and because even if Israel were successful, the Soviet Union would undoubtedly arm the Arab countries in similar fashion. Tolkowsky's view was supported by the majority of senior professional soldiers in Israel who thought it wise that the Middle East be kept bomb-free. Peres, on the other hand, was extremely keen to have the bomb and had been saying he was sure that he could get it from the French. Ben-Gurion's view was that Israel should first concentrate on a nuclear reactor for atomic power but might thereafter achieve her own bomb as a byproduct from it.[96]

American and British refusal to supply Israel with guided missiles and suspicion in Washington[97] and London regarding the use Jerusalem intended to make of such knowledge dictated Israel's continued dependence upon France's willingness to share such technology.

DE GAULLE AND THE NUCLEAR REACTOR

Some final aspects of the French-Israeli relationship in the context of nuclear arms are worth noting, for they further explain Israel's reluctance to view

France as a long-term strategic ally. The change in the nature of the relationship with Israel brought about by de Gaulle included a curtailing of cooperation on the nuclear plane. Aronson writes that by mid-1960, Ben-Gurion had to deal with an "unmitigated disaster," as the "tricky French were apparently deserting Israel in regard to Dimona."[98] This disaster was the French demand in May 1960 that Israel make public its nuclear plans and submit to inspection by the International Atomic Energy Agency (IAEA),[99] a demand Paris made after the United States disclosed that Israel was building a reactor with French help.[100]

Ben-Gurion met de Gaulle in France in June 1960. As a result of their discussions, de Gaulle agreed that the French would drop the demand for international safeguards at Dimona while disengaging themselves (publicly, at least) from Israel's nuclear development. The Israelis continued to build the Dimona reactor with French help, and in December 1960 Ben-Gurion announced the existence of the reactor to the Knesset, describing its purpose as "the peaceful development of the Negev desert."[101]

However, another result of the Ben Gurion–de Gaulle talks was a French decision to permit private French industry to collaborate with Israel on missile development.[102] This collaboration suggests that Ben-Gurion may indeed have intended, as noted in the document cited above, that Israel produce an atomic bomb as a byproduct of the "peaceful" operation of the reactor. French agreement on this cooperation further corroborates American and British suspicions that Israel could have intended such guided missiles only as the means of delivery for a nuclear warhead.

In fact, Israel never received guided missiles from the French. We have already noted that in 1958 and 1959 the Israelis turned to the United States and Britain in unsuccessful attempts to obtain guided missile technology. The turn was partly because of the French lag in missile development and partly because of Israel's doubts regarding continued French willingness to cooperate with Israel on such sensitive matters. Barnaby quotes "Western sources" that report that beginning in 1963, Israel collaborated on the development of a SSM with the French Dassault company. The result of this cooperation was the French MD-660, with a range of 450 kilometers, capable of delivering nuclear warheads.[103] The Israelis did not obtain this missile, despite their contribution to its development and the fact that the MD-660 is listed in the *Arms Trade Registers* as having been "developed on Israeli order."[104] Instead, the French halted all arms shipments to Israel following the Six-Day War of 1967.[105] The Israelis are alleged then to have developed a SSM with a maximum range of 500 kilometers, designated Jericho I, capable of carrying nuclear warheads and based on previous technological cooperation.[106]

It is unclear whether the aid in nuclear development that France secretly continued to provide Israel after 1960 was carried out with the knowledge of de Gaulle or was "behind his back."[107] The former seems likely, because Israel continued to receive conventional arms from France until early 1969.[108] The most important purchase of military hardware from France during this period was the Mirage-III-CJ interceptor, of which Israel received seventy-two between the years 1962 and 1964.[109] This, however, was the last Israeli purchase of jets from France. By February 1966, Israel had obtained American consent to the sale of forty-eight A-4H Skyhawk jets,[110] underscoring Israel's intention of purchasing U.S. military hardware whenever possible. Israel's desire to acquire American arms for political reasons[111] and the exigency of doing so because of the growing American technological advantage in arms development[112] thus actually presaged the end to the French-Israeli arms relationship brought about by the French arms embargo.

CONCLUSION

Between 1955 and 1967, Israeli expenditures on arms from France totaled more than an estimated $600 million, including $75 million for the Dimona reactor.[113] Yet Israel's continued efforts to acquire arms from the United States and the alacrity with which the Israelis moved to purchase these arms once the Americans agreed to their release strongly suggests that Israel always viewed the relationship with France as "second best" and temporary. Beyond arms deals, there was never more than a very narrow potential for any "special ties" between the two states.[114] However, Crosbie goes too far by claiming that "Israeli leaders tended to ignore all signs of [French] political disenchantment as long as the supply of essential arms continued," and she is mistaken in ascribing to the Israelis a "failure to recognize the dangers implicit in accepting short-sighted military goals as the barometer of the relationship."[115]

To some extent, the above interpretations of the views and goals of Israel's leadership regarding relations with France may be attributed to the unavailability of important documents when those authors wrote their accounts. In *A Tacit Alliance* (in which the author relies heavily upon personal interviews), Crosbie claims that until the mid-1960s, France and Israel were de facto allies and credits Shimon Peres with creating this "alliance."[116] Yet Peres's biographer, Matti Golan, writes that his subject "never saw France as the be-all and end-all of Israel's international relations."[117] Furthermore, the division of Israel's policy makers between those who called for close ties with the United States and "the guardians of a pro-French orientation" is highly tenuous.[118]

In fact, as we have seen, the Israelis (and especially Ben-Gurion) harbored few illusions regarding the relationship with France. In addition, rather than viewing France and West Germany together as the crux of a "European orientation," Israel saw in ties with the Federal Republic of Germany an additional source of arms and an alternative that might be of vital importance if France halted sales. Arms from the Federal Republic, in contrast with those from France, were nearly free, as they were covered by an item on aid to Israel inserted into West Germany's budget in 1962. Thus the Germans funded Israeli arms procurement in the Federal Republic through the extension of aid totaling $60 million.[119] The flow of arms from West Germany continued until 1965, when its discovery forced the Germans to halt deliveries. By then, however, the Federal Republic had provided Israel (mainly from German army surplus) with some 50 planes, helicopters, German Cobra antitank rockets, howitzers, and 150 M-48 tanks.[120]

Protocols of meetings of Mapai's Foreign Affairs and Central Committees, as well as Ben-Gurion's diary, shed additional light upon the Israeli attitude toward the relationship with France. These documents are particularly important in view of the paucity of material in the Israeli State Archive on the 1957–60 period in French-Israeli relations. While there is a great number of documents in the Israeli State Archives relating to the period up to the Suez-Sinai campaign, there are virtually none from the period following. This is attributable to the fact that during the latter period, the Israeli Defense Ministry dominated Israel's relationship with France and conducted a policy almost entirely independent of the Foreign Ministry.[121] The available documents afford a fairly complete picture of Israeli arms procurement from France. It is entirely possible, however, that Defense Ministry files from that period, which are still classified, deal with Israel's acquisition of a nuclear reactor from France in 1957 and the use which Israel intended to make of this reactor.

Michael Bar-Zohar's biography of Ben-Gurion also contains an incomplete account of the French-Israeli relationship, based largely upon Ben-Gurion's diary. Bar-Zohar attributes Ben-Gurion's reticence in pressing for an alliance with France to French disinterest alone,[122] rather than to the prime minister's reservations regarding any formal alliance. In the euphoria of French-Israeli cooperation in the fall of 1956, Ben-Gurion told Mapai's Central Committee that Israel would soon have a "true ally."[123] However, shortly after the Suez-

Sinai campaign he evinced a more sober view of these relations: In early March 1957, he told Mapai's Central Committee that "there is no treaty with that country [France] nor will there be."[124]

In Ben-Gurion's view, the peril in ties with France lay in the long-term, strategic implications of the unorthodox nature of the relationship. Israel had received arms from France, but only after having exhausted all possibilities of acquiring them in "orthodox" fashion.[125] The fact that most of these arms had been released against the wishes of the French Foreign Ministry put these sales in what Ben-Gurion termed the dubious category of "underground" transactions. No other country, noted the prime minister, would have sold arms in this manner. There was danger in the inherent instability of such a relationship. As we have seen, the French in 1957 called upon Israel to submit a long-term armament plan. Yet Ben-Gurion expressed his great reservations regarding ties with France by pointing out that French arms might not be forthcoming if Nasser attacked Israel one or two years hence.[126] Ben-Gurion's views contradict the assertion that it was with the fall of the socialist government of Guy Mollet in May 1957 that an "almost complete identification of interests that had characterized relations during the Socialists' government ceased to exist."[127] In truth, a complete identification of Israeli and French interests had never existed.

CONCLUSION

By the early 1950s, Israel's orientation in foreign policy was clearly Western. This did not mean that the internal debate over the country's direction in foreign policy had ceased completely. The anti-Semitism and anti-Zionism of the Eastern bloc, manifested in a campaign against the Jews that culminated in the Slansky Trials and the Doctors' Plot, had in the early 1950s seriously undermined the ideological position of the parties to the left of Mapai. Nevertheless, Ahdut Ha'avoda and Mapam continued to call for a more "balanced" approach in foreign policy. Their demands carried some weight in 1955, when Ben-Gurion set about forming a coalition with their participation. During those negotiations, Mapai and the two left-wing parties disagreed mainly over the question of what Israel would do if the United States agreed to grant it a security guarantee.

Ahdut Ha'avoda and Mapam made clear that should such a security guarantee be realized, they would leave the government coalition immediately. Ben-Gurion's view was that in any case the chances of obtaining such a guarantee were so slight that they did not pose a threat to the coalition. Indeed, an American security guarantee never materialized. The coalition crisis that Ahdut Ha'avoda and Mapam precipitated at the end of 1957 took place not on the background of relations with the United States but on that of ties Ben-Gurion pursued with the Federal Republic of Germany.

In the late 1950s, Ahdut Ha'avoda and Mapam continued to call for an abandonment of Israel's Western orientation in foreign policy, but their demands for an orientation that was at least neutral in terms of the East-West struggle had long ceased to pose a serious challenge to Mapai-dominated Israeli governments. The foreign policy challenges Israeli governments faced from the mid- to late 1950s were those of convincing the Western powers, especially the United States, of the permanence of Israel's Western direction and of achieving security through the arms the West granted regimes so oriented. Israel's problem was in bringing the West to recognize the validity of its call for arms to defend itself against Arab states whose Western-supplied arsenals were ostensibly for defense against the Soviet Union but in the Israeli view directed only against the Jewish state.

Paradoxically, the Soviet penetration of the Middle East in 1955, which entailed large shipments of arms first to Egypt and then Syria, also created a situation in which Israel was able to close the arms gap qualitatively, if not quantitatively. For although France supplied Israeli with arms in order to use it as a counterweight to Nasser's support of the rebels in Algeria as well as to gain a lucrative arms market, the justification France presented the NEACC for such sales was the Czech arms deal of September 1955. Israel viewed the beginning of Soviet involvement in the Middle East, and in the Arab-Israeli conflict in particular, as a highly dangerous development. Yet Soviet involvement in the region gradually brought the United States and Britain to view as valid Israel's demands for arms.

Despite Israel's failure to achieve a strategic relationship with the United States, certain researchers have termed the period following the Suez crisis a "golden age."[1] Indeed, Israel's gains from the 1956 round of fighting included a period of nearly eleven years of quiet on its southern border, unimpeded freedom of navigation through the Strait of Tiran, and a period of relative quiet on all fronts during which the country could concentrate on economic development.[2] By the end of the 1950s, the Israelis had achieved a modicum of security that allowed them to pursue extensive relations with Turkey, Iran, and other non-Arab states of the Middle East. It was this initiative, inter alia, that allowed Ben-Gurion to observe at the end of 1958 that Israel was now a "factor" and not merely an "object" on the international scene.[3]

Yet Israel's policy makers regarded the post–Suez crisis period as only a little less dangerous than that which preceded the conflict. Ben-Gurion, viewing the continued Soviet supply of arms to Egypt and Syria with the utmost gravity, rejected Chief-of-Staff Moshe Dayan's flippant observation in late 1956 that Israel had arms enough for a considerable period to come. The fact that France was then Israel's sole supplier of arms greatly heightened the prime minister's concern, because he fully expected the French to abruptly cut off this supply once they had resolved matters in Algeria.

Fears regarding the reliability of supply from France, the continued refusal of the United States to sell Israel arms, and the insignificant armament Britain sold Israel before late 1958 all contributed to the maintaining of intensive arms procurement efforts after as well as before the Suez-Sinai campaign.

These efforts included Israel's bid to augment its security through an attempt to associate with NATO, the quest to obtain intermediate-range surface-to-surface missiles, an arms connection with the Federal Republic of Germany, and, as posited by certain researchers, the development of a military nuclear option based on a reactor received from France.

The Israelis pressed their demand for arms to counter the Soviet-backed Arab threat with particular intensity during the British and American over-flights of Israel in 1958. The upheavals in Iraq, Jordan, and Lebanon in 1957–58 did not bring about a strategic relationship between Israel and the United States but did greatly mitigate the Anglo-American view that Israel was a stra-tegic impediment to the West, and this must be seen as a significant, albeit modest, turning point in Israel's strategic position. Indeed, Ben-Gurion's claim that the Israelis allowed the overflights of their territory in 1958 because they saw intrinsic value in aiding Western efforts should be accepted at face value, rather than viewed as an Israeli effort to extort arms from the Western powers. For the Israelis, permitting the use of their air space was an opportu-nity to demonstrate to the West the value of their foreign policy orientation.

During the overflights, Ben-Gurion repeated his demands that the United States grant Israel a security guarantee. Such a guarantee, he claimed, was vital in a situation in which Israel placed itself in danger vis-à-vis the Soviet Union for the sake of Western interests. Yet Ben-Gurion's view of such a guarantee remained consistent during the entire period covered in this work. Israel's orientation was Western, but it would remain free of military commit-ments to foreign powers. Ben-Gurion held that a guarantee of Israel's security would have to be in the framework of a bilateral agreement with the United States that did not contractually bind Israel or entail limitations upon Israel's ability to act freely in all matters of foreign policy and security. In his view, the main goal in Israel's foreign policy was augmentation of its security through the procurement of arms.

The Israelis were at the end of the 1950s no more willing to have foreign (even American) officials "poking around" Israel's military installations than they were at the beginning of the decade. Moreover, the protocols of the meetings of Mapai's committees show that reticence at entering into binding ties with any power was in fact the dominant view in that party. These de-liberations suggest that an Israeli government that chose to pursue binding ties with any foreign power would have faced considerable domestic politi-cal opposition. When Ben-Gurion spoke before Mapai's Central Committee at the end of 1957, he pointed out Israel's success in having remained free of such commitments.[4]

Yet ties with the United States were so important that the struggle within the Israeli political system over security policy before the Suez-Sinai campaign was marked by frequent reference to the effect of the practice of retaliation against the Arab states upon that relationship. We have seen that there were, in fact, three distinct views among the Israelis of what constituted the correct policy in relations with the United States. Sharett occupied a position not diametrically opposed to that of Ben-Gurion but at a point between Ben Gurion's "activist" (hawkish) views and the complete restraint in security matters that the Israeli embassy in Washington urged upon its government.

Despite the failure to obtain either arms or a security guarantee, the goal of a strategic relationship with the United States based on both of these elements remained the central goal of Israeli foreign policy. Moreover, the lack of success in obtaining either arms or a guarantee forced Israel to attempt to ensure its security through arms from both Britain and France. For as Pinhas Lavon told Mapai's Political Committee in October 1955, Israel would not "shoot only with American rifles and if they don't give them to us, recite *Kaddish*."[5]

During the years preceding the crisis of 1956, the Middle East was, despite the loss to the British Empire of India and Palestine, still of vital interest to Britain.[6] The birth of the state of Israel had in London's view undermined Britain's influence in the region. The British reaction to the Israeli victory in the war of 1948–49 was "unrelieved dismay." But in fact, Bevin's Labour government came to terms with the existence of the Jewish state and attempted to "cut the losses" it had incurred over Palestine by relying on "loyal allies" such as Jordan and Iraq and by viewing the Suez Canal as the "jugular vein of the Empire."[7] Indeed, the geostrategic exigencies of the Korean War further drove home to the British the vital nature of their military presence on the canal.[8]

The British presence protected the West's strategic interests in the Middle East, and with the British the Israelis had to talk if they wished to be integrated into Western defense of the Middle East. The Israelis had also to deal with Britain as the main arms supplier to the region, as well as a power having defense treaties with certain of Israel's Arab enemies. Israel's need for British arms and especially armor made reaching a modus vivendi with Britain imperative. Moreover, the American refusal to supply arms to Israel made the arms relationship with Britain a matter of great importance to Israel. Yet what we have seen is that Israel sought no alliance with Britain, and a military understanding between the two countries, which one scholar has posited began as early as 1951, did not in fact exist.[9]

Ben-Gurion was deeply suspicious of Britain, and the available foreign policy documents as well as Ben-Gurion's diary clearly demonstrate this suspicion in the case of the Israeli Foreign Ministry's brief flirtation with the idea of offering Britain bases in Israel. Ben-Gurion's evaluation of the danger to Israel of such an arrangement was correct, especially in view of Israeli-Jordanian relations. Moreover, the steady deterioration of the situation on the Israeli-Jordanian border from 1952 to 1956 jeopardized the very modest British supply of arms to Israel. Clashes such as the battle between Israeli and Jordanian forces at the West Bank town of Kalkilya in October 1956 threatened to bring about the involvement of British forces against Israel while also demonstrating that British-Israeli cooperation over Suez-Sinai was an "episode," not the culmination of a developing strategic entente.

Israel's leaders no more pursued a French "orientation" than a British one as a substitute for an alliance with the United States. A large number of documents in the Israeli State Archives demonstrate that Israel was exceedingly wary of close relations with France because of French interests in Syria, France's inherent weakness in the region, the instability of French governments, and the bureaucratic infighting in that country that made reliance on Paris for arms a highly dubious proposition. In Israeli eyes Britain was a declining power, but nevertheless one with considerable influence and a legitimate claim to represent the West's strategic interests in the region. The Israeli view was that France's assertion that it was in a similar position was unfounded.

The deep suspicions of France among the Israelis were not peculiar to the Israeli Foreign Ministry. The Foreign Ministry played a key role in arms procurement from France even while warning of the possible pitfalls of over-reliance upon the French. Key figures in the French government (especially the French Defense Ministry) who saw Israel as a counterweight to Egypt facilitated large arms deals with Israel in June and September 1956. But this French view of Israel was largely due to the support Nasser lent the rebels in Algeria, and the Israelis recognized that the circumstances in which they had obtained arms from the French and cooperated with them in the Suez-Sinai campaign was a temporary state of affairs.

Despite Israel's having acquired a large amount of arms from France in 1956, a strategic relationship with the United States remained the main goal of Israel's foreign policy after as well as before the Suez-Sinai campaign. The protocols of the debates that took place in Mapai's Central, Foreign Affairs, and Political Committees show that Israel's reticence at entering into a binding arrangement with the United States had not disappeared. Indeed, the Israelis wished to achieve a strategic relationship without a contractual bond. Thus Reuven Shiloah attempted to forge ties of a far-reaching nature with the United States that would have included scientific cooperation on sensitive military matters. The Americans were not receptive, and in early 1958 an Israeli embassy in Washington that had set its sights upon such enhanced American-Israeli cooperation, while assuming that economic aid was secure, was forced to deal with a State Department delay in the granting of an Exim Bank loan. And although the United States gave its blessing to the supply of a considerable level of armament to Israel by Western European countries, it maintained its policy of not selling offensive weapons to Israel. This meant that for Israel the purchase of arms from Britain and France remained salient during the post–Suez crisis period as well.

Following the Suez-Sinai campaign, Israel continued to expend great efforts both to forestall the supply of British arms to their Arab clients and to obtain the weapon Israel most wished to acquire from Britain, the Centurion tank. By mid-1958, Israel and Britain had transfigured their relationship from one of mutual suspicion and a still-present possibility of a clash because of Britain's treaty with Jordan to one of limited intelligence cooperation and the sale by Britain to Israel of sixty Centurion tanks as well as other arms. The British sale of such arms to Israel was a result of the end of Britain's influence in Iraq as well as a "reward" for Israel's permitting the Royal Air Force to overfly its territory. However, Britain did not provide Israel with arms as a result of an Israeli game of "brinkmanship," nor did the Israelis seek a strategic alliance with Britain.[10] In fact, Israel sought a strategic alliance only with the United States, and Ben-Gurion allowed the overflights because he perceived such assistance to Western efforts in the region to be in Israel's interest.

Although France sold Israel most of the arms that the Israelis acquired after the Suez crisis, Israel's leaders continued to harbor grave reservations regarding relations with Paris. Israel's policy makers never viewed France as a long-term alternative to close ties with the United States. Moreover, Ben-Gurion feared that France would "desert" Israel as soon as it solved its Algerian problem. The Israelis did not express these fears in public forums so as not to jeopardize relations with France, but both Ben-Gurion's diary and the protocols of meetings of Mapai's committees reveal the hope among Israel's leaders that they might replace dependence upon France for arms with a close relationship with the United States that would include the supply of American arms.

Finally, we have seen that certain researchers have posited that in the late 1950s Israel pursued a "European orientation" based on both France and the Federal Republic of Germany. In fact, Israel saw relations with West Germany as an alternative rather than ancillary to the relationship with France and hoped that ties with the Federal Republic might facilitate the procurement of arms from the United States. For Israel's leaders always believed that in the long-term, their relationship with the United States was paramount.

APPENDIX

THE CZECH ARMS DEAL

Memorandum from the Secretary of State's Special Assistant for Intelligence (Armstrong) to the Secretary of State

Washington, September 23, 1955

SUBJECT: Egyptian-Soviet Arms Purchase Agreement

. . . received a report . . . to the effect that on September 21 Egypt signed an "open agreement" with the USSR to run for five years, in which the Soviets committed to sell certain categories of arms and military equipment to Egypt. At the time of signing, Egypt is reported to have given the Soviets an initial order for the following items:

1. 200 jet aircraft (100 to be delivered by December 1955, comprising 37 medium jet bombers and the remainder MIG-15's).
2. 6 jet training planes.
3. 100 heavy tanks.
4. torpedo patrol boats.
5. 2 submarines.

The cost of the above order is reported to be 30 million pounds sterling Egyptian ($86 million), payable in Egyptian exports; all of the equipment is to be of Soviet manufacture, and the report states that the first shipment has left, or is about to leave Odessa by ship for Alexandria. The first shipment is said to have been inspected and accepted at Odessa by Egyptian military personnel.

. . . Soviet technicians will come to Egypt to assist in assembling the aircraft, but will stay only three months, and that no other Soviet personnel are to come to Egypt in connection with the agreement. . . . The Soviets are trying to get Nasser to use his influence with Syria and Saudi Arabia in favor of their purchasing Soviet arms.

. . . .

Comment: Other than for the heavy tanks, you will note that the list of equipment does not include artillery, which was reported as being offered by the USSR early in the summer. Nevertheless, receipt of the reported quantities of arms would, if Egyptians could man and maintain them, give Egypt a numerical superiority in jet aircraft and heavy tanks over Israel (Egypt now has 52 British jet fighters and about 350 jet pilots). Israel is not known to have medium jet bombers and to have only some 20 jet fighters, mainly French; Israel has no heavy tanks, but has about 300 medium and light tanks.

The terms of payment are only sketchily reported. Presumably, Egypt would ship cotton as the principal item in payment. The reported about would mean over 100,00 tons of cotton if it alone were used (cotton comprises over 80 per cent of Egypt's exports). Such an amount would take about one-third of Egypt's normal exportable cotton.

(*Source:* Department of State, Central Files, 774.56/9-2355. FRUS 14:507.)

TABLE 1. MILITARY STRENGTH OF MIDDLE EAST STATES, END OF 1949

WEAPON TYPE	ISRAEL	EGYPT	SYRIA	IRAQ	JORDAN
Tanks	35 Shermans	9 Centurions 120 Shermans[b]	A few very old French tanks	o	o
Artillery	12 25-pounders 70 75-mm 36 105-mm	24 25-pounders 4 18-pounders 16 3.7" Howitzers 4 4.5" Howitzers 6 6" Howitzers	4 105-mm	56 25-pounders 4 6" Howitzers 12 4.5" Howitzers 56 3.7" Howitzers	24 25-pounders 9 17-pounders
Fighters	30 Spitfires (5 ME-109s in reserve)	23 jets 72 piston-engines	24 mixed-type (piston-engines)	39 British (piston-engines)	o
Bombers	12	8 Halifax	3	o	o
Total aircraft[a]	105	130	68	68	9 assorted light aircraft

Source: British Foreign Office, 30 March 1950, PRO: FO/371 81966 E1194/2.

[a] Operational only

[b] The estimate of the British War Office was that only some twenty to thirty Egyptian tanks could take the field.

TABLE 2. AIRCRAFT STRENGTH OF MIDDLE EAST STATES, NOVEMBER 1953

TYPE OF AIRCRAFT	EGYPT	IRAQ	JORDAN	LEBANON	SAUDI ARABIA	SYRIA	ARAB STATES TOTAL	ISRAEL
Bombers								
Medium	17	0	0	0	0	0	17	3
Light	0	0	0	4	0	0	4	63
Fighters								
Jet	56	24	0	3	0	14	97	15
Piston	24	29	0	6	20	42	121	122
Trainers	156	46	2	19	12	71	306	171
Transport	48	10	6	2	0	7	73	24

Source: U.K. Ministry of Defense, 2 January 1954, PRO: FO/371 104229 E1192/283.

TABLE 3. TANK STRENGTH OF MIDDLE EAST STATES, 1 MARCH 1953

TYPE OF TANK	ISRAEL	REQUESTS RECEIVED U.K.	REQUESTS RECEIVED FRANCE	ISRAEL TOTAL	EGYPT	IRAQ	LEBANON	SYRIA
Medium								
Centurion	—	—	—	—	9	—	—	—
Churchill	2	—	—	2	—	—	—	—
Sherman	120	—	—	120	100	24	23 (8[a])	52
Total	122	—	—	122	109	24	31	52
Light								
Crusader (Centaur and Cromwell)	10	38	—	48	—	2	—	—
Renault R-35/Hotchkiss Ho39	—	—	—	—	—	—	22	—
German	—	—	—	—	—	—	—	30
Renault and miscellaneous	25	—	—	25	—	—	—	—
13-ton	—	—	40	40	—	—	—	—
Total	35	—	40	113	—	2	22	30

Source: U.K. Ministry of Defense, "Israeli Arms Requests," 23 June 1953; PRO: FO/371 104221 E1192/185.
[a]Prior commitment not yet delivered

TABLE 4. ARTILLERY STRENGTH OF ARAB STATES, 1 MARCH 1953

TYPE OF ARTILLERY	EGYPT	IRAQ	JORDAN	LEBANON	SAUDI ARABIA	SYRIA
Field (including self-propelled)						
155-mm	—	—	—	—	—	13
6-in	16	4	—	—	—	—
150-mm	—	—	—	—	—	9
5.5-inch	—	8	—	—	—	—
4.5-inch	4	8	—	—	—	—
25-pounder	76	84	48	—	8	—
105-mm	16	—	—	8	6	48 (24[a])
3.7-inch	12	60	15	—	—	—
18-pounder	4	4	—	—	4	—
75-mm	—	—	—	14 (5[a])	—	71
Total	126	168	63	27	18	165
Antitank artillery						
17-pounder	72	36	18	15	—	—
75-mm	—	—	—	—	4	—
6-pounder	77	48 (110[a])	48	—	18	—
57-mm	—	—	—	—	9	—
50-mm	—	—	—	—	—	36
47-mm	—	—	—	1	—	17
37-mm	—	—	—	34	—	—
25-mm	—	—	—	6	—	12 (50[a])
2-pounder	—	106	399	112	—	—
Total	149	194	66	50	31	53
Rocket launchers	0	0	0	0	86	500[a]
Antiaircraft artillery	264	66	65	60	0	200
Coastal artillery	36	0	0	0	0	0

Source: U.K. Ministry of Defense, 23 June 1953, PRO: FO/371 104221 E1192/185.
[a] Prior commitments not yet delivered

TABLE 5. ISRAELI ARTILLERY STRENGTH, 1 MARCH 1953

TYPE OF ARTILLERY	STRENGTH	REQUESTS RECEIVED U.S.	U.K.	FRANCE	TOTAL
Field (including self-propelled)					
155-mm	4	20	—	26	30
4.5-inch	0	—	14	—	14
105-mm	27	30	—	—	27
25-pounder	70	—	90	—	160
3.7-inch	5	—	14	—	19
77-mm	24	—	—	—	24
3-inch	0	12	—	—	0
75-mm	185	—	—	20	205
Total	315	—	—	—	479
Antitank artillery					
17-pounder	10	—	40	—	50
6-pounder	91	—	50[a]	—	141
57-mm	146[b]	—	—	—	146
50-mm	12	—	—	—	12
47-mm	28	—	—	—	28
37-mm	0	50	50	—	50
Total	287	—	—	—	427
Rocket launchers	0	—	—	500	500
Antiaircraft artillery	116	12	—	32[a]	148
Coastal artillery	0	—	—	—	0

Source: U.K. Ministry of Defense, 23 June 1953, PRO: FO/371 104221 E1192/185.

Note: The figures in the U.S. column are not included in the totals.

[a] Prior commitments not yet reported delivered

[b] Includes 75 reported as licensed for export by France, January and February 1953

TABLE 6. TOTAL OPERATIONAL AIRCRAFT STRENGTH OF MIDDLE EAST STATES, 1 NOVEMBER 1954

TYPE OF AIRCRAFT	EGYPT	IRAQ	JORDAN	LEBANON	SAUDI ARABIA	SYRIA	ARAB STATES TOTAL	ISRAEL
Night fighter	—	—	—	—	—	6[f]	6	6[h]
Day fighter—jet	32[a]	9[b]	—	2[c]	—	12[e]	55	11[g]
Day fighter—piston	16	36	—	—	—	32[i]	84	38
Fighter reconnaissance	12	—	—	—	—	—	12	—
Medium bomber	6	—	—	—	—	—	6	4
Light bomber	—	—	—	4	2[d]	—	6	18
Reconnaissance	—	11	5	—	15	11	42	8
Transport	35	2	7	1	—	7	52	12
Communications	—	10	—	3	—	—	13	17
Total	101	68[b]	12	10	17	68[i]	276	114[g]

Source: U.K. Ministry of Defense, PRO: FO/371 110816.

[a] 18 Vampire 5s; 10 Meteor 4s; 4 Meteor 8s
[b] Vampire 52s. The Iraqis also have 8 Venom FB1s, not yet operational.
[c] Vampire 52s
[d] B26 (Invader), not yet operational
[e] Meteor 8s
[f] Not yet operational as night fighters
[g] Meteor 8s, 7 more on order, also an uncertain number of Mystère IIs (apparently 6 early in 1955)
[h] Mosquito night fighter 30s
[i] Plus 20 Spitfire 22s recently delivered, not yet operational

TABLE 7. COMPARISON OF EQUIPMENT HOLDS OF MIDDLE EAST COUNTRIES, MAY 1955

TYPE OF WEAPON	ISRAEL	EGYPT	IRAQ	JORDAN	LEBANON	SYRIA	SAUDI ARABIA
Ground weapons							
Medium tanks	212	161	24	—	23	52	—
Light tanks	30	—	2	—	22	30	—
Armored cars	106	128	160	1,576	99	197	92
Carriers and scout cars	420	330	48		57	426	
Field artillery	460	138	168	77	34	127	30
Self-propelled	50	8	—	—	6	44	—
Antitank	789	149	340	672	168	77	142
Antiaircraft	230	392	66	77	60	200	—
Mortars	7,456	708	456	390	152	586	233
Machine guns (thousands)	21.7	3.6	2.1	2.3	0.6	3.0	0.5
Rifles (thousands)	170	100	26	34	7.5	69	26
Operational aircraft							
Jet night fighter	—	6	—	—	—	6	—
Jet day fighter	11	61	7	—	4	12	—
Piston night fighter	6	—	—	—	—	—	—
Piston day fighter	28	16	36	—	—	32	—
Reconnaissance	11	12	11	5	—	11	12
Medium bomber	3	6	—	—	—	—	—
Light bomber	18	—	—	—	4	—	6
Transport	12	38	4	2	—	6	—
Total front line	89	139	58	7	8	67	18

Source: U.K. Ministry of Defense, Arms Export Policy Commission: 21 May 1955, PRO: FO/371 115561 V1192/228.

TABLE 8. COMPARISON OF EQUIPMENT HOLDS OF MIDDLE EAST COUNTRIES, NOT INCLUDING THE CZECH ARMS DEAL, MAY 1955

TYPE OF WEAPON	ISRAEL	EGYPT	IRAQ	JORDAN	LEBANON	SYRIA	SAUDI ARABIA
Ground weapons							
Medium tanks	212[ac]	161[b]	24 12[d]	—	23	52	—
Light tanks	30 10	—	2	—	22	30	—
Armored cars	106	128	160	1,576	99	197	92
Carriers and scout cars	420	405	48			57	426
Field artillery	460	202	168	77	34	127	30
Self-propelled	50	8	—	—	6	44	—
Antitank	789	149	340	672	168	77	142
Antiaircraft	230	412	66	77	60	200	—
Mortars	7,456	708	456	390	152	586	233
Machine guns (thousands)	21.7	3.6	2.1	2.3	0.6	3.0	0.5
Rifles (thousands)	170	100	26	34	7.5	69	26
Operational aircraft							
Jet night fighter	6[a]	6	—	—	—	6	—
Jet day fighter	24[e]	61[f]	10	—	5	12	—
Piston night fighter	6	—	—	—	—	—	—
Piston day fighter	28	32[h]	36	—	—	32	—
Reconnaissance	11	12	11	5	—	11	12
Medium bomber	3	6	—	—	—	—	—
Light bomber	18	—	—	—	4	—	6
Transport	20	38	4	2	—	6	—
Total front line	116	155	61	7	9	67	18

Source: 10 November 1955, PRO: FO/371 115573 V1192/552.

[a] No Centurions

[b] 41 Centurions

[c] Sherman tanks for cannibalization

[d] 2 Centurions from U.K.; 10 Centurions from U.S.

[e] Meteors, including 6 now approved for delivery within six months

[f] Meteors and Vampires

[g] Meteors approved for delivery within next six months

[h] Includes 16 Sea Furies now approved for delivery within six months

NOTES

ABBREVIATIONS USED IN THE NOTES

BGA   Ben-Gurion Archives, Sde Boker, Israel
BJSM   British Joint Staffs Mission
BMEO   British Middle East Office
CIA   Central Intelligence Agency
FO   Foreign Office
FRUS   U.S. Department of State, *Foreign Relations of the United States*
IDF   Israeli Defense Forces
ISA   Israeli State Archives, Jerusalem
LPA   Labor Party Archives, Beit Berl, Israel
MAC   Mixed Armistice Commission
NA   National Archives, Washington, D.C.
NATO   North Atlantic Treaty Organization
NEACC   Near East Arms Coordinating Committee
PRO   Public Record Office, Kew, Surrey, United Kingdom
UNEF   United Nations Emergency Force

INTRODUCTION

1. Uri Bialer, *Between East and West: Israel's Foreign Policy Orientation, 1948–1956* (Cambridge: Cambridge University Press, 1990).

2. See Shlomo Slonim, "Origins of the 1950 Tripartite Declaration on the Middle East," *Middle Eastern Studies* 23, no. 2 (1987): 135–49.

3. Paul Jabber, *Not by War Alone* (Berkeley and Los Angeles: University of California Press, 1981), 97.

4. Steven Spiegel, *The Other Arab-Israeli Conflict* (Chicago: University of Chicago Press, 1985), 47.

5. Ibid.

6. Bialer, *Between East and West*, 256.

7. Spiegel, *Other Arab-Israeli Conflict*, 47.

8. Ibid., 51, 55.

9. Kollek to Shiloah, 26 July 1954, ISA 4374/19.

10. Bialer, *Between East and West*, 201.

11. Eldon Ricks, "United States Economic Assistance to Israel: 1949–60" (Ph.D. diss., Dropsie University, 1970), 64.

12. Ibid. Some 687,000 immigrants entered the country during the first three years of statehood. See figures on immigration in Aaron S. Klieman, *Israel and the World After Forty Years* (New York: Pergamon, 1990), 35.

13. Ricks, "United States Economic Assistance to Israel," 79.

14. Ibid., 87.

15. Percentage based on figures for Israel's capital imports during the period 1949–58 quoted in Bialer, *Between East and West*, 200.

16. Ibid., 79, 121.

17. *FRUS* 9:1593.

18. Kollek to Shiloah, 26 July 1954, ISA 4374/19.

CHAPTER ONE

1. Uri Bialer, *Between East and West: Israel's Foreign Policy Orientation 1948–1956* (Cambridge: Cambridge University Press: 1990), 197.

2. Ibid., 13.

3. Mordechai Gazit, "Ben Gurion's Attempts to Establish Military Ties with the United States," *Gesher* 32 (1986/7): 57 (Hebrew).

4. Bialer, *Between East and West*, 224, 228.

5. Ibid., 247.

6. For a detailed account of American policy toward Israel during the Eisenhower period see Isaac Alteras, *Eisenhower and Israel* (Gainesville: University of Florida Press), 1993.

7. Gazit, "Ben Gurion's Attempts to Establish Military Ties," 57.

8. Meir Avidan, *Principal Aspects of Israel-U.S.A. Relations in the 1950s* (Jerusalem: Leonard Davis Institute for International Relations, 1982), 32 (Hebrew).

9. Bialer, *Between East and West*, 264.

10. Ibid.

11. *New York Times*, 16 June 1955.

12. The most extensive critique of the effect upon events of Israeli "activism" is that of Benny Morris, *Israel's Border Wars* (New York: Clarendon Press), 1993.

13. Bialer, *Between East and West*, 264.

14. Ben-Gurion's diary, 2 and 11 July 1954, BGA.

15. Mordechai Bar-On, *The Gates of Gaza: Israel's Defense and Foreign Policy, 1955–1957* (Tel Aviv: Am Oved, 1992), 170–71 (Hebrew).

16. Moshe Sharett, *Personal Diary* (Tel Aviv: Ma'ariv, 1978), 1018.

17. Bialer, *Between East and West*, 268.

18. Ibid., 268–69.

19. For comparisons of the approaches of Ben-Gurion and Sharett, see Michael Brecher, *The Foreign Policy System of Israel* (London: Oxford University Press, 1972); Gabriel Sheffer, "Sharett, Ben Gurion and the 1956 War of Choice," *Medina, Mimshal Vihasim Benleumiyim* (State, Government and International Relations) 27 (Winter 1987) (Hebrew); Avi Shlaim, "Conflicting Approaches to Israel's Relations with the Arabs: Ben Gurion and Sharett, 1953–1956," *Middle East Journal* 37, no. 2 (1983).

20. According to Haggai Eshed, Shiloah, minister at the Israeli embassy in Washington from September 1953 until August 1957, believed in a complete identification of interests between the United States and Israel and rejected any move on the part of his government that he thought might jeopardize the American-Israeli relationship. See Haggai Eshed, *One Man Mossad* (Tel-Aviv: Edanim, 1988), 175 (Hebrew). Thus, as early as June 1954, Shiloah protested that the policy of retaliation damaged relations with the United States. Shiloah to Herzog, 10 June 1954, ISA 4374/20.

21. Sharett, *Personal Diary*, 794.

22. Ben-Dor to embassy in Washington, 23 August 1954; Avner to Ben-Dor, 27 August 1954, ISA 163/12.

23. See text of Sharett's speech at the commencement of consultations at the Foreign Ministry, 24 May 1955; a review of the conclusions of these consultations, 7 June 1955, ISA 2446/8; and Sharett's entry in *Personal Diary*, 1024–25.

24. Shiloah to Herzog, 10 June 1954, ISA 4374/20.

25. Bialer, *Between East and West*, 261.

26. Ibid., 262.

27. The evidence contradicts Michael B. Oren's claim that on instructions from Dulles, U.S. representatives at the NEACC vetoed Israeli orders for spare parts and surplus items. See Michael B. Oren, *The Origins of the Second Arab-Israeli War: Egypt, Israel and the Great Powers, 1952–1956* (London: Frank Cass, 1993), 83. The United States would not sell the Israelis tanks, jets, and heavy artillery, but it would acquiesce to limited British and French supplies of such items to Israel. Furthermore, while the United States would not sell Israel arms in the above-mentioned categories, it would license spare parts and ammunition for export to Israel. Thus, for example, in July 1953 the United States approved the sale to Israel of twelve ninety-millimeter aircraft guns with ammunition, assorted spare parts, and .50-caliber ammunition. See NEACC-US D-13, Israeli Arms Request, 22 July 1953, PRO: FO/371 104225. This policy is detailed in bimonthly British reports on the proceedings of the NEACC in PRO files FO/371 115552, 1955; 121325, 121340, 121354, and 121357, 1956.

28. Paul Jabber, *Not by War Alone* (Berkeley and Los Angeles: University of California Press, 1981), 97.

29. Shlomo Slonim, "Origins of the 1950 Tripartite Declaration on the Middle East," *Middle Eastern Studies* 23, no. 2 (1987): 135–49.

30. Report of the Foreign Office, "Supply of Arms to Israel," 2 July 1953, PRO: FO/371 104222 E1192/193.

31. British embassy in Washington to Foreign Office, 9 September 1953, PRO: FO/371 104225 E1192/263.

32. *FRUS* 9:1574.

33. Ibid.

34. Consultations on military aid, 23 July 1953, ISA 4373/15.

35. Herzog to Shiloah, 10 October 1954, ISA 4374/19; meeting, Mapai Central Committee, 13 May 1954, LPA.

36. Eban to United States Section, 29 January 1954, ISA 40/18/B.

37. For text, see *United States Treaties and Other International Agreements* UST: 5, 3:2497.

38. Lavon's report on his meeting with Trudeau, 17 May 1954, ISA 40/19/A.

39. Sending IDF units to fight outside the immediate arena of the Arab-Israeli conflict was in any case unfeasible from both a security and public opinion standpoint, but the American attitude troubled the Israelis nonetheless. See consultations at the Foreign Ministry, 30 May 1954, ISA 40/19/A.

40. Lavon's meeting with Trudeau, 17 May 1954, ISA 40/19/A.

41. In truth, the Iraqis received far less than the Israelis had thought they would. At the beginning of 1956, Iraq had only 36 medium tanks, compared with 222 for Israel. The Iraqis had only 2 light tanks; Israel had 50. Iraq would have been unable to deploy even this force against Israel; in early 1956, they had no transporters. Iraq had 10 jets to Israel's 30. American aid to Iraq in "lethal weapons" remained on a very small scale, most of U.S. aid being, by agreement with the British, cars and trucks. See "Present equipment holdings of Middle East countries," 2 January 1954, PRO: FO/371 121324 V1192/83A; embassy in Washington to Foreign Office, 28 October 1954, 110815 V1192/451; ibid., 24 and 26 May 1955, 115585 V1193/66, 66B; Minute of the War Office, 31 October 1955, 115588 V1193/154. Nevertheless, the alarm that plans for arming Iraq caused Israel should not be denigrated.

42. Embassy in Washington to Foreign Office, 6 February 1954, PRO: FO/371 110819 V1193/21.

43. *Department of State Bulletin*, 26 April 1954, 628, and 10 May 1954, 708.

44. Steven Spiegel, *The Other Arab-Israeli Conflict* (Chicago: University of Chicago Press, 1985), 63.

45. *FRUS* 9:1543.

46. Ibid., 1555–56.

47. Sharett, *Personal Diary*, 1018.

48. Consultations at the Foreign Ministry, 30 May 1954, ISA 40/19/A.

49. Ibid.

50. Shiloah to Sharett, 20 May 1954, ISA 4374/20. Shiloah claimed that poor relations with the United States were at least partly due to Sharett's lack of contact with the U.S. embassy in Tel Aviv. As a result, claimed Shiloah, Russell was receiving information from "Tel Aviv living rooms," and this was the reason his reports had become increasingly negative. Shiloah to Herzog, 10 June 1954, ISA 4374/20.

51. Meeting, Mapai Central Committee, 13 May 1954, LPA.

52. See a letter to Eban from A. C. Davis, Director of the Office of Foreign Military Affairs, U.S. Department of Defense, 9 July 1954, ISA 163/12.

53. See William Roger Louis, "The Tragedy of the Anglo-Egyptian Settlement of 1954," in *Suez 1956: The Crisis and Its Consequences*, ed. William Roger Louis and Roger Owen, 43–72 (Oxford: Oxford University Press, 1989).

54. *FRUS* 9:1574.

55. Sharett, *Personal Diary*, 560; also Bialer, *Between East and West*, 264.

56. Protocol of a meeting at the embassy in Washington, 6 August 1954, ISA 172/18.

57. *FRUS* 9:1621. Eban had in late February 1954 reported that there was a good chance that the United States would provide either arms or "other compensatory, balancing action." See his telegram no. 68 to the Foreign Ministry, 25 February 1954, ISA 40/18/B. Ben Gurion, however, was horrified to think that "American soldiers [might] spill blood in Israel's defense should she be attacked." Sharett, *Personal Diary*, 1355.

58. *FRUS* 9:1627–29. Russell warned that the treaty the Israelis wanted was one that they would be able to invoke on the occasion of a border incident. He also noted that "Israel still has as one of its principal goals release of as many as four million Jews behind the Iron Curtain and therefore cannot be uninhibited in its cooperation with the free world."

59. Sharett to embassy in Washington, 5 September 1954, ISA 40/19/B.

60. Eban's report of his meeting with Dulles, 15 September 1954, ISA 40/19/B.

61. *FRUS* 9:1667–69.

62. Ibid., 1671–72.

63. Ibid.

64. Herzog to Shiloah, 10 October 1954, ISA 4374/19.

65. Sharett, *Personal Diary*, 941.

66. Ibid., 691.

67. Ibid., 794.

68. Ibid., 691.

69. Bar-On, *Gates of Gaza*, 107–24; Shimon Shamir, "The Collapse of Project Alpha," in Louis and Owen, *Suez 1956*, 73–101.

70. Dulles's circular memo of 22 November 1954, *FRUS* 9:1695–1700. For a detailed analysis of the role of the Negev in the Arab-Israeli conflict see Ilan Asia, "Confrontation and War Over the Negev Corridor, 1949–1956" (Ph.D. diss., Bar-Ilan University, 1992) (Hebrew).

71. Shiloah to Herzog, 13 December 1954, ISA 40/18/B.

72. Shamir, "Collapse of Project Alpha," 78. For more detailed analyses of the Johnston Mission see Yoram Nimrod, *Mei Meriva* (Angry Waters) (Givat Haviva: Center for Arab and Afro-asian Studies, 1966); Michael Brecher, *Decisions in Israel's Foreign Policy* (London: Oxford University Press, 1974), 173–224; Eyal Kafkafi, "Ben Gurion, Sharett and the Johnston Plan," *Studies in Zionism* 13, no. 2 (1992): 165–86.

73. Levi Eshkol warned that a settlement entailing unpopular concessions could damage Mapai in the coming elections. Sharett, *Personal Diary*, 992. On 18 January 1954, Sharett predicted "difficult days to come in the discussions with Johnston." Ibid., 670.

74. Ibid., 677.

75. Kafkafi, "Ben Gurion, Sharett and the Johnston Plan," 176.

76. Sharett, *Personal Diary*, 688.

77. Ibid., 692.

78. Bialer, *Between East and West*, 265.

79. Sharett, *Personal Diary*, 667–68.

80. Summary of consultations at the Foreign Ministry, 1 March 1955, ISA 215/11; Sharett, *Personal Diary*, 683, 712.

81. Meeting, Mapai Central Committee, 17 February 1955, LPA.

82. Sharett, *Personal Diary*, 698; Sharett to Eban, 9 February 1955, ISA 215/11.

83. Sharett, *Personal Diary*, 726.

84. *FRUS* 14:55–56; Sharett, *Personal Diary*, 733.

85. Sharett, *Personal Diary*, 733.

86. Ibid., 805. Sharett's view that Israeli forces could predetermine the number of enemy dead in a retaliatory raid is odd.

87. Ibid., 837.

88. Bialer, *Between East and West*, 268–69.

89. *FRUS* 14:85.

90. Ibid., 6.

91. Ibid., 87.

92. Bialer, *Between East and West*, 267.

93. Sharett, *Personal Diary*, 998.

94. See Michael Bar-Zohar, *Ben Gurion: A Biography* (London: Weidenfeld and Nicolson, 1978), 218–19; Amos Perlmutter, *Military and Politics in Israel* (New York: Praeger, 1969); Sharett, *Personal Diary*, 816.

95. Sharett, *Personal Diary*, 794.

96. *FRUS* 14:93–94, 184.

97. Ibid.

98. Sharett, *Personal Diary*, 839.

99. Ibid., 872.

100. Ibid., 866. Ben-Gurion's proposed invasion would have been in response to a 24 March terrorist attack at Moshav Patish, on the Gaza border. *FRUS* 14:120.

101. *FRUS* 14:149–50.

102. Ibid.

103. Herzog to Sharett, 22 April 1955, ISA 4374/19.

104. *FRUS* 14:159–60.

105. Ibid.

106. Sharett, *Personal Diary*, 935.

107. Ibid., 938–39.

108. Ibid., 947.

109. Ben-Gurion's diary, 12 May 1955, BGA.

110. Sharett, *Personal Diary*, 989.

111. Ibid., 1003.

112. Ibid. Later the same day Teddy Kollek, director general of the prime minister's office, urged that Israel terminate all discussions with the United States except those connected with the Johnston Mission.

113. Ibid., 1031; *FRUS* 14:215.

114. Sharett, *Personal Diary*, 932, 947, 1018, 1048.

115. *FRUS* 14:170.

116. Sharett, *Personal Diary*, 985.

117. Peter Medding, *The Founding of Israeli Democracy, 1948–1967* (London: Oxford University Press, 1990), 48–53.

118. Perlmutter, *Military and Politics in Israel*, 84–85.

119. Medding, *Founding of Israeli Democracy*, 53.

120. Archives of Hakibbutz Hameuchad (Yad Tabenkin, Ramat Efal), 13B, 23, files 1 and 2; date is early 1954. See also Yitzhak Ben-Aharon's speech to the political committee of Ahdut Ha'avoda on 19 November 1954.

121. Medding, *Founding of Israeli Democracy*, 52.

122. Archives of Hakibbutz Hameuchad, 16 August 1955, 13/12, 6 (series 1), notebooks 1–9, 145–49.

123. Ibid., 12 August 1955, in a separate document titled "Main points of Ben Gurion's talks with Ahdut Ha'avoda delegation."

124. Ibid. At the same meeting, Ben Gurion informed the representatives of Ahdut Ha'avoda that he had already held similar talks with Mapam.

125. Sharett, *Personal Diary*, 1012.

126. Ibid., 1107.

127. Ibid., 1122.

128. *FRUS* 14:376.

129. Ibid., 297.

130. Sharett, *Personal Diary*, 1143.

131. Ibid., 1147–48.

132. Ibid., 1148. Neither Dayan nor Ben-Gurion in fact resigned. The American ambassador noted Sharett's resentment and dejection at Ben Gurion's insistence upon retaliation in this instance during his meeting on 1 September 1955, with Ben-Gurion, Sharett, and Elmore Jackson. Sharett defended the Israeli raid on Gaza of 28 February, but when Jackson explained that this was the basis of Nasser's complete abandonment of confidence in Israel's leaders, Sharett "never removed his eyes from Ben Gurion." *FRUS* 14:431–32.

133. *FRUS* 14:391–92.

134. Foreign Ministry consultations, 12 September 1955, ISA 194/8.

135. Quoted in Bialer, *Between East and West*, 271.

136. Shiloah to Herzog, 22 September 1955, ISA 4374/22.

137. See Bar-On, *Gates of Gaza*, 13–27.

138. For details of the Czech arms deal see table 9, appendix. It is difficult to determine precisely when these arms actually reached Egypt. Bar-On notes that according to Israeli military intelligence, the bulk of this weaponry reached Egypt by January 1956. See Bar-On, *Gates of Gaza*, 32. Safran notes that all of these arms were in Egyptian hands by summer 1956, although the Egyptian army had not succeeded in absorbing them. See Nadav Safran, *From War to War: The Arab-Israeli Confrontation, 1948–1967* (Indianapolis: Bobbs-Merrill, 1969), 209.

139. Sharett, *Personal Diary*, 1180.

140. *FRUS* 14:457.

141. Bialer, *Between East and West*, 272.

142. Sharett, *Personal Diary*, 1188. Sharett also recorded his surprise that the CIA was apparently pursuing a strategy so opposed to that of Dulles. There is no record of Eban's conversation with Dulles in the foreign policy documents of the United States National Archives.

143. Ibid., 1191, 1228.

144. Bar-On, *Gates of Gaza*, 58. The 23 October meeting between Ben-Gurion and Dayan took place on the same day that Sharett departed for Paris and Geneva to meet the foreign ministers of the four powers in an effort to obtain arms.

145. Ibid., 47, 58.

146. Ibid., 72. No record of the meeting was found in Sharett's diary. Of Mapai's ministers, Sharett and three others were opposed; joining them in rejecting the proposal were Mapam, the Progressives and the National Religious Party.

147. *FRUS* 14:578.

148. Ibid., 542.

149. Ibid.

150. Ibid., 638.

151. Ibid.

152. Bar-On, *Gates of Gaza*, 21.

153. Sharett, *Personal Diary*, 1248.

154. Ibid., 1249.

155. *FRUS* 14:657.

156. Sharett, *Personal Diary*, 1252.

157. Ibid., 1258.

158. Ibid., 1254.

159. *FRUS* 14:683.

160. Sharett, *Personal Diary*, 1266.

161. *FRUS* 14:683–84.

162. Ibid., 593. Emphasis added.

163. Sharett, *Personal Diary*, 1284.

164. Ibid., 1293.

165. *FRUS* 14:717.

166. Ibid., 698.

167. Ibid., 719.

168. Sharett, *Personal Diary*, 1294, 1303.

169. *FRUS* 14:784.

170. Ibid., 744.

171. Ibid., 719.

172. Ibid., 796.

173. Ibid., 683.

174. Ibid., 847.

175. Ibid., 848–49.

176. Bar-On terms this period in the Israeli campaign to obtain arms from the United States, which lasted until April 1956, "five months of illusions." Bar-On, *Gates of Gaza*, 184.

177. See Nissim Bar-Ya'acov, *The Israeli-Syrian Armistice: Problems of Implementation, 1949–1966* (Jerusalem: Magnes Press, 1967), 220–22; Howard Sachar, *A History of Israel: From the Rise of Zionism to Our Time* (New York: Knopf, 1976), 447.

178. *FRUS* 14:853.

179. Bar-On, *Gates of Gaza*, 179.

180. Ibid.

181. Sharett, *Personal Diary*, 1307.

182. Allen to Dulles, 13 December 1955, USNA: 784A.56.

183. *FRUS* 15:26–27.

184. Ibid., 72–74.

185. Ibid.

186. Ibid., 871. Freiberger notes that the United States excluded the British from this effort because by January 1956, a pattern of disagreements had emerged between the United States and the United Kingdom over Middle East policies. See Steven Z. Frei-

berger, *Dawn Over Suez: The Rise of American Power in the Middle East, 1953–1957* (Chicago: Ivan Dee, 1992), 133–34.

187. *FRUS* 15:352.

188. Ibid., 77–79.

189. Ibid., 163.

190. Ben-Dor to Herzog, 11 March 1956, ISA 193/1.

191. *FRUS* 15:258–59.

192. Ibid., 186.

193. Ibid., 342.

194. Ibid., 589.

195. Ibid., 269.

196. Sharett, *Personal Diary*, 1385–86.

197. Ibid., 1372–73.

198. Ibid., 1455–65.

199. "Munitions items licensed for export from the United States to Israel and the Arab states, March–April, 1956," in PRO: FO/371 121340; also July–August, 1956; 17 September 1956, FO/371 121357, V1192/1014.

200. Bar-On, *Gates of Gaza*, 186.

201. BJSM Washington to Ministry of Defense, 4 October 1956, PRO: FO/371 121354 V1192928.

202. Ibid., 184.

203. *FRUS* 15:198.

204. See details of the French-Israeli arms deals of 1956 in chapter 3.

205. Bar-On, *Gates of Gaza*, 185.

206. Bialer, *Between East and West*, 212, 244.

207. *FRUS* 14:265.

208. And not only in early 1956, as Bar-On states in *Gates of Gaza*, 185.

CHAPTER TWO

1. This period in Anglo-Israeli relations has elicited little attention from students of either British or Israeli policy. William Roger Louis, *The British Empire in the Middle East, 1945–1951* (Oxford: Clarendon Press, 1984) is a comprehensive study of Britain's policies in the region from 1945 to 1951. Louis's work includes a lengthy chapter on the Palestine question and the Arab-Israeli war of 1948 but little on Anglo-Israeli relations after that point. Ilan Pappé, *Britain and the Arab-Israeli Conflict, 1948–1951* (London: Macmillan Press, 1988) is primarily a study of Britain's role in the Israeli-Jordanian relationship during that period. Peter L. Hahn, *The United States, Great Britain and Egypt, 1945–1956* (Chapel Hill: University of North Carolina Press, 1991) provides valuable insight into the Anglo-Egyptian Agreement of 1954. Uri Bialer, *Between East and West: Israel's Foreign Policy Orientation 1948–1956* (Cambridge: Cambridge University Press, 1990) explores early Anglo-Israeli contacts on strategic cooperation and briefly explains why a British orientation in Israeli foreign policy was not possible. However, Bialer too leaves open the subject of Israel's relations with Britain from 1952 to 1956.

2. Undersecretary of State for Air to Foreign Office, 17 May 1955, PRO: FO/371 115561 V1192/218.

3. Louis, *British Empire in the Middle East*, 629–30.

4. Bialer, *Between East and West*, 231.

5. Ibid., 236.

6. British embassy in Washington to Levant department, 31 December 1954, PRO: FO/ 371 115553 V1192/4.

7. Ibid.

8. Ibid.

9. Ibid.

10. Gazit to Elath, 21 May 1954, ISA 40/14/B.

11. British embassy in Tel Aviv to Levant department, 16 February 1954, PRO: FO/371 110808 V1192/89.

12. British embassy in Tel Aviv to Foreign Office, 22 February 1955, PRO: FO/371 115818 VR/10317/1.

13. Ministry of Defense to Foreign Office, 31 May 1954, PRO: FO/371 110811 V1192/251.

14. British Commonwealth section to the Israeli embassy in London, 9 October 1955, ISA 330/3.

15. Schneerson to Avner, 12 July 1955, ISA 330/7.

16. Elath to Comay, 23 January 1953, ISA 42/13/A.

17. Pappé, *Britain and the Arab-Israeli Conflict*, 202.

18. Bialer, *Between East and West*, 258.

19. Ibid., 239.

20. Louis, *British Empire in the Middle East*, 583.

21. Paul Jabber, *Not by War Alone* (Berkeley and Los Angeles: University of California Press, 1981), 64.

22. Unsigned minute of the Foreign Office, 19 February 1953, PRO: FO/371 104218 E1192/82A. According to Hahn, London agreed in February 1950 to sell Egypt 158 war jets, 64 tanks, 264 artillery pieces, and some 3,600 vehicles over a period of four years. Hahn suggests that the abrupt British halt of arms shipments to Egypt in September 1950, which the British claimed was in order to meet its military needs in Korea, was in fact designed to put pressure on the Egyptian government to agree to accept London's proposals in the base negotiations. Hahn, *United States, Great Britain, and Egypt*, 97, 106.

23. Gazit to Elath, 25 August 1952, ISA 42/13.

24. See minutes by J. Wardrop, 9 June and 26 July 1953, PRO: FO/371 98295 E1225/5, 14.

25. Keith Kyle, *Suez* (London: Weidenfeld and Nicolson, 1991), 50. See also Elath's evaluation of British policy toward Egypt, based on his talks with Bowker of the Foreign Office, in his report to Sharett, 14 November 1952, ISA 42/13.

26. Unsigned minute of the Foreign Office, 19 February 1953, PRO: FO/371 104218 1192/82A.

27. Minute by J. E. Powell-Jones, 21 November 1952, PRO: FO/371 98285 E1194/96.

28. Minute by Wardrop, 9 June 1952, PRO: FO/371 98295 E1225/5.

29. Elath to Eytan, 10 November 1952, ISA 42/13.

30. In fact, the British themselves never completely resolved this question, either as a

matter of United Kingdom arms policy or in the framework of the NEACC. See Kyle, *Suez*, 36.

31. Yitzhak Steigman, *History of the Air Force: The Air Force from 1950 to 1956* (Tel Aviv: Israeli Ministry of Defense, 1986), 38 (Hebrew). In fact, in November 1953 the total number of fighter planes in the Arab air forces was 218, 97 of which were jets. The total number of fighters in the IAF was 137, but only 15 of these were jets. See table 2, appendix.

32. Ibid., 41.

33. Ibid., 52–54. Israel was interested in the American Sabre (F-86), the Swedish Saab J-29, and the French Mystère-2.

34. The British themselves admitted that their method of distribution compelled Israel to purchase the jets. See minute of Chadwick, 28 September 1952, in PRO: FO/371 98297 E1194/72.

35. Sharett's memo of 22 October 1952, ISA 42/13/A.

36. Sharett to Elath, 25 November 1952, ISA 42/13.

37. Elath to Foreign Ministry, 14 November 1952, ISA 42/13.

38. Michael Keren (counselor at the Israeli embassy in London), report on a meeting with William Strang, cable no. 3109, 8 January 1953, ISA 42/13. In fact, it was precisely the weakness of Arab regimes such as that of Syria which prompted the British to supply arms for "maintenance of internal security." See Gazit to Elath, 28 February 1955, ISA 330/7.

39. Salmon (Israeli military attaché in London) to Elath, 29 January 1953, ISA 42/13/A.

40. Elath to Sharett, 14 November 1952, ISA 42/13/A.

41. Keren to Comay, 9 January 1953, ISA 42/13/A.

42. British embassy in Tel Aviv to Foreign Office, 11 October 1952, PRO: FO/371 98295 E1194/78.

43. Elath to Comay, 23 January 1953, ISA 42/13/A.

44. Ibid.

45. For a full account of these clashes, see Aryeh Shalev, *Cooperation Under the Shadow of Conflict: The Israeli-Syrian Armistice Agreement, 1949–1955* (Tel Aviv: Ma'arachot, 1989) (Hebrew). Binyamin Givli, Israel's military intelligence chief, anxiously approached the British air attaché in Tel Aviv in December 1952 about rumors that the Syrians were negotiating a deal with Britain for between fifty and one hundred jets. See British embassy in Tel Aviv to Foreign Office, 20 December 1952, PRO: FO/371 98298 E1125/98. Actually, Glosters, the manufacturer of the Meteor, was holding Syria at arms length regarding any jets beyond the fourteen Meteors agreed upon. The Foreign Office was chary regarding the supply of additional jets to Damascus, because the total Syrian defense budget was six hundred thousand pounds, while the cost of the fourteen Meteors was five hundred thousand pounds. See the minute of J. E. Powell-Jones, 19 December 1952, PRO: FO/371 98298 E1225/97.

46. Sharett's memo of 22 October 1952, ISA 42/13/A.

47. Report of the Ministry of Supply, 23 December 1952, PRO: FO/371 98298 E1225/99. Israel had in fact received fifteen Meteors, not fourteen as originally planned.

48. Minute by Powell-Jones, 12 June 1953, PRO: FO/371 104220 E1192/166.

49. Unsigned minute of the Ministry of Supply, 20 August 1953, PRO: FO/371 104224 E1192/247.

50. See table 3, appendix, for relative tank strengths as of 1 March 1953.

51. Syria had several days earlier requested eighteen Centurions and seventy-five Daimler cars, and the Iraqis were to receive arms in accordance with Anglo-American regional defense plans. See British Middle East Office (BMEO) weekly political summary no. 22, 4 June 1953, in PRO: FO/371 104187 E1013/22, and Ross to Bulkeley of the War Office, 13 June 1953, PRO: FO/371 104220 E1192/166.

52. Ross to Bulkeley, 13 June 1953, PRO: FO/371 104220 E1192/166.

53. Ibid.

54. Minute by Falla, 7 October 1953, PRO: FO/371 104226 E1192/301.

55. Ibid.

56. John Glubb, British commander of the Jordanian Arab Legion, wrote a "powerful letter" to the British chiefs of staff protesting the possibility of the sale of Centurions to Israel. See Middle East Liasion Force (MELF) to War Office, 12 October 1953, PRO: FO/ 371 104226 1192/292A.

57. BMEO political summary no. 42, 21 October 1953, PRO: FO/371 104188 E1013/44.

58. Falla to Salisbury: Purchase of U.K. military stores by Israel, 19 September 1953, PRO FO/371 104226 E1192/279.

59. See tables 4 and 5, appendix.

60. Ibid.

61. Report of the Arms Working Party, 28 September 1953, PRO: FO/371 104226, E1192/287/A.

62. See Roger Allen's recommendation exactly one week before the Kibye operation, attached to a minute by Falla, that the Arab states receive arms before any more significant quantities be sold to Israel, 7 October 1953, PRO: FO/371 104226 E1192/301.

63. Foreign Office to British embassy in Washington, 2 December 1953, PRO: FO/371 104229 E1192/36.

64. PRO: FO/371 24 November 1953 104229 E1192/365.

65. Ben-Gurion's diary, 7 August 1954, BGA. The Shermans were the first item on Ben-Gurion's list, which included 250 half-tracks, 50 25-pounder guns, 5 155-mm guns, 5 French light tanks for trial purposes, 14 antiaircraft guns (caliber unspecified), 15 Mystères (Mark 2), 9 Meteors, 20 Mosquitos, 10 P-51 Mustangs, 2 destroyers, and 4 torpedo boats.

66. Note by the Joint Secretary of the Joint War Production Committee, Ministry of Defense, 4 December 1953, PRO: FO/371 104229 E1192/373.

67. Falla to Evans, 27 August 1954, PRO: FO/371 110813 V1192/346. The Israelis became increasingly aware that some sort of tripartite consultation on arms was taking place, but, despite British pronouncements precisely to this effect, seem never to have fully grasped the extent to which French arms to Israel, along with British determination to adhere to a certain balance, affected Britain's arms policies.

68. Elath to Sharett, 12 November 1953, ISA 225/5.

69. Ibid.

70. Gazit to British Commonwealth Section, 27 January 1954, ISA 41/14. The possibility that Britain might move troops into the West Bank was particularly worrisome to the IDF. Yehoshafat Harkabi, deputy chief of military intelligence, requested clarification on this from the director general of the Foreign Ministry. The answer was that according

to the rules of international law, British entry into the West Bank, including East Jerusalem, was legal. See Harkabi to Eytan, 29 October 1953, and response provided by the legal counsel of the Foreign Ministry, 23 December 1953, both in ISA 41/14.

71. Michael Brecher, *Decisions in Israel's Foreign Policy* (London: Oxford University Press, 1974), 255.

72. Gazit to Elath, 16 February 1955, ISA 220/3.

73. Unsigned minute of the Foreign Office, 9 September 1954, PRO: FO/371 111065 VR1072/167.

74. Jabber, *Not by War Alone*, 98–99. Jabber notes that the sale of Meteors to Egypt at the end of 1952 was a temporary relaxation of that embargo.

75. Bialer, *Between East and West*, 263.

76. Gazit to Elath, 16 February 1955, ISA 220/3.

77. British embassy in Tel Aviv to the Foreign Office, 30 October 1954, PRO: FO/371 110816, V1192/453.

78. Bialer, *Between East and West*, 259.

79. Avner to the embassy in Washington, 28 April 1954, ISA 40/18/B.

80. Bialer, *Between East and West*, 259.

81. Report by Paul Falla, "Defense Cooperation with Israel," 19 February 1954, PRO: FO/371 111118 VR1195/1.

82. Elath to Sharett, 4 November 1954, ISA 40/18/A; Sharett to Elath, 7 November 1954, ISA 40/14/B; Elath to Sharett, 8 November 1954. See also Ben-Gurion's short note to Sharett on Eden's intentions in Moshe Sharett, *Personal Diary*, 601.

83. Sharett, *Personal Diary* (Tel Aviv: Ma'ariv, 1978), 601.

84. Ibid.

85. Gazit to Elath, 31 December 1954, ISA 40/18/A. The call for a security guarantee from Britain and the attempt to force the Foreign Office to explain publicly and in detail its refusal to grant one was a public relations ploy aimed at stymying efforts to push Israel into territorial concessions. See Sharett to Elath, 8 January 1956, ISA 330/3.

86. Minute by Tripp, 22 September 1954, PRO: FO/371 111118 VR1192/4.

87. Falla to Tripp and Powell-Jones, 10 September 1954, PRO: FO/371 111118 VR1195/4.

88. Minute by Tripp, 22 September 1954, PRO: FO/371 111118 VR 1195/4.

89. Minute by Powell-Jones, 24 September 1954, PRO: FO/371 111118 VR1195/4.

90. See Lurie's report of 14 February 1954, ISA 41/14. Arab raids caused 137 Israeli casualties in 1951, 147 in 1952, 162 in 1953, and 180 in 1954. During those years, most of the casualties were on the Jordanian border. See Brecher, *Decisions in Israel's Foreign Policy*, 229.

91. Howard Sachar, *A History of Israel* (New York: Knopf, 1986), 445.

92. *FRUS* 9:1497.

93. Ibid., 1510.

94. Avner to Rafael, 5 August 1954, ISA 40/14/B.

95. Gazit to British Commonwealth Section, 3 September 1954, ISA 40/14/B.

96. See details on the proposals for local commanders' talks in *FRUS* 9:1610–11.

97. Gazit to British Commonwealth Section, 17 September 1954, ISA 40/14/B.

98. *Divrei Haknesset* (Knesset Hearings) (Hebrew), 1 September 1954, 16:2547–51.

99. Elath to Sharett, 22 September 1954, ISA 39/22/B.

100. Minute of Falla, 24 September 1954, PRO: FO/371 10814 V1192/366. For a brief

analysis of the divergent views of the Middle East arms balance among the British ministries which dealt with weapons transfers, see Yoav Tenemboim, "British Policy Towards Israel and the Arab-Israeli Dispute, 1951–1954" (Ph.D. diss., Oxford University, 1991).

101. Gazit to Elath, 31 December 1954, ISA 40/18/A.

102. Ibid.

103. Report by Beith of a conversation with Pierre Maillard, 26 November 1954, PRO: FO/371 110817. The purchase of 30 Mystères (15 Mystère-2s and another 15 Mystère-2s or Mystère-4s) was part of Dayan's plan to increase the IDF's strength to 100 jets and 300 tanks. Ben Gurion's diary, 26 November, 1954, BGA. According to Foreign Office sources, Israeli tank strength as of 1 November 1954 was 150 (Shermans) and jet fighter strength 11 (Meteors). See table 6, appendix.

104. Ministry of Defense to BJSM Washington, 24 September 1955, PRO: FO/371 115568 V1192/381B.

105. Ibid.

106. Gazit to Elath, 31 December 1954, ISA 40/18/A.

107. BMEO to Foreign Office, 28 April 1955, PRO: FO/371 115560 V1192/199.

108. See Gazit to British Commonwealth section, 25 November 1955, ISA 330/7.

109. Sharett, *Personal Diary*, 967.

110. Schneerson to Elath, 8 and 9 May 1955, ISA 330/7.

111. Gazit to British Commonwealth Section, 25 November 1955, ISA 330/7.

112. Ibid.; 16 February 1955, ISA 220/3.

113. BJSM Washington to Ministry of Defense, 9 March 1955, PRO: FO/371 115557 V1192/124D.

114. Ben-Dor to Western Europe Section, 20 May 1955, ISA 194/4, and Avner to Ben-Dor, 26 May 1955, ISA 194/4.

115. British embassy in Tel Aviv to Foreign Office, 30 June 1955, PRO: FO/371 115564 V1192/276.

116. Ibid., 259.

117. Evelyn Shuckburgh, *Descent to Suez* (London: Weidenfeld and Nicolson, 1986), 267.

118. Ben-Gurion's diary, 2 May, 1955, BGA.

119. *FRUS* 14:229.

120. Elath to British Commonwealth Section, 29 June 1955, ISA 330/7.

121. British embassy in Tel Aviv to Foreign Office, 30 June 1955, PRO: FO/371 115564 V1192/275.

122. Foreign Office to British embassy in Tel Aviv, 22 August 1955, PRO: FO/371 115567 V1192/350G.

123. Schneerson's report of a meeting between Peres and Nicholls, at which he was present, 15 August 1955, ISA 330/3. By November 1955, Egypt had forty-one Centurion tanks. See table 8, appendix.

124. Ibid. The request for 200 half-tracks should be viewed in light of the fact that in January 1955, the British were still considering a previous Israeli request for only 25 half-tracks. Almog to Elath, 21 January 1955, ISA 330/7. In May 1955, Israel had 106 and Egypt 128. See table 7, appendix.

125. Ministry of Defense to MELF dated July 1955, PRO: FO/371 115566.

126. By the end of 1955, Israel had received twenty Ouragans. See Air Ministry to Foreign Office, 10 December 1955, PRO: FO/371 115579 V1192/723. Israel bought the Ouragan as a stop-gap measure until the Mystère could be acquired. It was superior to the Meteor but inferior to the MiG-15. See Steigman, *History of the Air Force*, 64.

127. British embassy in Tel Aviv to Foreign Office, 30 June 1955, PRO: FO/371 115564 V1192/275.

128. Such as thirty additional Meteors, which the British assumed Israel had acquired from either Belgium or Denmark and shipped through France. Rose to Beith, 6 February 1956, PRO: FO/371 121324 V1192/100.

129. Schneerson to Elath, 15 August 1955, ISA 330/3.

130. Unsigned minute of the Foreign Office, 30 June 1955, PRO: FO/371 115564 V1192/280.

131. Avner to Schneerson, 14 July 1955, ISA 330/7.

132. Breene to Gethin, 8 December 1955, PRO: FO/371 115572 V1192/490.

133. U.K. arms and ammunition exports to Egypt and Israel from January 1953 to December 1954 actually favored Israel. The total value for that period is £1,164,830 for Egypt, £1,523,935 for Israel. However, the discrepancy which developed in 1955 is clear from the figures for the first half of 1955 alone: £1,273,449 for Egypt, £590,951 for Israel. See Foreign Office to Ministry of Defense, 12 July 1955, PRO: FO/371 121346 V1192/718. The figures in pounds sterling for the second half of 1955 were not found. However, the Foreign Office at the end of 1955 noted that "even if we go back to January 1953 for overall releases to the Israelis, the total would still come to less than what we have agreed to release to the Egyptians in the last nine months. Furthermore, there have been no releases of major weapons to Israel since the Gaza incident." Breene to Gethin, 8 December 1955, PRO: FO/371 115572 V1192/490.

134. Elath to British Commonwealth Section, 29 September 1955, ISA 330/7.

135. Ibid., 6 July 1955, ISA 330/7.

136. Gazit to British Commonwealth Section, 25 November 1955, ISA 330/7.

137. Sharett, *Personal Diary*, 1251.

138. Robert Rhodes James, *Anthony Eden* (London: Weidenfeld and Nicolson, 1986), 429. The British code named this plan Operation Cordage. For a brief description of Cordage and of the failed Templer mission of early 1956, see Kyle, *Suez*, 92–93.

139. Research section to British Commonwealth Section, 27 December 1955, ISA 192/41.

140. Sharett, *Personal Diary*, 1251. This is the source of the following account of the Sharett-Macmillan meeting of 26 October 1955.

141. On 14 October 1955, Shuckburgh wrote, "We must not compensate Israel for the increased strength which the Soviet bloc arms give to Egypt. To do so would bring about a situation in which the West was arming Israel and the Russians Egypt. The concept of a 'balance' no longer has any reality and will have to disappear from our vocabulary." PRO: FO/371 115480 V1054/5.

142. Sharett met Macmillan again on 31 October, ostensibly to discuss the results of Sharett's talks with Soviet foreign minister Molotov. Sharett noted in his diary that Shuckburgh, "the guard-dog," was not present, and the meeting was more cordial. There were, however, no concrete results. See Sharett, *Personal Diary*, 1275.

143. Israeli consulate in Nicosia to Foreign Ministry, 15 November 1955, ISA 192/41.

144. Sharett's belief that this might have been Eden's intent emerged in a conversation he had with Nicholls in early 1956. See Schneerson's account of the conversation, 4 January 1956, ISA 330/3.

145. Herzog to Foreign Ministry, 17 November 1955, ISA 330/7. See also Lawson's account in *FRUS* 14:785. Lawson omits Ben-Gurion's reference to the RAF planes Israel shot down during its 1948 War of Independence.

146. Sharett to Elath, 19 January 1956, ISA 331/7.

147. Israeli embassy in London to Foreign Ministry, 2 January 1956, ISA 331/7, and British embassy in Washington to Foreign Office, 29 January 1956, PRO: FO/371 121324 V1192/76.

148. Gazit to British Commonwealth Section, 5 January 1956, ISA 331/7.

149. Ibid.

150. See a report by J. G. S. Beith: "Mysteres for Israel," 26 November 1954, PRO: FO/371 110817, and a report by A. A. Duff of his conversation with Fernand Laurent of the Quai d'Orsay, 9 December 1954, PRO: FO/371 110817 1191/221/54. In early 1955, the Foreign Office was disturbed at the idea that the Israelis may have been aware of British protests to the French over the sale of Mystères. See a minute by Powell-Jones, 1 March 1955, PRO: FO/371 115557, V1192/21. Documents of the Israeli Foreign Ministry give no such indication.

151. British Commonwealth Section to Avner, 27 April 1956, ISA 330/7.

152. Unsigned minute of the Levant Department, 28 February 1956, PRO: FO/371 121330 V1192/251.

153. This was Omega. Alpha was to be allowed to wither, negotiations on the Aswan Dam were to languish, and arms shipments to Egypt were to be denied export licenses. See Kyle, *Suez*, 99.

154. Embassy in London to Foreign Ministry, 14 May 1956, ISA 330/7.

155. Avner to Meroz, 15 May 1956, ISA 330/7.

156. Minute by Shuckburgh, 14 October 1955, PRO: FO/371 115480 V1054/5.

157. See table 6, appendix.

158. Kyle, *Suez*, 93–94.

159. Elath to British Commonwealth Section, 6 March 1956, ISA 330/7.

160. In point of fact, as of November 1955, Iraq had no tank transporters. See a minute of the War Office, 31 October 1955, PRO: FO/371 115588 V1192/154. There is no indication in the available NEACC records of 1956 that Iraq received these transporters.

161. James, *Anthony Eden*, 430.

162. Bar-On, *Security and Foreign Policy of Israel, 1955–1957*, 198–215.

163. British embassy in Tel Aviv to Lloyd, 12 July 1956, PRO: FO/371 121367 V1192/56G. In order to deter the possibility of an Israeli strike against Jordan, the British embassy in Tel Aviv recommended that Britain promise Israel between six and twelve Centurions to be delivered in 1957, precisely to give the Israelis the impression that they were not yet at peak strength.

164. Ibid., 12 July 1956, PRO: FO/371 121367 V1192/56G.

165. Ibid.

166. See details of NEACC meeting, BJSM Washington to Ministry of Defense, 5 July

1956, PRO: FO/371 121345 V1192/696; Circular memo of Kirkpatrick, 4 July 1956, PRO: FO/371 121345 V1192/702.

167. British Commonwealth Section to Elath, 9 August 1956; Elath to British Commonwealth Section, 10 August 1956, ISA 328/22.

168. Elath to British Commonwealth Section, 17 August 1956, ISA 328/22.

169. British embassy in Tel Aviv to Foreign Office, 3 September 1956, PRO: FO/371 121369 V1195/24.

170. The Israelis employed tanks and planes in this operation, which approached open warfare. See Sachar, *History of Israel*, 490.

171. British Commonwealth Section to embassy in London, 19 October 1956, ISA 329/5.

172. Michael Bar-Zohar, *Ben Gurion* (Tel Aviv: Zmora, Bitan, 1978), 1227 (Hebrew).

173. *FRUS* 16:622.

174. Ibid., 675–76.

175. Bar-Zohar, *Ben Gurion*, 1227.

176. Elath to Meir, 12 October 1956, ISA 331/1.

177. Elath to British Commonwealth Section, 11 October 1956, ISA 331/8.

178. British Commonwealth Section to Israeli embassy in London, 15 October 1956, ISA 329/5.

179. British embassy in Tel Aviv to Foreign Office, 18 October 1956, PRO: FO/371 121356 V1192/977.

180. Elath to British Commonwealth Section, 11 October 1956, ISA 331/8.

181. Elath to Meir, 18 August 1956, ISA 328/22.

182. Air Ministry to Ministry of Defense, 22 October 1956, PRO: FO/371 121355 V1192/957.

183. Commonwealth Relations Office, 1 November 1956, PRO: FO/371 121356 V1192/992.

184. Kyle, *Suez*, 314.

185. Ben-Gurion's diary, 25 September 1956, BGA.

186. Ben-Gurion's diary, 27 September 1956, BGA.

187. Michael B. Oren, *Origins of the Second Arab-Israeli War: Egypt, Israel and the Great Powers, 1952–1956* (London: Frank Cass, 1993), 140.

188. W. Scott Lucas, *Divided We Stand: Britain, the US and the Suez Crisis* (London: Hodder and Stoughton, 1991), 244–47.

CHAPTER THREE

1. Meeting, Mapai Foreign Affairs Committee, 7 May 1957, LPA.

2. Ben-Gurion's diary, 10 March 1957, BGA.

3. The researcher has access to a large number of recently declassified documents of the Israeli Foreign Ministry from the pre–Sinai crisis period. Most of these documents pertain to the years 1953–56, reflecting the growing salience of France as a potential source of arms from the end of 1952. The archives of the Israeli and French Defense Ministries remain closed to researchers. However, declassified British documents which deal with the workings of the NEACC allow us to fill in most of the gaps regarding French arms deals in the Middle East. In addition, the researcher has access to the diaries of David

Ben-Gurion, Moshe Sharett, and the Israeli ambassador to France, Yaakov Tsur. See Yaakov Tsur, *An Ambassador's Diary in Paris* (Tel-Aviv: Am Oved, 1968) (Hebrew). Three secondary sources which deal with French-Israeli relations in the 1950s also provide important background to this study: Sylvie Crosbie, *A Tacit Alliance: France and Israel from Suez to the Six Day War* (Princeton, N.J.: University Press, 1974); Michael Bar-Zohar, *Bridge Over the Mediterranean: French-Israeli Relations, 1947–1963* (Tel-Aviv: Am Hasefer, 1965) (Hebrew); Mordechai Bar-On, *The Gates of Gaza* (Tel-Aviv: Am Oved, 1992) (Hebrew).

4. Shimon Peres, *David's Sling* (Jerusalem: Weidenfeld and Nicolson, 1970), 31 (Hebrew).

5. Crosbie, *Tacit Alliance*, 39–50, 62–67.

6. Meeting, Mapai Central Committee, 3 January 1957, LPA.

7. Najar to Tsur, 23 April 1954, ISA 179/9-A; Tsur's circular memo, 28 April 1954, ISA 164/2; Tsur to Najar, 29 October 1954, ISA 164/2; Tsur to Western Europe Section, 13 January 1956, ISA 194/3.

8. Crosbie, *Tacit Alliance*, 3.

9. Bar-On, *Gates of Gaza*, 210.

10. Peres, *David's Sling*, 31; Moshe Dayan, *Story of My Life* (Jerusalem: Edanim, 1976), 207–9 (Hebrew).

11. In a speech on 18 January 1957, Prime Minister David Ben-Gurion suggested that Moshe Sharett and the Foreign Ministry had not done everything possible to obtain arms from France. See an article which presents Sharett's version of events: Mordechai Gazit, "Sharett, Ben Gurion and the Arms Deal with France in 1956," *Gesher* 108 (Winter 1983): 86–100 (Hebrew).

12. Paul Jabber, *Not by War Alone* (Berkeley and Los Angeles: University of California Press, 1981), 97.

13. Bar-Zohar, *Bridge Over the Mediterranean*, 25.

14. For a study of French relations with the prestate Yishuv and with Israel to 1949, see David Lazar, "Israel and France: The Beginning of Relations." *State, Government and International Relations* A, no. 2 (1971) (Hebrew).

15. Crosbie, *Tacit Alliance*, 34.

16. Bar-Zohar, *Bridge Over the Mediterranean*, 32.

17. Ibid., 34.

18. Avner to Ben-Dor, 18 February 1955, ISA 192/41.

19. See text of consultations which took place at the Israeli Foreign Ministry between 17 and 23 July 1950, ISA 2463/2: 22.

20. Crosbie, *Tacit Alliance*, 7.

21. Divon to Najar, 23 August 1953; Divon to Western Europe Section, 28 August 1953, ISA 177/7.

22. Ben-Dor to Tsur, 10 February 1955, ISA 192/41.

23. See Shlomo Slonim, "Origins of the 1950 Tripartite Declaration on the Middle East," *Middle Eastern Studies* 23, no. 2 (1987): 135–49.

24. William Roger Louis, *The British Empire in the Middle East, 1945–1951* (Oxford: Oxford University Press, 1984), 585.

25. Jabber, *Not by War Alone*, 97.

26. Embassy in Beirut to embassy in Washington, 15 July 1952, PRO: FO/371 98283 E1194/46.

27. Embassy in Damascus to Foreign Office, 20 November 1951, PRO: FO/371 91229 E1192/339.

28. Chapman-Andrews to Furlonge, 14 August 1951, PRO: FO/371 91188 E1027/11.

29. Embassy in Damascus to Foreign Office, 15 December 1953, PRO: FO/371 104230 E1192/406.

30. Rough estimate based upon quarterly reports of United States arms sales to the Middle East in PRO: FO/371 91232 E1193.

31. Embassy in Washington to Foreign Office, 18 September 1951, PRO: FO/371 91233 E1193/29.

32. Embassy in Damascus to Foreign Office, 15 December 1953, PRO: FO/371 104230 E1192/406.

33. Jabber, *Not by War Alone*, 112.

34. *The Arms Trade Registers*, Stockholm International Peace Research Institute (SIPRI) (Cambridge, Mass.: MIT Press, 1975), 55.

35. Foreign Office to Ministry of Defense, 12 July 1955, PRO: FO/371 121346 V1192/718.

36. The latter figure is that given by Shimon Peres quoted in Crosbie, *Tacit Alliance*, 42. Crosbie confuses the sums of Israel's arms purchases with those of its total defense expenditures and erroneously notes that Israel between 1950 and 1955 spent between $50 and $100 million per annum on arms.

37. Crosbie, *Tacit Alliance*, 41–43.

38. Najar to Divon, 19 July 1953, ISA 177/7.

39. Yitzhak Steigman, *History of the Air Force: The Air Force from 1950 to 1956* (Tel Aviv: Israeli Ministry of Defense, 1986), 52–54 (Hebrew).

40. Minute by J. E. Powell-Jones, 21 November 1952, PRO: FO/371 98285 E1194/96. In the Non-Substitution Agreement of December 1945, the French and British governments affirmed "their intention of taking no steps to usurp the interests which each possesses and the responsibilities which each recognizes the other to have in the Middle East." British embassy in Paris to Strang, 29 September 1952, PRO: FO/371 98284 E1194/73. The British justified this sale by noting that the Non-Substitution Agreement did not conform to reality. The French no longer had the power or the influence to require British adherence and in any case, both Syria and Lebanon had turned to Britain for arms. Memo by Falla, 22 September 1953, PRO: FO/371 104191 E1025/10.

41. Sharett's memo of 22 October 1952, ISA 42/13/A.

42. British Middle East Office (BMEO) weekly political summary no. 49, 10 December 1953, PRO: FO/371 104188 E1013/51.

43. Embassy in Damascus to Foreign Office, 15 December 1953, PRO: FO/371 104230 E1192/406.

44. Ibid., 15 January 1953, PRO: FO/371 104216 E1192/30. See also BMEO weekly political summary no. 22, 4 June 1953, PRO: FO/371 104187 E1013/22.

45. Embassy in Paris to Foreign Office, 4 December 1953, PRO: FO/371 104229 E1192/36.

46. Divon to Western Europe Section, 10 July 1953, ISA 177/7; embassy in Paris to Foreign Office, 7 October 1952, PRO: FO/371 98285 E1194/77.

47. Bar-Zohar, *Bridge Over the Mediterranean*, 59.

48. Embassy in Paris to Foreign Office, 6 October 1953, PRO: FO/371 104226 E1192/300.

49. Divon to Najar, 23 August 1953, ISA 177/7.

50. British embassy in Washington to Foreign Office, 9 September 1953, PRO: 104225 E1192/263.

51. Bar-Zohar, *Bridge Over the Mediterranean*, 59.

52. Crosbie, *Tacit Alliance*, 44.

53. Tsur, *Ambassador's Diary*, 15.

54. Bar-Zohar, *Bridge Over the Mediterranean*, 43.

55. One of these interests was French negotiations with the Syrians for the purchase of French AMX tanks. The French military attaché in Damascus recommended to his government that it sell these tanks for twenty thousand pounds each, about 33 percent less than the original price, in the hopes of "beneficial political repercussions." U.K. military attaché in Damascus to War Office, 8 December 1953, PRO: FO/371 110807 V1192/8.

56. Western Europe Section to Tsur, 20 December 1953, ISA 172/8.

57. Bar-Zohar, *Bridge Over the Mediterranean*, 60.

58. Crosbie, *Tacit Alliance*, 49.

59. Bar-Zohar, *Bridge Over the Mediterranean*, 60–61.

60. Bar-On, *Gates of Gaza*, 204.

61. Crosbie, *Tacit Alliance*, 58.

62. Interview with Yehoshafat Harkabi, 22 July 1990, Jerusalem.

63. Crosbie, *Tacit Alliance*, 45.

64. The Quai d'Orsay was attempting to retain the French influence which remained following the fall of the relatively pro-French Adib Shishakli on 27 February 1954. See Patrick Seale, *The Struggle for Syria* (London: Oxford University Press, 1965), 141.

65. Tsur to Western Europe Section, 8 August 1954, ISA 163/1; British embassy in Paris to Levant department, 9 August 1954, PRO: FO/371 111123 VR1204/14.

66. Ben-Dor to Western Europe Section, 13 August 1954, ISA 163/12.

67. Israeli Foreign Ministry officials recognized that the volatile Israeli-Syrian border endangered French-Israeli relations and considered the chief-of-staff's assurances to the French to be irresponsible. See Avner to Ben-Dor, 27 August 1954, ISA 163/12. In fact, there had been major exchanges of fire between Israel and Syria at the northeastern shore of Lake Kinneret on 15 March and 30 June 1954 and minor flareups throughout 1954 and 1955. See Nissim Bar-Ya'acov, *The Israeli-Syrian Armistice: Problems of Implementation, 1949–1966* (Jerusalem: Magnes Press, 1966), 217, 219.

68. Embassy in Paris to Foreign Office, 4 December 1954, PRO: FO/371 110817 V1192/521. In fact, the French told the British that they would not release the six Mystère-2s before mid-1955. Ibid., 11 August 1954, PRO: FO/371 110813 V1192/332A.

69. Ibid., 11 August 1954, PRO: FO/371 110813 V1192/332A.

70. Ibid., 10 August 1954, PRO: FO/371 110813 V1192/332.

71. Ibid., 25 September 1954, PRO: FO/371 110815 V1192/409.

72. Ibid., 10 August 1954, PRO: FO/371 110813 V1192/332.

73. Ben-Dor to Western Europe Section, 14 September 1954, ISA 163/12.

74. Embassy in Paris to Foreign Office, 11 August 1954, PRO: FO/371 110813 V1192/332.

75. Embassy in Paris to Levant Department, 11 August 1954, PRO: FO/371 110813 V1192/332A.

76. Report on discussions at the Foreign Ministry regarding relations with France, 21 September 1954, ISA 164/4.

77. Deputy director general of the Israeli Defense Ministry; appointed head of Israel's arms purchasing commission in Europe based in Paris in January 1955.

78. Bar-Zohar, *Bridge Over the Mediterranean*, 65.

79. Najar to Tsur, 11 January 1955, ISA 192/41.

80. Ben-Dor to Najar, 22 October 1954, ISA 188/1.

81. Najar to Sharett, 13 October 1954, ISA 163/12.

82. Report on discussions at the Foreign Ministry regarding relations with France, 21 September 1954, ISA 164/4.

83. Moshe Sharett, *Personal Diary* (Tel Aviv: Ma'ariv, 1978), 712 (Hebrew).

84. Ben-Dor to Tsur, 10 February 1955, ISA 192/41.

85. According to Bar-Zohar, Israel's reticence at opposing the pact provided the French Foreign Ministry with an additional excuse for not providing arms. Bar-Zohar, *Bridge Over the Mediterranean*, 70.

86. Najar to Tsur, 2 March 1955, ISA 194/3.

87. Western Europe Section to Tsur, 23 February 1955, ISA 192/41.

88. Western Europe Section to embassy in Paris, 20 December 1954, ISA 180/1. See also an evaluation by the British embassy in Washington, 31 December 1954, PRO: FO/371 110817 V1192/4.

89. Ben-Dor to Tsur, 10 February 1955, ISA 192/41.

90. Bar-Zohar, *Bridge Over the Mediterranean*, 65.

91. Western Europe Section to embassy in Paris, 20 December 1954, ISA 180/1.

92. Ibid.

93. British Joint Staffs Mission (BJSM) in Washington to Ministry of Defense, 7 December 1955, PRO: FO/371 115579 V1192/713.

94. See Bar-Zohar, *Bridge Over the Mediterranean*, 75–76. Bar-Zohar's account is corroborated by documents in PRO files FO/371 115560, 115562, 115563.

95. Nahmias to Peres, 8 March 1955; Ben-Dor to Najar, 30 March 1955; Ben-Dor to Najar, 1 April 1955, ISA 188/1.

96. Armaments fournis par la France aux états Arabes et à Israël au cours des mois de janvier et fevrier 1956; 29 March 1956, PRO: FO/371 121336 V1192/465.

97. Ibid.

98. *Arms Trade Registers*, 46.

99. On 20 July 1955, the Israelis requested that all of the Mystères for which they had applied be of the Mark-4 type. Bar-Zohar, *Bridge Over the Mediterranean*, 87.

100. Ben-Dor to Najar, 31 March 1955, ISA 188/1.

101. Undersecretary of State for Air to Foreign Office, 28 July 1955, PRO: FO/371 115565 V1192/323.

102. The available records make it difficult to determine whether at this point the Israelis thought these would be Mystère-4s. The French assured the British that they did not intend to supply Israel with the Mystère-4. Embassy in Paris to Foreign Office, 22 August 1955, PRO: FO/371 115566 V1192/345/A.

103. The French had requested NEACC authorization to sell Israel an additional nine Mystères, bringing the total number which France intended to transfer to the Israelis to fifteen. Jeffery to Tupman (Ministry of Defense), 16 September 1955, PRO: FO/371 115568 V1192/381.

104. Minute by Shuckburgh, 2 September 1955, PRO: FO/371 115568 V1192/388.

105. British embassy in Paris to Foreign Office, 7 October 1955, PRO: FO/371 115570 V1192/452.

106. Bar-On, *Gates of Gaza*, 189. The French Foreign Ministry denied rumors that there was an explicit agreement that France not send any more arms to Israel in exchange for an end to hostile Egyptian radio broadcasts to Algeria. Embassy in Paris to Foreign Office, 16 November 1955, PRO: FO/371 115577 V1192/540. However, the Israelis already suspected such a deal; officials of the Quai d'Orsay had told them that France could sell heavy arms to Egypt because the Egyptians were not transfering those to North Africa. Ben-Dor to Tolkovsky, 22 July 1955, ISA 188/1.

107. Avni to Rafael, 2 September 1955, ISA 194/4; Ben-Dor to Western Europe Section, 10 October 1955, ISA 192/41; Navon to Shek, 20 October 1955, ISA 192/41.

108. Tsur, *Ambassador's Diary*, 179.

109. Gazit, "Sharett, Ben Gurion and the Arms Deal," 94.

110. Tsur to Western Europe Section, 24 June 1955, ISA 188/1. Pierre Maillard, head of the Levant desk at the Quai d'Orsay, told Tsur that many of the French defense officials willing to supply Israel with arms did so out of narrow financial interests and "blind hatred of the Arabs" and were in fact openly anti-Semitic. Tsur to Western Europe Section, 11 January 1956, ISA 193/1.

111. Gazit, "Sharett, Ben Gurion and the Arms Deal," 90.

112. Peres, Harkabi, and Laskov called for asking Faure for Mystère-4s instead of Mystère-2s, forty Super-Sherman tanks and five hundred bazookas. Sharett, *Personal Diary*, 1239.

113. The Faure government fell on 25 November 1955. Bar-On, *Gates of Gaza*, 191.

114. Ben-Dor to Avner, 18 October 1955, ISA 192/41.

115. Gazit, "Sharett, Ben Gurion and the Arms Deal," 95.

116. Sharett, *Personal Diary*, 1251.

117. The list included sixty AMX-13 tanks, 500 bazookas, forty Super-Sherman tanks and one thousand SS-10 antitank missiles. The Quai d'Orsay effectively prevented violation of United States offshore procurement regulations, which forbade sale of this item before July 1956. Bar-On, *Gates of Gaza*, 188–91.

118. Tsur feared "fallout" from what many French perceived as Israeli meddling in their internal affairs and wished to lower Israel's "profile" before the 2 January 1956 elections in France. Thus when at the end of 1955 Peres brought a plan to launch an "assault" in France in order to recruit politicians to Israel's cause, Tsur insisted that he refrain from interfering in French domestic matters. Tsur, *Ambassador's Diary*, 201–2, 205. Nevertheless, as Bar-On notes, Peres during this period forged "invaluable ties" with future French leaders. Bar-On, *Gates of Gaza*, 193.

119. Tsur to Najar, 13 January 1956, ISA 194/3.

120. Najar to Sharett, 5 January 1956, ISA 193/1.

121. Bar-On, *Gates of Gaza*, 193.

122. Tsur, *Ambassador's Diary*, 208.

123. Minute of Levant department, 28 February 1956, PRO: FO/371 121330 V1192/251; embassy in Washington to Foreign Office, 7 March 1956, PRO: FO/371 121331 V1192/280. Bar-On refers to a "short-lived" French arms embargo on Israel.

124. Sharett, *Personal Diary*, 1323.

125. Ibid., 1312.

126. Ibid., 1309.

127. Circular memo by Pinay, 21 December 1955, Archives des affaires étrangères de la France, 1955, 2:966–67.

128. Tsur to Eytan, 15 November 1955, ISA 194/4.

129. Record of conversation between Marc Jarblum (head of the French section of the World Jewish Congress) and Maillard, 5 January 1956, ISA 193/1.

130. Najar to Sharett, 9 January 1956, ISA 193/1. This is also what the French military attaché in Tel Aviv told Peres two days later, when Peres expressed his anxiety and apprehension over the French decision to withold arms. Livry to Billotte, 11 January 1956, Archives des affaires étrangères de la France, 1956, 1:33.

131. Najar to Tsur, 11 January 1956, ISA 193/1.

132. Ibid.

133. Tsur to Najar, 3 February 1956, ISA 193/1.

134. Sharett, *Personal Diary*, 1350–51.

135. Bar-On, *Gates of Gaza*, 195.

136. Minute by Hadow, 9 November 1955, PRO: FO/371 115576 V1192/600.

137. BJSM, Washington to Ministry of Defense, 10 January 1956, PRO: FO/371 121322 V1192/26.

138. Tsur to Western Europe Section, 11 January 1956, ISA 193/1.

139. Bar-Zohar, *Bridge Over the Mediterranean*, 94–97.

140. This list included eight 155-mm howitzers, twenty 75-mm guns for mounting on Sherman tanks, and thirty AMX-13 tanks. The French foreign minister did not elaborate upon his decision but only informed de Courcel, France's permanent secretary general for national defense, that he saw no point in continuing the embargo. See Pineau to de Courcel, 2 February 1956, Archives des affaires étrangères de la France, 1956, 1:146–7.

141. The United States had authorized release of the jets from NATO but not their sale to Israel. Bar-Zohar, *Bridge Over the Mediterranean*, 97. See also Abel Thomas, *Comment Israël Fut Sauve* (Paris: Albin-Michel, 1978).

142. Minute of Levant department, 28 February 1956, PRO: FO/371 121330 V1192/251. A report on a NEACC meeting at the beginning of October indicates that the French later decided not to supply Israel with napalm bombs. BJSM, Washington to Ministry of Defense, 4 October 1956, PRO: FO/371 121354 V1192/928.

143. Ibid.

144. Bar-On, *Gates of Gaza*, 197.

145. The Syrians received twenty-five MiG-15 jets and one hundred BTR-152 armored personnel carriers from the Soviet Union in 1956. *Arms Trade Registers*, 64–65. In late May, the British embassy in Damascus reported that the Syrians were to receive twenty MiGs at an unspecified date. Embassy in Damascus to Foreign Office, 23 May 1956, PRO: 121340 V1192/554. Yaacov Roi notes that in June 1956, Soviet Foreign Minister Shepilov visited Syria. It was reported that during his visit (an unspecified number of) Soviet

planes, tanks and other weapons were unloaded at the port of Latakia. Yaacov Roi, *From Encroachment to Involvement: A Documentary Study of Soviet Policy in the Middle East, 1945–1973* (New York: John Wiley and Sons, 1974), 227.

146. Tsur to Western Europe Section, 7 June 1956, ISA 193/1; Ben-Dor to Tsur, 29 June 1956, ISA 192/2. Nevertheless, the new political situation in Syria did not dampen Quai enthusiasm for peddling arms to Damascus in order to curry influence. On 22 May, the British Joint Staffs Mission in Washington reported a French request to supply Syria with a long list of military items, including twelve 155-mm guns, forty 81-mm mortars, twenty 120-mm mortars, and large amounts of ammunition. BJSM, Washington to Ministry of Defense, 22 May 1956, PRO: 121340 V1192/561.

147. Bar-On, *Gates of Gaza*, 200.

148. Gazit presents Mollet's demand as proof that the embassy in Paris was not, as Ben-Gurion claimed, operating in complete accordance with diplomatic protocol. Gazit, "Sharett, Ben Gurion and the Arms Deal," 90.

149. Bar-On, *Gates of Gaza*, 200–202.

150. Interview with Gershon Avner, 21 October 1989, Jerusalem.

151. Sharett, *Personal Diary*, 1385–86. Sharett later wrote Ben-Gurion of his "deep resentment . . . at the utter disregard for the decisive role of the Foreign Ministry in the entire operation." Gazit, "Sharett, Ben Gurion and the Arms Deal," 95. In fact, one month after Sharett's resignation in June 1956, Tsur was informed of the secret agreement between the two Ministries of Defense. See Bar-On, *Gates of Gaza*, 207.

152. Nadav Safran, *Israel, The Embattled Ally* (Cambridge, Mass.: Belknap Press, 1981), 352.

153. Selwyn Ilan Troen, "The Sinai War as a 'War of No Alternative': Ben Gurion's View of the Israel-Egyptian Conflict," in *The Suez-Sinai Crisis 1956, Retrospective and Reappraisal*, ed. Selwyn Ilan Troen and Moshe Shemesh (London: Frank Cass, 1990), 183–84.

154. Gazit, "Sharett, Ben Gurion and the Arms Deal," 91.

155. Ben-Dor to Tsur, 11 March 1956, ISA 193/1.

156. Tsur to Eban, 22 May 1956, ISA 194/3.

157. Bar-On, *Gates of Gaza*, 205.

158. Ibid.

159. Ibid.

160. Ibid., 207.

161. Shimon Peres. "The Road to Sèvres: Franco-Israeli Cooperation," in Troen and Shemesh, *Suez-Sinai Crisis 1956*, 140.

162. Bar-On, *Gates of Gaza*, 207.

163. Ibid., 204.

164. Jean-Paul Cointet, "Guy Mollet, the French Government and the SFIO," in Troen and Shemesh, *Suez-Sinai Crisis 1956*, 133.

165. Bar-On, *Gates of Gaza*, 207.

166. Tsur to Western Europe Section, 15 June 1956, ISA 194/3.

167. Ben-Dor to Western Europe Section, 28 June 1956, ISA 194/3. It was not possible to determine the number of guns the French wished to sell Egypt.

168. Tsur to Western Europe Section, 28 June 1956, ISA 194/3.

169. Tsur to Meir, 2 July 1956, ISA 330/7.

170. Embassy in Washington to Foreign Office, 5 July 1956, PRO: FO/371 121348 V1192/755.

171. Minute by Hadow, 1 June 1956, PRO: FO/371 121339 V1192/519E.

172. Embassy in Washington to Foreign Office, 5 and 6 July 1956, PRO: FO/371 121348 V1192/755, V1192/763.

173. Ibid., 20 June 1956, PRO: FO/371 121341 V1192/581.

174. Ben-Dor to Tsur, 11 March 1956, ISA 193/1.

175. Bar-On, *Gates of Gaza*, 207.

176. Ibid., 220–21.

177. Ibid., 224–34.

178. Ben-Gurion's diary, 25 September 1956, BGA.

179. Ibid.

180. Peres, "The Road to Sèvres," 143.

181. Ibid.

182. Bar-On, *Gates of Gaza*, 268.

183. Ibid., 261–62.

184. Ibid.

185. Ibid.

186. Najar to Tsur, 1 February 1956, ISA 193/1.

187. Crosbie, *Tacit Alliance*, 82.

CHAPTER FOUR

1. This account draws largely upon the narrative of Mordechai Bar-On, *The Gates of Gaza: Israel's Defense and Foreign Policy 1955–1957* (Tel Aviv: Am Oved, 1992), 294–318 (Hebrew).

2. Mordechai Bar-On, "The Influence of Political Considerations on Operational Planning in the Sinai Campaign," in *The Suez-Sinai Crisis 1956: Retrospective and Reappraisal*, ed. Selwyn Troen and Moshe Shemesh (London: Frank Cass, 1990), 213.

3. Isaac Alteras, *Eisenhower and Israel* (Gainesville: University of Florida Press), 214.

4. Bar-On, *Gates of Gaza*, 308.

5. Ibid., 309.

6. Ibid., 309; Keith Kyle, *Suez* (London: Weidenfeld and Nicolson, 1991), 369–70.

7. Alteras, *Eisenhower and Israel*, 237.

8. Bar-On, *Gates of Gaza*, 313.

9. Ibid., 313–14.

10. Ibid., 315.

11. Ibid.

12. For a full account of this American pressure, see Diane Kunz, *The Economic Diplomacy of the Suez Crisis* (Chapel Hill: University of North Carolina Press, 1991).

13. Bar-On, *Gates of Gaza*, 317.

14. Casualties included 180 Israelis and 2,000 Egyptians killed. Israel captured Egyptian arms and war material the value of which was estimated to be over $50 million. This included seven thousand tons of ammunition, five hundred thousand gallons of fuel, one

hundred Bren carriers, two hundred artillery pieces, one hundred tanks, and over one thousand other vehicles. Figures quoted in Howard M. Sachar, *A History of Israel* (New York: Knopf, 1986), 501.

CHAPTER FIVE

1. Ben-Gurion's speech before the Central Committee of Mapai, 30 December 1957, LPA.

2. Ibid.

3. Ben-Gurion's diary, 24 November 1956, BGA.

4. Meir Avidan, *Principal Aspects of Israel-U.S.A. Relations in the 1950s* (Jerusalem: Leonard Davis Institute for International Relations, 1982) 76 (Hebrew).

5. Steven Spiegel, *The Other Arab-Israeli Conflict* (University of Chicago Press, 1985), 76.

6. Mordechai Bar-On, *The Gates of Gaza: Israel's Defense and Foreign Policy 1955–1957* (Tel Aviv: Am Oved, 1992), 345 (Hebrew).

7. Spiegel, *Other Arab-Israeli Conflict*, 78.

8. Isser Harel, *Security and Democracy* (Tel Aviv: Edanim, 1989), 407 (Hebrew).

9. Ben-Gurion's diary, 24 November 1956, BGA.

10. Ibid., 1 December 1956.

11. Harel, *Security and Democracy*, 403. Harel's account suggests that Israel did in fact pass this information on to the CIA.

12. Ben-Gurion's diary, 24 November and 1 December 1956, BGA.

13. *FRUS* 16:1231.

14. Memorandum of conversation, Department of State, 30 November 1956, USNA: 684A.86/11-3056.

15. Ibid.

16. Ibid., 84; Bar-On, *Gates of Gaza*, 348.

17. Haggai Eshed, *One Man Mossad* (Tel Aviv: Edanim, 1988), 250 (Hebrew).

18. Keith Kyle, *Suez* (London: Weidenfeld and Nicolson, 1991), 538.

19. Bar-On, *Gates of Gaza*, 356.

20. *FRUS* 17:393.

21. Spiegel, *Other Arab-Israeli Conflict*, 84–85.

22. *FRUS* 17:393.

23. Meeting, Mapai Foreign Affairs Committee, 24 March 1957, LPA.

24. Archives of Hakibbutz Hameuchad, Yad Tabenkin, Ramat Efal: 23 May 1957, 13, 5, file 5.

25. Meeting, Mapai Foreign Affairs Committee, 7 April 1957, LPA.

26. Shiloah's probe was disingenuous, since he knew that the joint chiefs of staff were still working out details of contingency plans regarding which bases and which U.S. forces were to be employed. Only at a later stage would the Americans contact the region's countries, and even then it would be the Baghdad Pact states they would first consult. See Arad's memo of 8 March 1957, ISA 3089/7.

27. Meeting, Mapai Foreign Affairs Committee, 7 April 1957, LPA.

28. Ibid.

29. Ibid.

30. British embassy in Washington to Hadow, 12 February 1957, PRO: FO/371 127741 V10345/76.

31. Meeting, Mapai Foreign Affairs Committee, 7 April 1957, LPA.

32. Spiegel, *Other Arab-Israeli Conflict*, 79.

33. On 2 April Dulles approved the recommendation that the United States implement the $25-million Development Assistance and Technical Assistance programs, release local currency and counterpart funds when an agreement had been reached on their use, authorize meeting to some extent Israel's request for a P.L. 480 Title I program and notify the Export-Import Bank that political conditions were satisfactory for the dispatch of a study mission to Israel. *FRUS* 17:505.

34. Meeting, Mapai Foreign Affairs Committee, 7 April 1957, LPA.

35. Ibid.

36. *FRUS* 17:552.

37. Sherman to Eban, 15 April 1957, ISA 409/3.

38. See a report by Meir Sherman, 10 April 1957, ISA 409/3.

39. Circular memo by Arad, 18 April 1957, ISA 409/3.

40. Sherman to Eban, 10 April 1957, ISA 409/3.

41. Ben-Gurion's diary, 8 April 1957, BGA.

42. Eban to Meir, 18 May 1957, ISA 3088/3-I.

43. Spiegel, *Other Arab-Israeli Conflict*, 85.

44. Meroz to United States Section, 27 March 1957, ISA 3089/7.

45. Meir's report of her meeting with Lawson, 19 April 1957, ISA 330/3.

46. Circular memo by Meroz, 30 May 1957, ISA 330/2.

47. Circular memo by Arad, 22 May 1957, ISA 409/3.

48. Eban to Meir, 18 May 1957, ISA 3088/3-I. In fact, on 22 April the State Department decided to postpone indefinitely Richards's visits to Jordan, Syria, and Egypt. *FRUS* 17:566.

49. Eban to Meir, 18 May 1957, ISA 3088/3-I.

50. See protocol of the meeting between Meir and Richards, 3 May 1957, ISA 3088/3-1; *FRUS* 17:597.

51. Protocol, Meir-Richards meeting, 3 May 1957, ISA 3088/3-1.

52. British embassy in Tel Aviv to Foreign Office, 9 May 1957, PRO: FO/371 VR10348/6.

53. *FRUS* 17:600.

54. Herzog to Eban, 13 May 1957, ISA 3088/3I.

55. *FRUS* 17:597.

56. Herzog to Eban, 13 May 1957, ISA 3088/3I.

57. Meeting, Mapai Foreign Affairs Committee, 7 May 1957, LPA.

58. On 23 March, the United States joined the military committee of the Baghdad Pact. The Israelis feared that the United States would join the pact itself and afford the Arabs even greater influence in Washington. See memo by Arad, 10 June 1957, ISA 3089/7.

59. Ibid.

60. Ibid.

61. Eban to Meir, 18 May 1957, ISA 3088/3-I.

62. Ibid.

63. Ibid.

64. Ibid.

65. *FRUS* 17:603.

66. For the texts of the statements see circular memo of the Hasbara (information) Section of the Foreign Ministry, 22 May 1957, ISA 3088/3-I.

67. Ibid.

68. See *FRUS* 17:642, 654–56, 663, 698.

69. *FRUS* 17:597–601.

70. Meeting, Mapai Foreign Affairs Committee, 7 May 1957, LPA.

71. Ben-Gurion's speech to the Knesset, 3 June 1957, in *Divrei Haknesset* (Knesset Hearings) 22 (Hebrew); also British embassy in Tel Aviv to Levant Department, 13 June 1957, PRO: FO/371 128100 VR10345/11.

72. Patrick Seale, *The Struggle for Syria* (London: Oxford University Press, 1965), 285.

73. Ibid., 291.

74. During the course of 1957, the Syrians received the following items from the Soviet Union: sixty MiG-17s, ten Yak-11s, and seven Mi-1s. *The Arms Trade Registers*, Stockholm International Peace Research Institute (SIPRI) (Cambridge, Mass.: MIT Press, 1975), 64. The bulk of these arms appear to have been delivered in a major transaction between the Soviet Union and Syria in late October 1957.

75. Seale attributes these "rumors" to "lurid reports" published in American, British, and Israeli newspapers of "the arrival in force of Soviet officers and technicians." *Struggle for Syria*, 288.

76. *Divrei Haknesset* 22 (3 June 1957).

77. *FRUS* 17:701.

78. Eshed, *One Man Mossad*, 252.

79. Ben-Gurion's diary, 9 September 1957, BGA. At one point during the summer of 1957, a Syrian-Israeli clash seemed imminent and Chief-of-Staff Moshe Dayan warned of a severe Israeli response. In an address on 13 July 1957, Dayan noted that he had invited the Russians to Israel's border with Syria to witness the absence of aggressive Israeli intentions. The Russians were not interested. Instead, they were "looking for a tune to please the riff-raff in Damascus and Kalkilya." Dayan warned that "if we have to stand up to one or more of the Arab states, supported in their attack by the Soviet Union, the United States will not necessarily help us." British embassy in Tel Aviv to Levant department, 18 July 1957, PRO: FO/371 128090 VR1022/5.

80. Foreign Ministry to Eban, 15 September 1957, ISA 329/3.

81. *FRUS* 17:712.

82. Foreign Ministry to Eban, 15 September 1957, ISA 329/3.

83. Rundall to Lloyd, 11 November 1957, PRO: FO/371 128090 VR1022/14.

84. *FRUS* 17:727.

85. Ibid., 748.

86. Avidan, *Principal Aspects*, 85.

87. Ben-Gurion's diary, 15 August 1957, BGA.

88. The British ambassador reported that "the Israelis are genuinely worried about the deterioration of their position during recent months and they are desperately searching for a way to deal with Russian penetration before it actually laps around them."

British embassy in Tel Aviv to Foreign Office, 25 November 1957, PRO: FO/371 128125 VR1079/2.

89. Eshed, *One Man Mossad*, 258–65. The author describes Shiloah's role (minister at the embassy in Washington until September 1957 and afterward head of the newly formed political committee of the Foreign Ministry) as chief promulgator and catalyst of Israel's attempts to forge ties with NATO. Eshed cites almost no sources and claims that his account is based upon "interviews and private archives." In fact, he relies upon only a few of the documents available in the Israeli State Archives, cited in this work below.

90. Moshe Sharett *Personal Diary* (Tel-Aviv: Ma'ariv, 1978), 2309 (Hebrew).

91. British embassy to Foreign Office, 12 October 1957, PRO: FO/371 128090 VR1022/9; Ben-Gurion's diary, 30 September 1957, BGA; Shiloah's memo relating how he had succeeded in convincing the prime minister, Shiloah to Eban, 2 October 1957, ISA 4374/26. Eshed claims that Shiloah then realized that Israel would not be able to gain membership in NATO and accepts at face value Shiloah's account of his meeting with Ben-Gurion on 30 September 1957. See Eshed, *One Man Mossad*, 253; Shiloah to Eban, 2 October 1957, ISA 4374/26.

92. Ben-Gurion's diary, 30 September 1957, BGA.

93. Eshed, *One Man Mossad*, 259. This document is not available to other researchers at the Israeli State Archives, but Sasson's reply leaves little doubt that Shiloah favored membership in NATO.

94. Sasson to Shiloah, 22 October 1957, ISA 219/10.

95. Eshed's biography is uncritical of its subject and perpetuates the idea that Ben-Gurion accepted Shiloah's proposals without reservation. Bar-Zohar's biography of Ben-Gurion does not mention Shiloah's role. See Michael Bar-Zohar, *Ben Gurion* (Tel-Aviv: Zmora, Bitan, 1987), 1320–21 (Hebrew).

96. Shiloah to Eban, 2 October 1957, ISA 4374/26.

97. Ibid.

98. Ibid.

99. Foreign Ministry to Meir, 6 October 1957, ISA 2450/8.

100. Herzog to Foreign Ministry, 8 October 1957, ISA 2450/8; British embassy in Washington to Foreign Office, 12 October 1957, PRO: FO/371 128090 VR1022/9; *FRUS* 17:759; British embassy in Tel Aviv to Foreign Office, 14 October 1957, PRO: FO/371 128090 VR 1022/10.

101. Ben-Gurion's diary, 24 October 1957, BGA; *FRUS* 17:772.

102. Eliav's circular memo, 6 November 1957, ISA 409/4.

103. Shiloah to Eban, 16 November 1957, ISA 4374/26.

104. Ben-Gurion's diary, 14 November 1957, BGA.

105. Shiloah to Eban, 16 November 1957, ISA 4374/26.

106. Ibid. Shiloah noted that on 2 October 1950, a year and a half before being accepted as a member of NATO, Turkey was brought into the "Middle East military planning committee" of the organization.

107. Ibid.; unsigned Foreign Ministry memo: "Preparations for the NATO Convention," 19 November 1957, ISA 416/21.

108. British embassy in Washington to Foreign Office, 6 November 1957, PRO: FO/371 128107 VR1052/29.

109. Unsigned Foreign Ministry memo: "Preparations for the NATO Convention," 19 November 1957, ISA 416/21.

110. United States section to Foreign Ministry, 25 November 1957, ISA 3088/2.

111. Rountree to Dulles, 29 November 1957, USNA: 784A.00/11-2957.

112. On 6 December, the Near East Affairs office recommended for "political reasons" that the Exim Bank not extend to Israel the loan it had requested. Among the considerations were the absence of Israeli cooperation on the refugee problem and the fact that a loan of $40 million would bring the level of U.S. aid to Israel during fiscal year 1958 to $100 million; in the eyes of Rountree, this was too great a sum. *FRUS* 17:845.

113. Unsigned Foreign Ministry memo: "Preparations for the NATO Convention," 19 November 1957, ISA 416/21.

114. Meroz to Shiloah, 13 November 1957, ISA 2456/11.

115. Memo by Shiloah, 3 December 1957, ISA 2456/11.

116. Bergmann to Comay, 5 December 1957, ISA 2456/11.

117. Comay to Meir, 26 November 1957, ISA 2456/11.

118. Bergmann to Comay, 5 December 1957, ISA 2456/11.

119. Ibid.

120. Comay to Meir, 26 November 1957, ISA 2456/11.

121. Ibid., 3 February 1958, ISA 2456/11.

122. Interview with Pinchas Eliav, 9 November 1992, Jerusalem.

123. Memo by Shiloah, 3 December 1957, ISA 2456/11.

124. Thus, when on 25 December the embassy in Washington drew up further plans for an approach to the United States on American-Israeli scientific cooperation of a military nature, the question of how this could be squared with relations with France was given due consideration. Unsigned memo of the embassy in Washington, 25 December 1957, ISA 2456/11.

125. Protocol of a meeting at the Foreign Ministry, 31 December 1957, ISA 4374/26.

126. Shiloah to Meir, 7 January 1958, ISA 3105/13.

127. Ben-Gurion's diary, 25 April 1958, BGA.

128. United States section to Shiloah, January 1958 (precise date not cited), ISA 3088/6-II.

129. Eshed, *One Man Mossad*, 261. This was an Israeli plan to create a framework for cooperation among the either non-Arab or non-Moslem countries of the Middle East. The original intent of this plan was to include Iran, Turkey, Sudan, Ethiopia, the Maronites of Lebanon, and Cyprus in an informal pact which would serve as a counterweight to Nasser's pan-Arabism. In practice, Israel succeeded in forging ties mainly with Iran and Turkey. The Israelis hoped that the United States would provide political and economic support to the countries involved in this periphery alliance. However, it was not until the end of 1958 that the Israelis were able to devote much attention to this initiative. See Bar-Zohar, *Ben Gurion*, 1321. For details of Israeli contacts with Ankara during the months preceding the NATO conference, see ISA files 3125/4,5,6,8 and 11; 234/12B.

130. United States section to Shiloah, January 1958 (precise date not cited), ISA 3088/6-II.

131. Eban's memo to Dulles, 9 January 1958, ISA 2456/10.

132. Comay to Elath, 17 January 1958, ISA 3098/10.

133. Eban to Shiloah, 3 February 1958, ISA 228/6/A.

134. The sum of $24.2 million was considerably less than the Israelis had hoped for. The original sum Israel had requested was $75 million, and the sum discussed by the State Department in August 1957 was $40 million. Eldin Ricks, "United States Economic Assistance to Israel: 1949–1960" (Ph.D. diss., Dropsie University, 1970), 68.

135. United States section to embassy in Washington, 26 February 1958, ISA 228/6/A.

136. Circular memo by Yariv, Israeli military attaché in Washington, 22 April 1958, ISA 3088/6-II.

137. Avner to Sasson, 6 March 1958, ISA 228/6/A. The only arms the United States transfered to Iraq during this period were forty M-24 Chafee eighteen-ton light tanks, manufactured in 1945. *Arms Trade Registers*, 52.

138. Ben-Gurion's diary, 5 March 1958, BGA.

139. Shiloah to Ben-Gurion, 2 March 1958, ISA 3085/1.

140. Ben-Gurion's diary, 5 March 1958, BGA.

141. Ibid., 31 December 1957, 11 March 1958, 3 April 1958.

142. Embassy in Tel Aviv to Dulles, 25 April 1958, USNA: 784A.00/4-2558.

143. Avner to Herzog, 9 April 1958, ISA 3088/6-II. Emphasis added.

144. As Michael B. Oren claims in "The Test of Suez: Israel and the Middle East Crisis of 1958," *Studies in Zionism* 12, no. 1 (1991): 74.

145. Avner to Herzog, 12 August 1958, ISA 3088/6-II.

146. Ibid.

147. Ben-Gurion's diary, 24 July 1958, BGA.

148. Ibid.

149. Herzog to Avner, 21 August 1958, ISA 3088/6-II.

150. Ibid.

151. Herzog to Eytan, 21 August 1958, ISA 3085/13A.

152. Eban's cicular memo, 3 October 1958, ISA 334/23. Eban argued that not only had Israel now received arms from the United States; it had in fact also had a security guarantee during the period of the overflights. Eban cited Arthur Dean's insistence that the Israelis had ignored Eisenhower's commitment to defend Israel if attacked which was not different, claimed the American attorney, from a formal guarantee. Eban to Meir, 11 October 1958, ISA (file number not cited).

153. Avner to Gazit, 15 September 1958, ISA 3088/5.

154. Ben-Gurion's diary, 7 October 1958, BGA.

155. Eban's circular memo, 3 October 1958, ISA 334/23.

156. Ibid.

157. Ibid.

158. Ibid.

159. Mordechai Gazit, "Israel's Military Procurement from the United States," (Jerusalem: Leonard Davis Institute, Hebrew University, 1983), 17 (Hebrew).

160. Avner to Meroz, 21 December 1958, ISA 3088/6-II.

161. Oren attempts to magnify the significance of the sale by erroneously terming the recoilless rifle "an offensive weapon." See "Test of Suez," 80.

162. Gazit, "Israel's Military Procurement," 23.

163. Ibid., 327.

164. Avner to Meroz, 21 December 1958, ISA 3088/6-II.

165. Rountree's briefing of Ambassador Ogden R. Reid, 11 June 1959, USNA: 611.84A/6-1159.

166. As indicated by Ben-Gurion's conversation with Lawson dealing with the intelligence and military aspects of Israel's relations with Turkey. Avner to Herzog, 28 October, 1958, ISA 3088/5. Efforts by this writer to obtain documents pertaining to the activities of James Angleton, who headed the Israel desk of the CIA, have been to no avail.

167. Rountree to Dulles, 17 January 1959, USNA: 611.84A/1-1759; Ben-Gurion's diary, 7 and 23 December 1958, BGA.

168. Ben-Gurion's diary, 7 December 1958, BGA.

169. For an analysis of this period in American-Israeli relations, see Mordechai Gazit, *President Kennedy's Policy Toward the Arab States and Israel*, Studies Series (Tel Aviv: Shiloah Center, Tel Aviv University, 1983) (Hebrew).

170. Protocol of meeting of Mapai Central Committee, 11 September, 1958, LPA.

171. Ibid.

172. Ben-Gurion's diary, 29 December 1958, BGA.

173. Avidan, *Principal Aspects*, 85.

174. Ben-Gurion's speech before the Central Committee of Mapai, 30 December 1957, LPA.

175. Ibid.

176. Ibid.

177. *FRUS* 13:358–61.

178. Nadav Safran *Israel, The Embattled Ally* (Cambridge, Mass.: Belknap Press, 1978), 360.

179. Spiegel, *Other Arab-Israeli Conflict*, 89–90.

180. Ben-Gurion's speech at a bond drive conference. BBC summary of broadcasts, daily series no. 646, 5 September 1958, PRO: FO/371 133822.

181. Gazit, "Israel's Military Procurement," 22.

182. Eshed, *One Man Mossad*, 250.

183. Avidan, *Principal Aspects*, 77.

184. Ben-Gurion's diary, 1 December 1956, BGA.

185. *FRUS* 17:597–601.

186. Ben-Gurion's speech before the Central Committee of Mapai, 30 December 1957, LPA; Rundall's report to Selwyn Lloyd: "Trends in Israel's Foreign Policy," 4 November 1957, PRO: FO/371 128090 VR1022/14.

CHAPTER SIX

1. Foreign Office to United Kingdom delegation to the United Nations, 22 November 1956, PRO: FO/371 121358.

2. Jordan received fifty M-47/48 Patton tanks from the United States in 1957 and twelve Hawker Hunter jets from the United Kingdom in 1958. In 1957, Iraq received twenty Centurion tanks from the United Kingdom and in 1957 and 1958, fifteen Hawker Hunters. In 1957, Syria received the following aircraft from the Soviet Union: sixty MiG-17 fighters, eight Il-4 transport planes, ten Yak-11 trainers, and seven Mi-1 helicopters. In 1958, the

Syrians received ten Yak-18 transports and ten Mi-4 helicopters. See *The Arms Trade Registers*, Stockholm International Peace Research Institute (SIPRI) (Cambridge, Mass.: MIT Press, 1975), 50–52, 56–57, 63–65.

3. Foreign Office memo: "Arms for Israel," 22 December 1956, PRO: FO/371 121359, V1192/1101.

4. Elath to British Commonwealth Section, 4 January 1957, ISA 413/3.

5. Avner to British Commonwealth Section, 15 February 1957, ISA 329/2.

6. Foreign Office to United Kingdom delegation to the United Nations, 22 November 1956, PRO: FO/371 121358.

7. Minute by Kirkpatrick, 3 December 1956, PRO: FO/371 121359 V1192/1075.

8. Elath to British Commonwealth Section, 21 and 22 November 1956, ISA 328/22. Reilly to Kirkpatrick, 21 November 1956, PRO: FO/371 121358 V1192/1061.

9. Mordechai Bar-On, *The Gates of Gaza: Israel's Defense and Foreign Policy, 1955–1957* (Tel Aviv: Am Oved, 1992), 333 (Hebrew).

10. Ibid., 334.

11. Main items discussed in the framework of an NEACC meeting of 22 November, 1956: France was to supply 175 75-mm guns, 60 AMX and 40 Sherman tanks, 100,000 antitank mines, 40 105-mm self-propelled guns, 24 additional Mystère-4s and 60 Fouga jet trainers. The only British items on the list were 10 Meteor MK-7 trainers. It is not clear when the French items were in fact delivered to Israel. Minute by Rose, 23 November 1956, PRO: FO/371 121359 V1073/1093.

12. Ben-Gurion's diary, 7 January 1957, BGA.

13. Elath to British Commonwealth Section, 4 January 1957, ISA 413/3.

14. Elath to Eytan, 8 February 1957, ISA 328/22.

15. Neither side could annul the treaty unilaterally. The Anglo-Jordanian Treaty was thus terminated in a joint declaration on 13 February, 1957. See text of declaration in ISA 329/2.

16. Elath to British Commonwealth Section, 8 January 1957, ISA 329/2.

17. Ibid.

18. Avner to British Commonwealth Section, 15 February 1957, ISA 329/2.

19. Embassy in Tel Aviv to Foreign Office, 12 June 1957, PRO: FO/371 127781 V1194/99.

20. Elath to Foreign Ministry, 18 February 1957, ISA 331/8. In exchange, the Israelis offered to refrain from publicizing details of the Jordanian "fiasco." See M. Ofer's account of his conversation with Westlake of the British embassy in Tel Aviv, 20 February 1957, ISA 329/2.

21. Rundall to Ross, 12 June 1957, PRO: FO/371 127781 V1194/97.

22. Ibid.

23. Elath to Foreign Ministry, 15 March 1957, ISA 329/2.

24. Unsigned minute of the Foreign Office, 16 January 1957, PRO: FO/371 127781.

25. Minute by Rose, 18 March 1957, PRO: FO/371 127781 V1194/65.

26. Unsigned minute of the Foreign Office, 16 January 1957, PRO: FO/371 127781.

27. Foreign Office report, February 1957, in PRO: FO/371 128114.

28. Secretary of State to Minister of Defense, April 1957, PRO: FO/371 127781 V1194/94.

29. M. Palgi to Elath, 15 February 1957, ISA 331/8.

30. Ibid.

31. British Commonwealth Section to embassy in Britain, 18 June 1957, ISA 330/3.

32. Minute by Rose, "Middle East talks, stage III," 17 June 1957, PRO: FO/371 127757; Schneerson to embassy in Britain, 7 June 1957, ISA 330/3.

33. Elath to British Commonwealth Section, 4 January 1957, ISA 413/3.

34. Minute by Rose, 17 June 1957, PRO: FO/371 127757.

35. Elath to Foreign Ministry, 22 May 1957, ISA 331/8.

36. Schneerson to embassy in Britain, 20 June 1957, ISA 330/3.

37. Minute of the Levant Department, 17 June 1957, PRO: FO/371 128199 VR1531/13.

38. British Commonwealth Section to embassy in Britain, 15 July 1957, ISA 331/8.

39. Scneerson to embassy in London, 20 June 1957, ISA 330/3.

40. Elath to Meir, 15 July 1957, ISA 328/22.

41. Ibid.

42. Record of a meeting held in the prime minister's room, House of Commons, 1 August 1957, PRO: FO/371 128107.

43. Minute of the Levant Department, 17 June 1957, PRO: FO/371 128199 V1531/13.

44. M. Ofer, record of conversation with Westlake and Higgins of the British embassy in Tel Aviv, 19 July 1957, ISA 3098/4.

45. Rundall to Rose, 15 August 1957, PRO: FO/371 128181 VR1151/42.

46. "Arms for Israel," 5 August 1957, PRO: FO/371 127783 V1194/133.

47. Ibid., 25 July 1957, PRO: FO/371 127782 1194/126.

48. Rundall to Rose, 15 August 1957, PRO: FO/371 128181 VR1151/42. According to the embassy in London, Rundall was "astonished at the depth of anti-British feeling in Israel." Avner to Ofer, 16 July 1957, ISA 331/8.

49. Ibid.

50. Embassy in Tel Aviv to Foreign Office, 27 August 1957, PRO: FO/371 128090 VR1022/6.

51. Elath to Foreign Ministry, 21 August 1957, ISA 328/22.

52. "Arms for Israel," 25 July 1957, PRO: FO/371 127782 V1194/126.

53. Elath to Foreign Ministry, 5 September 1957, ISA 328/22. The Jordanians in fact received the jets, but not the Centurions.

54. Avner to Foreign Ministry, 22 October 1957, ISA 3098/1.

55. Comay to Elath, 4 September 1957, ISA 328/22.

56. Comay to Foreign Ministry, 28 August 1957, ISA 330/3.

57. Avner to Elath, 10 October 1957, ISA 331/1.

58. Rundall to Rose, 6 November 1957, PRO: FO/371 128107 VR1052/31.

59. Shek to British Commonwealth Section, 25 November 1957, ISA 3098/15.

60. Elath to Meir, 10 December 1957, ISA 413/3.

61. Lloyd to Rundall (Foreign Office telegram no. 1016), 10 December 1957, PRO: FO/ 371 128107.

62. Elath to Meir, 10 December 1957, ISA 413/3.

63. Lloyd to Rundall (Foreign Office telegram no. 1016), 10 December 1957, PRO: FO/ 371 128107.

64. The theme of Israel's fear of Guildhall and the Alpha plan recurs frequently in Israeli documents. British Commonwealth section to Foreign Ministry, 11 March 1957, ISA 331/

8; Avner to Foreign Ministry, 15 March 1957, ISA 329/2; Elath to British Commonwealth Section, 5 April 1957, ISA 331/8.

65. Embassy in London to Foreign Ministry, 22 October 1957, ISA 3098/1.

66. Rundall to Hadow, 23 December 1957, PRO: FO/371 128118 VR1072/144.

67. United States Section to embassy in Washington, 26 December 1957, ISA 3098/12.

68. Hadow to Rundall, 3 January 1958, PRO: FO/371 128118 VR1072/144.

69. United States Section to embassy in Washington, 26 December 1957, ISA 3098/12.

70. Embassy in Tel Aviv to Foreign Office, 19 December 1957, PRO: FO/371 128118 VR1072/12.

71. British Commonwealth Section, 2 January 1958, ISA 334/28.

72. Rundall to Lloyd, 6 January 1958, PRO: FO/371 134267 VR1014/1.

73. British Commonwealth Section to Comay, 24 January 1958, ISA 3098/15.

74. In January 1958, Israel had 128 fighter planes, 56 of which were Mystère-4As. See a 6 February report on Israel's air strength in PRO: FO/371 134349 VR1223/1.

75. Shek to British Commonwealth Section, 21 April 1958, ISA 3098/15.

76. British Commonwealth Section to Shiloah, 13 June 1958, ISA 3098/15.

77. This union was in answer to the United Arab Republic, which Egypt and Syria formed on 1 February 1958. Britain intended to strengthen the Iraqi-Jordanian union in every possible way. Thus, the Levant Department noted that "the first priority should be to help our friends. This means military and economic aid to the Arab Union. . . . The Americans have promised to provide eighteen F-86s to Iraq and twelve Hunter-6s to Jordan." Unsigned memo, 6 June 1958 in PRO: FO/371 133823.

78. Michael B. Oren stresses the confrontational nature of Anglo-Israeli relations, noting that Ben-Gurion had on 3 February made clear to the British that "if foreign troops approach the river Jordan, we will reserve our freedom to act." Oren also quotes Ben-Gurion's warning in May to Dag Hammarskjold, the UN secretary general, that "Hussein cannot be allowed to blackmail [Israel] because of his difficult internal situation. We must establish a limit to what we will endure." Oren, "Test of Suez," 63–64.

79. Rundall to Lloyd, 27 January 1958, PRO: FO/371 134291 VR1072/19.

80. British Commonwealth Section to embassy in London, 2 March 1958, ISA 3098/4.

81. Ofer to Comay, 6 March 1958, ISA 3098/4. The embassy in London considered this such valuable information that it requested that the Research Section of the Israeli Foreign Ministry reciprocate by passing on intelligence reports to the Foreign Office. Shek to British Commonwealth Section, 5 March 1958, ISA 334/6.

82. British Commonwealth Section to embassy in London, 22 June 1958, ISA 334/6; Foreign Office memo, "Israel and the Iraq/Jordan Union," 27 February 1958, PRO: FO/371 134293 VR1073/3.

83. Rundall to Lloyd, 24 June 1958, PRO: FO/371 134292 VR1072/19.

84. Shek to British Commonwealth Section, 10 June 1958, ISA 334/6.

85. Ibid.

86. See an account of the overflights based on Ben-Gurion's diary in Michael Bar-Zohar, *Ben Gurion* (Tel Aviv: Zmora-Bitan, 1987), 1333–34 (Hebrew). Documents of the Israeli State Archives add little of substance to the material in Ben-Gurion's diary. However, recently released documents of the British Foreign Office shed new light on the overflights affair.

87. See King Hussein's memoirs, *Uneasy Lies the Head* (London, 1962), 86–95.

88. Record of conversation between Ben-Gurion and Barbara Salt of the British embassy, 15 July 1958, ISA 334/23.

89. Ben-Gurion's diary, 4 August 1958, BGA. Michael B. Oren advances the thesis that Israel's primary goal during the crisis was the attainment of a strategic alliance with Britain and that Ben-Gurion pursued this goal by employing a strategy of "brinkmanship." Oren, "Test of Suez," 67.

90. For a definition of the concept of brinkmanship in international relations, see Thomas C. Schelling, *Arms and Influence* (New Haven: Yale University Press, 1966), 91, 99–125. Schelling describes brinkmanship as the technique of compellence, the creation of risk, usually a shared risk, and a competition in risk taking.

91. Oren makes these claims in "Test of Suez."

92. Memorandum of conversation, Department of State, 27 April 1957, USNA: 784A.5411/4-2757.

93. Israeli sensitivity was not, as Oren suggests, simply a matter of respect for Israel's sovereignty. As U.S. undersecretary of state Christian Herter noted, "Israeli resistance was due partly to the fact that in overflights made from Cyprus, the British did not observe the ordinary courtesies of notifying them when and where planes were going to overfly, sticking to a corridor. The Israelis are naturally terribly nervous for fear that there may be mixed in with these planes, Egyptian or other planes which could suddenly destroy the whole of Israel." See record of proceedings of the U.S. Senate Foreign Relations Committee, executive session of the Senate, 22 July 1958, in the John Foster Dulles Papers, Princeton University.

94. Embassy in Tel Aviv to the political representative with the Middle East Forces, Cyprus, 7 May 1958, PRO: FO/371 134345 1223/58G.

95. Ibid.

96. Minute of the Foreign Office, 15 July 1958, PRO: FO/371 134347 VR1222/48.

97. Ben-Gurion's note to MacMillan, 17 July 1958, ISA 334/23. The Israelis wanted to know where the United States stood on the matter before giving their consent. See embassy in Tel Aviv to Foreign Office, 17 July 1958, PRO: FO/371 134345 VR1222/6.

98. MacMillan's note to Ben-Gurion, 18 July 1958, ISA 3098/4.

99. Oren, "Test of Suez," 67.

100. Foreign Office to embassy in Washington, 17 July 1958, PRO: FO/371 134345 VR1222/7.

101. MacMillan's note to Ben-Gurion, 18 July 1958, ISA 3098/4.

102. Ben-Gurion's diary, 19 July 1958, BGA.

103. In the British evaluation, in the event of a coup the Israelis would move as quickly as possible to the Jordan River in order to arrive before the Iraqis or the Egyptians. Rundall to Hoyer-Millar, 5 August 1958, PRO: FO/371 134313 VR1093/5.

104. Thus when the CIA warned Eisenhower that Israel might grab the West Bank, it attributed the possibility to radical influences on Ben-Gurion. Bar-Zohar, *Ben Gurion*, 1334.

105. Rundall to Foreign Office, 23 July 1958, PRO: FO/371 134284 VR/1051/15.

106. Ben-Gurion's diary, 16 July 1958, BGA.

107. Rundall to Foreign Office, 17 July 1958, PRO: FO/371 134345 VR1222/6.

108. Ibid., 27 July 1958, PRO: FO/371 134271 VR1022/6G.

109. Ben-Gurion's diary, 19 July 1958, BGA.

110. Embassy in Tel Aviv to Foreign Office, 19 July 1958, PRO: FO/371 134284 VR1051/12G.

111. Ibid.

112. Ibid.

113. Ibid., 26 July 1958, PRO FO/371 134286 VR1061/37G.

114. Lloyd to Rundall, 21 July 1958, PRO: FO/371 134284 VR1051/13.

115. Embassy in Tel Aviv to Foreign Office, 15 August 1958, PRO: FO/371 134286 VR1061/37G.

116. Foreign Office to Washington, telegram no. 4892, 20 July 1958, PRO: FO/371 134284.

117. Embassy in Tel Aviv to Foreign Office, 21 July 1958, PRO: FO/371 134346, VR1222/25G.

118. Minute of the Foreign Office, 26 July 1958, PRO: FO/371 134286 VR1061/37G.

119. Brief for the secretary of state titled "Mrs. Meir's visit," 9 August 1958, PRO: FO/371 134285.

120. British Commonwealth Section to Elath, 22 July 1958, ISA 334/23.

121. Oren, "Test of Suez," 73.

122. Oren writes that the note, which he claims originated with Krushchev, is still classified. Bar-Zohar, however, cites the content of the *aide memoire* sent by Soviet Deputy Foreign Minister Zorin, in which the Soviet Union claimed that British troops were overflying Israel as part of an "invasion" of Arab countries, and in which the Soviets threatened Israel's "national interests." Bar-Zohar, *Ben Gurion*, 1340.

123. Ibid.

124. Circular memo by Elissar, 5 August 1958, ISA 3085/13/A. Israel authorized a continuation of American flights for supply purposes until 10 August. See Bar-Zohar, *Ben Gurion*, 1341. According to Oren, Ben-Gurion was not certain as to the seriousness of the Soviet threat. Oren also claims that the Soviet threat strengthened Ben-Gurion's hand, since he could tell the United States and Britain that without arms and guarantees, he could no longer expose his people to undue risks. Oren, "Test of Suez," 74. In fact, Ben-Gurion realized well before receiving the Russian note that the overflights put Israel in a precarious position vis-à-vis the Soviet Union. Ben-Gurion's diary, 24 July 1958, BGA.

125. Ben-Gurion was reported to have been "deeply hurt" at Dulles's assumption that he was frightened by the Soviet note. See Herter to Dulles, Department of State telegram, 5 August 1958, USNA: 784A.00/8-558.

126. Ibid.

127. Oren, "Test of Suez," 75.

128. Tel Aviv to Foreign Office, 4 August 1958, PRO: FO/371 134347 V1222/60B.

129. British Commonwealth Section to embassy in London, 5 August 1958, ISA 3098/15.

130. Embassy in Tel Aviv to Foreign Office, 2 August 1958 PRO: FO/371 134347 VR1222/55G, and 4 August, VR1222/60G.

131. A list which Elath presented included two hundred Centurion tanks, three hundred half-tracks, antitank and antiaircraft guided missiles, three fighter squadrons, two bomber squadrons, and two submarines. Foreign Office to Tel Aviv, telegram no. 590, 8 August 1958, PRO: FO/371 134285.

132. Foreign Office to embassy in Tel Aviv, tel. no. 590, 7 August 1958, PRO: FO/371 134285.

133. British embassy in Paris to Foreign Office, 8 August 1958, PRO: FO/371 134285 VR1051/27B.

134. Ibid., 6 August 1958, PRO: FO/371 134274 VR10317/8.

135. See memos by Shuckburgh; Ross and Hayter, 28 July, 3 August 1958, PRO: FO/371 134285 VR1051/35G, and Hoyer-Millar, 5 August 1958, 134285 VR1051/21.

136. Foreign Office to embassy in Amman, telegram no. 3456, 1 October 1958, PRO: FO/371 133858. Emphasis added.

137. Ibid.

138. British Commonwealth Section to Elath, 22 July 1958, ISA 334/23.

139. Conversation between Lloyd and Meir, 11 August 1958, PRO: FO/371 134285 VR1051/29.

140. Shek to British Commonwealth Section, 20 August 1958, ISA 3098/5.

141. Livran to Elath, 11 November 1958, ISA 334/23.

142. Ben-Gurion's diary, 6 November 1958, BGA.

143. Embassy in Tel Aviv to Foreign Office, 10 September 1958, PRO: FO/371 134286 V1192/72G.

144. Ibid., 20 September 1958, PRO: FO/371 134286 V1041/58.

145. British Commonwealth Section to Elath, 14 December 1958, ISA 334/23.

146. Ben-Gurion's diary, 12 August 1958, BGA.

147. Shek to British Commonwealth Section, 23 December 1957, ISA 3098/15.

148. Foreign Office to embassy in Washington, 27 August 1958, PRO: FO/371 133858 V1194/189.

149. Ben-Gurion's diary, 28 October 1958, BGA. Earlier that month, the Foreign Office approved the sale to Israel of two submarines and one hundred half-tracked vehicles. The United States approved the sale to Israel of one hundred recoilless rifles. Embassy in Tel Aviv to Foreign Office, 9 October 1958, PRO: FO/371 133858 V1194/261; "United Kingdom Middle East arms policy," 17 October 1958, 134295.

150. Foreign Office to embassy in Washington, 27 August 1958, PRO: FO/371 133858 V1194/189. Oren is mistaken in claiming that "Britain and the United States maintained that their arms sales to Israel were one-time transactions, and not indicative of any departure from previous policy." Oren, "Test of Suez," 81.

151. Foreign Office to embassy in Washington, 27 August 1958, PRO FO/371 133858 V1194/189.

152. In early October, Israel was short some $10 million required to pay for the initial consignment of Centurions. Ben-Gurion proposed delaying delivery of the tanks until Israel could find the money. Ben-Gurion's diary, 7 October 1958, BGA.

153. Foreign Office to Washington, telegram no. 6149, 28 August 1958, PRO: FO/371 133858.

154. Ibid. Approximately one hundred each in Iraqi and Syrian possession and two hundred in Egyptian possession.

155. Minute of the Foreign Office, 24 April 1959, PRO: FO/371 142293 V1192/33.

156. Edward Luttwak and Dan Horowitz, The Israeli Army (New York: Harper and Row, 1975), 171. For a breakdown of Israel's purchases, see Arms Trade Registers, 55.

157. Ibid. From 1964 to 1966, Israel acquired two hundred M-48 tanks from the United States, France, and the Federal Republic of Germany.

158. Ben-Gurion's diary, 13 December 1956, BGA.

159. Ibid., 28 February 1957. Ben-Gurion did not restrict the confidence of his fears to his diary. The State Department learned that he was alleged to be "increasingly doubtful as to the value of Israeli-French ties and was considering withdrawing Shimon Peres from his mission in France." Whitney to Dulles, 24 April 1957, USNA: 684A.86/4-2457.

160. Memorandum of conversation, Department of State, 30 June 1958, USNA: 611.84A/6-3058.

161. Ibid.

162. Bar-On, *Gates of Gaza*, 333.

163. Ibid.

164. British Commonwealth Section to embassy in London, 2 March 1958, ISA 3098/4.

165. United States Section to Meroz, 26 December 1957, ISA 3098/12; embassy in Tel Aviv to Foreign Office, 19 December 1957, PRO: FO/371 128118 VR1042/12.

166. Ibid., 50–52.

CHAPTER SEVEN

1. Sylvie Crosbie, *A Tacit Alliance* (Princeton, N.J.: Princeton University Press, 1974), 101.

2. Michael Bar-Zohar, *Bridge Over the Mediterranean: French-Israeli Relations 1947–1963* (Tel Aviv: Am Hasefer, 1965), 192 (Hebrew).

3. Mordechai Bar-On, *The Gates of Gaza: Israel's Defense and Foreign Policy 1955–1957* (Tel Aviv: Am Oved, 1992), 359 (Hebrew).

4. Ibid.

5. Crosbie, *Tacit Alliance*, 90.

6. Bar-On, *Gates of Gaza*, 364.

7. Ben-Gurion's diary, 28 February 1957, BGA.

8. Meeting, Mapai Central Committee, 3 March 1957, LPA.

9. Ibid., 14 March 1957. Committee member Yehudit Ginsburg pressed Meir to explain the significance of the relationship with France and to predict its duration. The foreign minister answered that "the French tell us we don't have too many friends." That, she said, was the best basis for friendship.

10. Ben-Gurion shared these misgivings. In April 1957 the Political and Security Affairs Section of the U.S. Office at the United Nations reported a "highly confidential" conversation in which Ben-Gurion was said to be "increasingly doubtful of the value of Israeli-French ties." The prime minister was supposed to have considered withdrawing Peres's arms procurement mission from Paris. Presumably, he did not do this because all other arms procurement channels were blocked. U.S. Office of the United Nations to Dulles, 25 April 1957, USNA: 684A.86/4-2457.

11. Meeting, Mapai Central Committee, 2 March 1957, LPA.

12. Nicholls to Lloyd, 11 February 1957, PRO: FO/371 128093 VR 10317/3.

13. Ibid.

14. Ben-Gurion's diary, 31 May 1958, BGA.

15. Edward Luttwak and Dan Horowitz, *The Israeli Army* (New York: Harper and Row, 1975), 170.

16. *The Arms Trade Registers*, Stockholm International Peace Research Institute (Cambridge, Mass.: MIT Press, 1975), 53.

17. Ben-Gurion's diary, 3 April 1958, BGA.

18. Ibid. Ben-Gurion noted that the price of one Super-Mystère was four hundred thousand dollars. These were delivered in 1959. *Arms Trade Registers*, 53.

19. Michael Bar-Zohar, *Ben Gurion* (Tel Aviv: Zmora, Bitan, 1978), 1348.

20. Ben-Gurion's diary, 27 May 1957, BGA.

21. Meeting, Mapai Central Committee, 3 January 1957, LPA.

22. Meeting, Mapai Foreign Affairs Committee, 7 May 1957, LPA.

23. Ibid.

24. Crosbie, *Tacit Alliance*, 98.

25. Ben-Gurion's diary, 11 May 1957, BGA.

26. Bar-Zohar, *Bridge Over the Mediterranean*, 180.

27. Ben-Gurion's diary, 1 October 1957, BGA.

28. Michael Bar-Zohar, *Ben Gurion* (Tel-Aviv: Zmora, Bitan, 1987), 1347 (Hebrew).

29. Meeting, Mapai Foreign Affairs Committee, 7 May 1957, LPA.

30. Ibid.

31. Ben-Gurion's diary, 10 March 1957, BGA.

32. Meeting, Mapai Foreign Affairs Committee, 27 June 1957, LPA.

33. Ben-Gurion's diary, 16 July 1958, BGA.

34. Crosbie, *Tacit Alliance*, 142.

35. Ibid.

36. Meeting, Mapai Foreign Affairs Committee, 2 September 1958, LPA.

37. Ben-Gurion's diary, 29 December 1957, BGA.

38. Ibid., 31 December 1957, 10 January 1958.

39. Crosbie, *Tacit Alliance*, 123.

40. Bar-Zohar, *Ben Gurion*, 1351.

41. Ibid.

42. Shlomo Aronson with Oded Brosh, *The Politics and Strategy of Nuclear Weapons in the Middle East* (Albany, N.Y.: SUNY Press, 1992), 150.

43. Meeting, Mapai Central Committee, 30 December 1957, LPA.

44. Ben-Gurion's diary, 17 June 1958, BGA.

45. Meeting, Mapai Foreign Affairs Committee, 27 June 1957, LPA.

46. Bar-Zohar, *Ben Gurion*, 1357.

47. Ben-Gurion's diary, 29 December 1957, BGA. In fact, by 1963, French-German cooperation on this project had failed. By the time the Germans fielded the forty-ton main battle tank designated Leopard (1966), Israel had already purchased a full complement of British Centurions and American Pattons. Israel received 200 M-48 Patton tanks between 1964 and 1966. *Arms Trade Registers*, 55, 146. According to Deutschkron, the Federal Republic of Germany supplied some 150 of these with American approval. Inge Deutschkron, *Bonn and Jerusalem* (Philadelphia: Chilton, 1970), 274.

48. Meeting, Mapai Central Committee, 30 December 1957, LPA; British embassy in Bonn to Foreign Office, 30 December 1957, PRO: FO/371 134275 VR10318/1.

49. Bar-Zohar, *Ben Gurion*, 1352.

50. Meeting of Mapai Central Committee, 30 December 1957, LPA.

51. Ibid., 11 September 1958. Ben-Gurion may have thought it would be easier for the Germans to divert both arms and technology to Israel than it would be for the French, since the Germans were doing more to intensify military cooperation with the United States than with France. Thus, for example, by 1958 the FRG had decided to purchase certain weapon systems from the United States rather than from France, such as the F-104-G Starfighter rather than the Mirage-III (jet aircraft). Wilfrid Kohl, *French Nuclear Diplomacy* (Princeton, N.J.: Princeton University Press, 1971), 281.

52. Bar-Zohar, *Ben Gurion*, 1352–53.

53. Protocol of a meeting on 31 May 1957 at the German Defense Ministry, 3 June 1957, ISA 3099/25A. This was small arms ammunition.

54. Ben-Gurion's diary, 29 December 1957, BGA. On the German side, Adenauer approved the sole handling of defense matters vis-à-vis Israel by Strauss. War materials and arms were excluded from the German-Israeli Reparations Agreement. British embassy in Bonn to Foreign Office, 30 December 1957, PRO: FO/371 134275 VR10318/9-A.

55. Embassy in Bonn to Foreign Office, 23 December 1957, PRO: FO/371 128094 10319/13.

56. Ibid., 30 December 1957, PRO: FO/371 134275 VR10318/9-A.

57. Ibid. In fact, Israel in 1958 purchased submarines from Britain, not Germany.

58. *Daily Telegraph* (London), 28 December 1957, in PRO: FO/371 134275 VR10318/9-A.

59. Embassy in Tel Aviv to Foreign Office, 7 January 1958, PRO: FO/371 134268 VR1015/4.

60. Aronson, *Politics and Strategy of Nuclear Weapons*, 150.

61. As suggested by Bar-Zohar in *Ben Gurion*, 1357.

62. Ben-Gurion's diary, 30 December 1957, BGA.

63. Bar-Zohar, *Ben Gurion*, 1354.

64. Parker to Greenhough, 30 December 1957, PRO: FO/371 134268.

65. The switch may have been in deference to Dayan's reported reluctance to be identified with an unpopular issue which might damage his future political ambitions. Embassy in Tel Aviv to Foreign Office, PRO: FO/371 134275 VR10318/4.

66. Ben-Gurion's diary, 29 December 1957, BGA.

67. Peter Medding, *The Founding of Israeli Democracy, 1948–1967* (London: Oxford University Press, 1990), 99; Bar-Zohar, *Ben Gurion*, 1355.

68. *Arms Trade Registers*, 54.

69. Ibid., 54, 144–45.

70. Ben-Gurion's diary, 25 August 1954, BGA.

71. Frank Barnaby, *The Invisible Bomb* (London: I. B. Tauris, 1989), 22.

72. Aronson, *Politics and Strategy of Nuclear Weapons*, 61–62.

73. Ibid.

74. Matti Golan, *Shimon Peres* (London: Weidenfeld and Nicolson, 1982), 65.

75. Meeting, Mapai Central Committee, 30 December 1957, LPA.

76. Barnaby, *Invisible Bomb*, 7.

77. Ibid., 4.

78. Aronson, *Politics and Strategy of Nuclear Weapons*, 62.

79. Crosbie, *Tacit Alliance*, 120–21.

80. Barnaby, *Invisible Bomb*, 8. Barnaby writes that in fact, the reactor was upgraded to a capacity far above 24 megawatts, and that Dimona eventually reached a capacity of 150 megawatts. See p. 40.

81. Aronson, *Politics and Strategy of Nuclear Weapons*, 61.

82. Ibid., 63.

83. Golan, *Shimon Peres*, 64.

84. In fact, a "German option" with regard to missiles was no more relevant than a French one, as long as their "research pool" lagged behind the United States and Britain in development in this field.

85. Barnaby, *Invisible Bomb*, 8.

86. Kohl, *French Nuclear Diplomacy*, 64.

87. Golan, *Shimon Peres*, 63.

88. Minute by Hadow, 4 March 1959, PRO: FO/371 142363 VR1192/23. The Foreign Office reported that the French were "studying" a SSM with a 150-kilometer range.

89. The British view was that "in spite of close ties . . . , we need not assume that the French would be very keen to encourage the Israelis in this line of development." Foreign Office to embassy in Washington, 12 March 1959, PRO: FO/371 142363 VR1192/23.

90. Embassy in Washington to Foreign Office, 17 March 1959, PRO: FO/371 142363 VR1192/27. The Western Electric Nike Ajax, developed in the early 1950s, had a range of forty kilometers. The Nike Hercules, developed in 1958, had a range of one hundred kilometers. *Arms Trade Registers*, 145. Both were surface-to-air guided missiles; procurement efforts suggest that Israel may have intended to use this technology in order to produce a guided SSM.

91. Foreign Office to embassy in Washington, 12 March 1959, PRO: FO/371 142363 VR1192/23.

92. Minute by Tesh, 20 February 1959, PRO: FO/371 142363 VR1192/28.

93. Foreign Office to embassy in Washington, 12 March 1959, PRO: FO/371 142363 VR1192/23.

94. Minute by Rothnie, 15 February 1959, PRO: FO/371 142363.

95. Embassy in Tel Aviv to Foreign Office, 10 April 1959, PRO: FO/371 142379 VR1192/59.

96. Ibid.

97. *FRUS* 13:393.

98. Aronson, *Politics and Strategy of Nuclear Weapons*, 68.

99. Ibid., 62.

100. Crosbie, *Tacit Alliance*, 161.

101. Aronson, *Politics and Strategy of Nuclear Weapons*, 70–71.

102. Crosbie, *Tacit Alliance*, 157.

103. *Arms Trade Registers*, 144.

104. Ibid.

105. Luttwak and Horowitz, *Israeli Army*, 218, 311. The arms stoppage became a total embargo following an Israeli retaliatory raid on the Beirut airport on 28 December 1968.

106. Barnaby, *Invisible Bomb*, 22–23.

107. Aronson, *Politics and Strategy of Nuclear Weapons*, 69.

108. France placed a total embargo on all arms to Israel on 3 January 1969, the result of heavy Arab pressure. See Edward Kolodziej, *Making and Marketing Arms* (Princeton, N.J.: Princeton University Press, 1987), 344.

109. *Arms Trade Registers*, 53.

110. Steven Spiegel, *The Other Arab-Israeli Conflict* (Chicago: University of Chicago Press, 1985), 134. Israel took delivery of these jets in 1968. *Arms Trade Registers*, 55.

111. Mordechai Gazit, *Israel's Military Procurement from the United States* (Jerusalem: Leonard Davis Institute, Hebrew University, 1983), 22 (Hebrew).

112. Crosbie, *Tacit Alliance*, 230.

113. J. C. Hurewitz, *Middle East Politics: The Military Dimension* (New York: Praeger, 1969), 442.

114. Crosbie, *Tacit Alliance*, 222.

115. Ibid., 226.

116. Avner Yaniv, "The French Connection: A Review of French Policy Towards Israel," *Jerusalem Journal of International Relations* 1, no. 3 (Spring 1976): 120.

117. Golan, *Shimon Peres*, 69.

118. Crosbie, *Tacit Alliance*, 225.

119. Deutschkron, *Bonn and Jerusalem*, 270.

120. Ibid., 270. According to Deutschkron, the fifty planes Israel received from Germany were Noratlas transport, Dornier-27 monoplanes, and Fouga Magister jet trainers. See also n. 61.

121. Bar-Zohar, *Bridge Over the Mediterranean*, 191.

122. Bar-Zohar, *Ben Gurion*, 1347.

123. Quoted in Crosbie, *Tacit Alliance*, 71.

124. Meeting, Mapai Central Committee, 2 March 1957, LPA.

125. Ibid., 3 January 1957.

126. Ben-Gurion's diary, 10 March 1957, BGA.

127. Crosbie, *Tacit Alliance*, 122.

CONCLUSION

1. For example, Michael Bar-Zohar, *Ben Gurion* (Tel-Aviv: Zmora, Bitan, 1987) (Hebrew), and Haggai Eshed, *One Man Mossad* (Tel-Aviv: Edanim, 1988) (Hebrew). Alteras also ascribes to the period of the second Eisenhower administration a greater warming between the United States and Israel than in fact took place. See Isaac Alteras, *Eisenhower and Israel* (Gainesville: University of Florida Press, 1993).

2. Yitzhak Rabin, "The Sinai Campaign and the Limits of Power," in *The Suez-Sinai Crisis, 1956: Retrospective and Reappraisal*, ed. Selwyn Ilan Troen and Moshe Shemesh (London: Frank Cass, 1990), 239.

3. Meeting, Mapai Central Committee, 9 September 1958, LPA.

4. Ibid., 30 December 1957, LPA.

5. Meeting, Mapai Political Committee, 16 October 1955, LPA. Lavon in fact made these remarks in the context of Israeli consideration of a request to the Soviet Union for arms in the wake of the Czech deal. *Kaddish* is the Jewish prayer recited for the dead.

6. Ibid., ix.

7. William Roger Louis, *The British Empire in the Middle East 1945–1951* (Oxford: Clarendon Press, 1984), 556, 740–41.

8. Ibid.

9. Ilan Pappé, *Britain and the Arab-Israeli Conflict, 1948–1951* (London: Macmillan Press, 1988), 202.

10. As suggested by Michael B. Oren, "The Test of Suez: Israel and the Middle East Crisis of 1958," *Studies in Zionism* 12, no. 1 (1991).

BIBLIOGRAPHY

ARCHIVES

Archives des affaires étrangères de la France, Imprimerie Nationales, Paris
Archives of Ahdut Ha'avoda and Mapam, Yad Tabenkin, Ramat Ef'al
Ben Gurion Archives, Sde Boker, Israel
John Foster Dulles Papers, Princeton University
Israeli Labor Party (Mapai) Archives, Beit Berl
Israeli State Archives, Jerusalem
National Archives of the United States, Washington, D.C.
Public Record Office, Kew, Surrey, United Kingdom

OTHER DOCUMENTARY SOURCES

The Arms Trade Registers. Stockholm International Peace Research Institute (SIPRI).
   Cambridge, Mass.: MIT Press, 1975.
Declassified Documents Quarterly. Rutgers University.
De Novo, John A. "The Eisenhower Doctrine." In *Encyclopedia of American Foreign
   Policy: Studies of the Principal Movements and Ideas*, edited by Alexander De Conde,
   1:292–301. New York: Scribner's, 1978.
Divrei Haknesset (Knesset Hearings). Israel's Parliamentary Records, Jerusalem (He-
   brew).
Ro'i, Yaacov. *From Encroachment to Involvement: A Documentary Study of Soviet Policy
   in the Middle East, 1945–1973*. New York: John Wiley and Sons, 1974.
U.S. Department of State, *Foreign Relations of the United States*. Washington, D.C.:
   Government Printing Office.

MEMOIRS AND PERSONAL ACCOUNTS

Dayan, Moshe. *Story of My Life*. Jerusalem: Edanim, 1976 (Hebrew).
Eden, Anthony. *Full Circle: The Memoirs of Sir Anthony Eden*. London: Cassell, 1960.
Eisenhower, Dwight D. *Mandate for Change: Memoirs, 1953–1956*. London: Heine-
   mann, 1963.
———. *Waging Peace: Memoirs, 1956–1961*. London: Heinemann, 1965.
Harel, Isser. *Security and Democracy*. Tel Aviv: Edanim, 1989 (Hebrew).

Hussein I, King of Jordan. *Uneasy Lies the Head.* London: Bernard Geis, 1962.

MacMillan, Harold. *Riding the Storm, 1956–1959.* New York: Harper and Row, 1971.

Nutting, Anthony. *No End of a Lesson: The Story of Suez.* New York: Potter, 1967.

Peres, Shimon. *David's Sling.* London: Weidenfeld and Nicolson, 1970 (Hebrew).

Sharett, Moshe. *Personal Diary.* Tel Aviv: Ma'ariv, 1978 (Hebrew).

Shuckburgh, Evelyn. *Descent to Suez: Diaries, 1951–1956.* London: Weidenfeld and Nicolson, 1986.

Tsur, Yaakov. *An Ambassador's Diary in Paris.* Tel Aviv: Am Oved, 1968 (Hebrew).

BOOKS AND PAMPHLETS

Alteras, Isaac. *Eisenhower and Israel: U.S.-Israeli Relations, 1953–1960.* Gainesville: University of Florida Press, 1993.

Aronson, Shlomo, with Brosh, Oded. *The Politics and Strategy of Nuclear Weapons in the Middle East.* Albany: SUNY Press, 1992.

Avidan, Meir. *Principal Aspects of Israel-U.S. Relations in the 1950s.* Jerusalem: Leonard Davis Institute for International Relations, 1982 (Hebrew).

Bar-On, Mordechai. *The Gates of Gaza: Israel's Defense and Foreign Policy, 1955–1957.* Tel Aviv: Am Oved, 1992 (Hebrew).

Bar-Ya'acov, Nissim. *The Israeli-Syrian Armistice: Problems of Implementation, 1949–1966.* Jerusalem: Magnes Press, 1967.

Bar-Zohar, Michael. *Ben Gurion: A Biography.* Tel Aviv: Zmora, Bitan, 1987 (Hebrew).

———. *Bridge Over the Mediterranean: French-Israeli Relations, 1947–1963.* Tel Aviv: Am Hasefer, 1965 (Hebrew).

Baylis, John. *Anglo-American Defence Relations, 1939–1980: The Special Relationship.* New York: St. Martin's Press, 1981.

Bialer, Uri. *Between East and West: Israel's Foreign Policy Orientation, 1948–1956.* Cambridge: Cambridge University Press, 1990.

Brecher, Michael. *Decisions in Israel's Foreign Policy.* Oxford: Oxford University Press, 1974.

———. *The Foreign Policy System of Israel.* Oxford: Oxford University Press, 1972.

Burns, William J. *Economic Aid and American Foreign Policy Toward Egypt, 1955–1981.* Albany: SUNY Press, 1985.

Childers, Erskine B. *The Road to Suez: A Study of Western-Arab Relations.* London: MacGibbon and Gee, 1962.

Cooper, Chester L. *The Lion's Last Roar: Suez, 1956.* New York: Harper and Row, 1978.

Crosbie, Sylvie. *A Tacit Alliance: France and Israel from Suez to the Six Day War.* Princeton, N.J.: Princeton University Press, 1974.

Deutschkron, Inge. *Bonn and Jerusalem.* Philadelphia: Chilton, 1970.

Divine, Robert A. *Eisenhower and the Cold War.* New York: Oxford University Press, 1981.

Eshed, Haggai. *One Man Mossad.* Tel Aviv: Edanim, 1988 (Hebrew).

Eveland, Wilbur Crane. *Ropes of Sand: America's Failure in the Middle East.* New York: Norton, 1980.

Freiberger, Steven Z. *Dawn Over Suez: The Rise of American Power in the Middle East, 1953–1957.* Chicago: Ivan Dee, 1992.

Gazit, Mordechai. "Israel's Military Procurement from the United States." Jerusalem: Leonard Davis Institute, Hebrew University, 1983 (Hebrew).

———. *President Kennedy's Policy Toward the Arab States and Israel.* Studies Series. Tel Aviv: Shiloah Center, Tel Aviv University, 1983.

Genco, Stephen J. "The Eisenhower Doctrine: Deterrence in the Middle East." In *Deterrence in American Foreign Policy: Theory and Practice,* edited by Alexander L. George and Richard Smoke, 309–62. New York: Columbia University Press, 1974.

Golan, Matti. *Shimon Peres.* London: Weidenfeld and Nicolson, 1982.

Hahn, Peter L. *The United States, Great Britain and Egypt, 1945–1956.* Chapel Hill: University of North Carolina Press, 1991.

Hurewitz, J. C. *Middle East Politics: The Military Dimension.* New York: Praeger, 1969.

Jabber, Paul. *Not by War Alone.* Berkeley and Los Angeles: University of California Press, 1981.

Jackson, Elmore. *Middle East Mission: The Story of a Major Bid for Peace in the Time of Nasser and Ben Gurion.* New York: Norton, 1983.

James, Robert Rhodes. *Anthony Eden.* London: Weidenfeld and Nicolson, 1986.

Klieman, Aaron S. *Israel and the World After Forty Years.* New York: Pergamon Press, 1990.

Kohl, Wilfrid. *French Nuclear Diplomacy.* Princeton, N.J.: Princeton University Press, 1971.

Kolodziej, Edward A. *Making and Marketing Arms: The French Experience and Its Implications for the International System.* Princeton, N.J.: Princeton University Press, 1987.

Kunz, Diane B. *The Economic Diplomacy of the Suez Crisis.* Chapel Hill: University of North Carolina Press, 1991.

Kyle, Keith. *Suez.* London: Weidenfeld and Nicolson, 1991.

Lenczowski, George. *The Middle East in World Affairs.* 4th ed. Ithaca: Cornell University Press, 1980.

Louis, William Roger. *The British Empire in the Middle East, 1948–1951.* Oxford: Oxford University Press, 1984.

Louis, William Roger, and Roger Owen, eds. *Suez 1956: The Crisis and Its Consequences.* Oxford: Oxford University Press, 1989.

Lucas, W. Scott. *Divided We Stand: Britain, the U.S. and the Suez Crisis.* London: Hodder and Stoughton, 1991.

Luttwak, Edward, and Dan Horowitz. *The Israeli Army.* New York: Harper and Row, 1975.

Mansfield, Peter. *The British in Egypt.* London: Weidenfeld and Nicolson, 1971.

Medding, Peter. *The Founding of Israeli Democracy, 1948–1967.* Oxford University Press, 1990.

Monroe, Elizabeth. *Britain's Moment in the Middle East.* 2nd ed. Baltimore: Johns Hopkins University Press, 1981.

Morris, Benny. *Israel's Border Wars.* New York: Clarendon Press, 1993.

Nimrod, Yoram. *Mei Meriva* (Angry Waters) Givat Haviva: Center for Arab and Afro-Asian Studies, 1966 (Hebrew).

Oren, Michael B. *The Origins of the Second Arab-Israeli War: Egypt, Israel and the Great Powers, 1952–1956*. London: Frank Cass, 1993.

Pappé, Ilan. *Britain and the Arab-Israeli Conflict, 1948–1951*. London: Macmillan Press, 1988.

———. *The Making of the Arab-Israeli Conflict, 1947–1951*. London: Tauris, 1992.

Peres, Shimon. *Kela David* (David's Sling). Jerusalem: Weidenfeld and Nicolson, 1970 (Hebrew).

Perlmutter, Amos. *Military and Politics in Israel*. New York: Praeger, 1969.

Rabinovich, Itamar. *The Road Not Taken: Early Arab-Israeli Negotiations*. Oxford: Oxford University Press, 1991.

Robertson, Terence. *Crisis: The Inside Story of the Suez Conspiracy*. New York: Atheneum, 1965.

Sachar, Howard. *A History of Israel: From the Rise of Zionism to Our Time*. New York: Knopf, 1976.

Safran, Nadav. *From War to War: The Arab-Israeli Confrontation, 1948–1967*. Indianapolis: Bobbs-Merrill, 1969.

———. *Israel, The Embattled Ally*. Cambridge, Mass.: Belknap Press, 1978.

Schelling, Thomas C. *Arms and Influence*. New Haven: Yale University Press, 1966.

Schoenbaum, David. *The United States and the State of Israel*. Oxford: Oxford University Press, 1993.

Seale, Patrick. *The Struggle for Syria*. New Haven: Yale University Press, 1987.

Shalev, Arieh. *Cooperation Under the Shadow of Conflict: The Israeli-Syrian Armistice Agreement, 1949–1955*. Tel Aviv: Ma'arachot, 1989 (Hebrew).

Shwadran, Benjamin. *The Middle East, Oil and the Great Powers*. 2nd ed. Boulder, Colo.: Westview Press, 1985.

Spiegel, Steven. *The Other Arab-Israeli Conflict*. University of Chicago Press, 1985.

Steigman, Yitzhak. *History of the Air Force: The Air Force from 1950 to 1956*. Tel Aviv: Israeli Ministry of Defense, 1986 (Hebrew).

Thomas, Abel. *Comment Israël Fut Sauve*. Paris: Albin-Michel, 1978.

Troen, Selwyn Ilan, and Moshe Shemesh, eds. *The Suez-Sinai Crisis 1956, Retrospective and Reappraisal*. London: Frank Cass, 1990.

Urquhart, Brian. *Hammerskjold*. New York: Knopf, 1973.

Vatikiotis, P. J. *The History of Egypt*. 2nd ed. Baltimore: Johns Hopkins University Press, 1980.

———. *Nasser and His Generation*. New York: St. Martin's Press, 1978.

Williams, Ann. *Britain and France in the Middle East and North Africa, 1914–1967*. New York: St. Martin's Press, 1968.

ARTICLES, RESEARCH PAPERS, AND DISSERTATIONS

Asia, Ilan. *Confrontation and War Over the Negev Corridor, 1949–1956*. Ph.D. diss., Bar-Ilan University, 1992 (Hebrew).

Dooley, Howard J. "Great Britain's 'Last Battle' in the Middle East: Notes on Cabinet

Planning during the Suez Crisis of 1956." *International History Review* 11 (August 1989): 486–517.

Gazit, Mordechai. "Ben Gurion's Attempts to Establish Military Ties with the United States." *Gesher* 32 (1986/7) (Hebrew).

———. "Sharett, Ben Gurion and the Arms Deal with France in 1956." *Gesher* 108 (Winter 1983) (Hebrew): 86–100.

Golani, Motti. "The Historical Place of the Czech-Egyptian Arms Deal, Fall 1955." *Middle Eastern Studies* 31, no. 4 (October 1995): 803–827.

Hahn, Peter L. "Containment and Egyptian Nationalism: The Unsuccessful Effort to Establish the Middle East Command, 1950–53." *Diplomatic History* 11 (Winter 1987): 23–40.

Holsti, K. J. "National Role Conceptions in the Study of Foreign Policy." *International Studies Quarterly* 14, no. 1 (September 1970): 233–309.

Kafkafi, Eyal. "Ben Gurion, Sharett and the Johnston Plan." *Studies in Zionism* 13, no. 2 (1992): 165–86.

Lazar, David. "Israel and France: The Beginning of Relations." *State, Government and International Relations* A, no. 2 (1971) (Hebrew).

Levey, Zach. "Anglo-Israeli Strategic Relations, 1952–56." *Middle Eastern Studies* 31, no. 4 (October 1995): 772–802.

———. "Israel's Pursuit of French Arms, 1952–58." *Studies in Zionism* 14, no. 2 (Autumn 1993): 183–210.

———. "Israel's Quest for a Security Guarantee from the United States, 1952–54." *British Journal of Middle Eastern Studies* 22, no. 1 (1995): 43–63.

Little, Douglas. "The Making of a Special Relationship: The United States and Israel, 1957–1968." *International Journal of Middle East Studies* 25 (1993): 563–85.

Oren, Michael B. "The Test of Suez: Israel and the Middle East Crisis of 1958." *Studies in Zionism* 12, no. 1 (1991): 55–83.

Ricks, Eldin. *United States Economic Assistance to Israel: 1949–1960.* Ph.D. diss., Dropsie University, 1970.

Sheffer, Gabriel. "Sharett, Ben Gurion and the 1956 War of Choice." *State, Government and International Relations* 27 (Winter 1987) (Hebrew).

Shlaim, Avi. "Conflicting Approaches to Israel's Relations with the Arabs: Ben Gurion and Sharett, 1953–56." *Middle East Journal* 37, no. 2 (1983): 180–201.

Slonim, Shlomo. "Origins of the 1950 Tripartite Declaration on the Middle East." *Middle Eastern Studies* 23, no. 2 (1987): 135–49.

Tal, David. "The American-Israeli Security Treaty: Sequel or Means to the Relief of Israeli-Arab Tensions, 1954–1955." *Middle Eastern Studies* 31, no. 4 (October 1995): 828–48.

———. "Israel's Road to the 1956 War." *International Journal of Middle East Studies* 28 (1996): 59–81.

Tenemboim, Yoav. *British Policy Towards Israel and the Arab-Israeli Dispute, 1951–1954.* Oxford: Oxford University Press, 1991.

Wishart, David. "The Breakdown of the Johnston Negotiations Over the Jordan Waters." *Middle Eastern Studies* 26 (October 1990): 536–46.

Yaniv, Avner. "The French Connection: A Review of French Policy Towards Israel." *Jerusalem Journal of International Relations* 1, no. 3 (Spring 1976): 115–31.

INDEX